I KNOW THAT NAME!

I KNOW THAT NAME!

*The People Behind Canada's
Best-Known Brand Names
From Elizabeth Arden
to Walter Zeller*

Mark Kearney *and*
Randy Ray

A HOUNSLOW BOOK
A MEMBER OF THE DUNDURN GROUP
TORONTO · OXFORD

Publisher: Anthony Hawke
Copy-Editor: Jennifer Bergeron
Design: Jennifer Scott
Printer: AGMV Marquis

National Library of Canada Cataloguing in Publication Data

Kearney, Mark, 1955–
    I know that name! : the people behind Canada's best-known brand names from Elizabeth Arden to Walter Zeller / Mark Kearney and Randy Ray.

Includes bibliographical references.
ISBN 1-55002-407-8

1. Businesspeople — Canada — Biography. 2. Business names — Canada — History.
I. Ray, Randy, 1952– II. Title.

HF3224.5.K42 2002   338.092'271   C2002-902283-5

1   2   3   4   5   06   05   04   03   02

THE CANADA COUNCIL | LE CONSEIL DES ARTS
FOR THE ARTS | DU CANADA
SINCE 1957 | DEPUIS 1957

Canada

ONTARIO ARTS COUNCIL
CONSEIL DES ARTS DE L'ONTARIO

We acknowledge the support of the **Canada Council for the Arts** and the **Ontario Arts Council** for our publishing program. We also acknowledge the financial support of the **Government of Canada** through the **Book Publishing Industry Development Program** and **The Association for the Export of Canadian Books**, and the **Government of Ontario** through the **Ontario Book Publishers Tax Credit** program.

Care has been taken to trace the ownership of copyright material used in this book. The author and the publisher welcome any information enabling them to rectify any references or credit in subsequent editions.

J. Kirk Howard, President

Printed and bound in Canada.
Printed on recycled paper.
www.dundurn.com

Dundurn Press
8 Market Street
Suite 200
Toronto, Ontario, Canada
M5E 1M6

Dundurn Press
73 Lime Walk
Headington, Oxford,
England
OX3 7AD

Dundurn Press
2250 Military Road
Tonawanda NY
U.S.A. 14150

I KNOW THAT NAME!

Table of Contents

Introduction

Like most Canadians, you probably pop into Loblaws or Sobeys once a week to buy groceries. You tip back the occasional Labatt Blue, Sleeman lager, or Molson Export. Maybe you like to sip a glass of whisky distilled by Hiram Walker or Seagram's, and no doubt you've stopped into Harvey's for a hamburger and munched on Miss Vickie's potato chips or a McIntosh apple.

You buy clothes at Holt Renfrew, Jack Fraser, or Reitmans, and you have fond memories of shopping trips to Eaton's, Simpson's and Woodward's. You grab your morning coffee and donut at Tim Hortons, shop for a new chesterfield at Leon's, pick up office supplies at Grand & Toy, buy chocolates at Laura Secord, have your film developed at Black's, and purchase CDs at Sam the Record Man.

For years, the names of these and dozens of other Canadians have been in the public eye in one way or another. They're displayed on signs, labels, packaging, transport trucks, coffee cups, bus shelters, and clothing. They're in our kitchen pantries, on products found in supermarkets and hardware stores, and in magazines, on roadside billboards, and Web sites. Many are seen or heard regularly on radio and television.

The names are familiar, but how much do we as Canadians know about the people behind them? We're the beneficiaries of their innovation and expertise, we use their products and services regularly, and millions have been employed by them, but how many of us have paused to consider who these people were, or are?

That's what we wondered.

In this, our sixth book, we introduce readers to more than one hundred Canadians whose names have been woven into the fabric of Canadian history and are as much a part of our collective national consciousness as maple syrup, hockey, and the CBC.

They are names most of us recognize but can't put a face to. Where did these people grow up? What was the inspiration for the businesses, services, and products that have found their way into the lives of generations of Canadians? What obstacles did they overcome? Why did they succeed where others failed? What kind of people were they away from their businesses? In short, what did they do to get their names into lights?

We uncovered fascinating stories about dozens of remarkable Canadians who put Canada on the map with their creativity, intelligence, innovation, and sheer drive, often against incredible odds.

Some were handed their businesses on a silver platter, but most started from scratch, as solo entrepreneurs or as part of mom and pop operations or tiny family businesses that were launched at a kitchen table, in a workshop, or in a cramped rented office. Often, they began with little more than a few bucks and an idea; somehow they managed to turn their plans and dreams into major successes, en route to becoming household names. Many became millionaires; some are billionaires whose names are known around the globe.

For many, the road to the top was rocky, often littered with missed opportunities, personal tragedies, economic crises, and skirmishes with militant workers, government policies, and competitors. Many saw their premises levelled by fire — sometimes more than once; a number struggled through the Great Depression and several wars. Yet they persevered.

While most were business people first and foremost, there was more to life than long hours in the family store, factory, or office. Long before they started the enterprises that bear their names, some had already made names for themselves in other endeavors, as athletes, inventors, and, in at least one case, as a canal builder.

Once successful in business, several moved on to make their mark in other areas, including local, provincial, and federal politics, philanthropy, and different ventures, such as insurance and shipping. Others gave generously to charitable causes, or put their weight behind world-class events such as Expo 86 in Vancouver and the Santa Claus Parade in Toronto.

By now you may be wondering how we came up with the names we've written about in this book. Nearly everyone you'll read about has at some point had his or her name prominently displayed on a well-known business or product. That's why we wrote about grocers Theodore Loblaw and Frank Sobey, but not IGA supermarkets or Buy-Low Foods. Coles Books made the book, but Chapters did not. You'll read about Tim Hortons Donuts, but not Dunkin' Donuts.

Introduction

Our focus is on names of national or regional prominence, such as Mark's Work Wearhouse, Bata Shoes, Ganong Chocolates, and Brick Beer. Unfortunately, that meant we didn't include local businesses like Jane's Florist Shop, Bill's Auto Repair, or your favourite hairdresser.

All of our subjects have significant Canadian ties. That's why we profiled picklemakers Walter and Jeanna Bick and chocolate bar maker William Neilson, but not the Americans behind Heinz ketchup or Hershey's chocolate — even though Heinz and Hershey are names found on the shelves of virtually every grocery store in Canada. There's a story on Walter Zeller but not L.L. Bean, and you'll learn how Harvey's hamburgers got its name but not how Wendy's or McDonald's came to be; you'll meet pasta maker Carlo Catelli but not Chef Boyardee.

Many of these personalities were born in Canada and had their success here; others were born outside Canada, in countries such as Russia, Ireland, and the United States, and often didn't achieve greatness until they set up shop on Canadian soil and became residents of Canada. Some were born here but soon after moved elsewhere to hit the big time, often returning home later in life. A handful merely passed through on their way to bigger and better things, but because of some interesting link with Canada, we thought readers would like to know their stories.

On occasion when we thought there was a person behind a name, such as Robin's Donuts, and there wasn't, we told that tale, too.

Although successive generations often played a key role in making a business or product thrive, our aim was to concentrate on the founders who planted the seeds and lent their names to the many companies and products that to this day are known around the world. Had they not started the ball rolling, who knows if later generations would have made their names as prominent as they are today?

We were delighted to find Canadian ties to such internationally known enterprises as Elizabeth Arden, Fuller Brush, Dow Chemical, Schick shaving products, and Smith Brothers cough drops. We were at times disappointed to learn about Canadian enterprises that closed their doors after many years in business or were swallowed by huge multinational corporations, often based outside Canada. Sadly, this usually meant their names were erased from Canada's business landscape.

But we were buoyed by the many Canadian companies that have resisted takeovers and held onto their names. Today, these firms are as Canadian as they were the day they earned their first dollar. Their founders would be impressed.

We were able to contact some of the people we've written about to let them tell their story. In other cases that was not possible, so our research relied on the recollections of relatives, former employees, neighbours, and those who run their companies today. Sometimes we found these people close to home, other times we tracked them down as far away as Nashville, Tennessee; Phoenix, Arizona; and Delray Beach, Florida. Along the way, we spent many hours on the telephone and the Internet; we contacted or visited countless libraries, archives, and museums, and we pored over thousands of pages of company and family histories, trade journals, annual reports, books, and faded newspaper clippings to unearth the stories behind these icons.

Our book doesn't pretend to tell the full story about each of these Canadians; we haven't included everyone whose name has appeared on a product or sign — space doesn't allow it; and we aren't the first to profile such people as John Molson, Joseph-Armand Bombardier, and Elizabeth Arden. Several sources from which we drew information have done that, and for their help and for readers who want to learn more about certain individuals, we've compiled a lengthy bibliography at the back of our book.

But we feel we have broken new ground by introducing you to a host of exceptional Canadians whose stories until now have been buried in company histories, university and government archives, microfilm cabinets, and obscure trade journals, where few Canadians will ever read them.

Those of you who have read our Canadian trivia books know we like to dig up fascinating facts about Canada that surprise and educate. In this book, we present an array of tantalizing tidbits that we hope you'll enjoy. They're woven into our stories and found under the Name Droppers heading at the end of many of our profiles. Did you know, for instance, that Tim Horton ran two other businesses before he got into donuts? Or that John Molson built Canada's first railway? We didn't.

The names you will read about have always been familiar. We hope our book will better acquaint you with each of these Canadians and help you appreciate their accomplishments. Perhaps you'll also draw inspiration from their stories.

We're confident you will enjoy meeting the people behind the names as much as we did.

Mark Kearney and Randy Ray

James Aikenhead

Aikenhead's Hardware

Generations of Toronto-area do-it-yourselfers and contractors didn't simply go to the hardware store — they went to Aikenhead's, a chain founded in the 1800s by James Aikenhead.

The myriad of goods peddled over the years by Aikenhead and members of his family include nuts, bolts, nails, hinges, hearth brushes, candlesticks, ship spikes, rope mats, plumbing and electrical fixtures, lawnmowers, paint, ladders, and tools.

These and a vast array of other supplies and gadgets were used to build homes, offices, and institutional buildings across the city, including landmarks such as the Royal York Hotel, old City Hall, Casa Loma, buildings at the University of Toronto campus, and the Commerce Court office tower complex in the heart of Toronto's financial district.

"The Aikenhead Hardware Company ... played a very significant role in providing for the early settlers to this country the tools and equipment necessary to clear the land and build their homes and businesses," says a document obtained from the Trent University Archives in Peterborough, Ontario.

Aikenhead was born in 1816 in Dublin, the son of Irish merchants. Some time after coming to Canada in 1830, he landed a job as a window cleaner at Joseph Ridout's ironmongery/hardware shop in York, an Upper Canada community of about three thousand people, which in 1834 was incorporated as Toronto.

James Aikenhead

Courtesy of the Aikenhead family.

With dollars and cents not yet in use, the business, which was located in a red brick building at King and Yonge streets, accepted bartering, as well as pounds, shillings, and pence as payment for its goods.

After working at various jobs, Aikenhead and fellow employee Alexander Crombie in 1868 became partners in the company, which was renamed Ridout, Aikenhead & Crombie. In 1893, Aikenhead bought out his partners, and his name appeared alone on the store's signs.

Aikenhead was known as a conscientious entrepreneur who provided customers with the best product knowledge and service. The official Aikenhead history describes him as "a man of keen discernment and sound business judgment. His sterling qualities and outstanding business ability were the moulding influence that was to form the inspiration for a great business enterprise in Toronto."

Energy and enterprise were among the many qualities he would hand down to his descendants who would play a role in the company.

In 1902, under the direction of James's son, Thomas Edward Aikenhead, the company, now known as Aikenhead Hardware Co., moved to Adelaide Street in Toronto and two years later to Temperance Street.

Shortly after James Aikenhead's death in 1903, Thomas became president. In later years, his sons James and John Wilfrid ran the busi-

The first Aikenhead store at Yonge and King in Toronto.

Courtesy of the Aikenhead family.

ness, and eventually their sons were involved. When World War I broke out, the company operated a Winnipeg retail and contracting business, which was closed because every man on its staff went to war.

In 1940, there were three Aikenhead stores in Toronto and in 1946 sales topped $1 million. By the 1960s, Aikenhead's had twenty-two Ontario outlets, including stores in Brampton, Sudbury, St. Catharines, Kitchener, and Markham. Annual sales were $22 million.

In its heyday, Aikenhead's was known for its phenomenal selection, expert service, and competitive prices. At its downtown Toronto stores, the fasteners section was the most popular department. "Bins upon bins of nails, screws, nuts and other fasteners rival the best-stocked farmers' co-op. In fact, one can buy a single screw at Aikenhead's. No need for 12 screws encased in plastic and cardboard," writer Clark Hoskin wrote in the January/February 1991 issue of *Hardware Merchandising* magazine.

Many do-it-yourselfers have fond memories of Aikenhead's six-storey Temperance Street store, which was the company's head office until 1963.

"People went to that store because they knew they could find things no one else had," recalls Tom Ross, former executive director of the Canadian Retail Hardware Association. Former customers and suppliers still refer to the Temperance Street location as a "tool mecca" for its knowledgeable staff and wide array of hand and power tools.

In 1971, Molson Industries Ltd. bought control of Aikenhead's with the intention of merging the company with its Beaver Home Centres subsidiary, a plan that was later abandoned. By 1992, with the Aikenhead's chain pared down to a single store in downtown Toronto, Molson's launched Aikenhead's Improvement Warehouse Inc., with outlets in southern Ontario; Edmonton and Calgary, Alberta; and Surrey, British Columbia.

The Aikenhead name was erased from Canada's retail landscape in 1994 when Home Depot purchased a 75 percent interest in the company.

Peter Lymburner Robertson

Robertson screwdriver

The Robertson screwdriver is among the tools found at hardware stores and building supply outlets across Canada.

The screwdriver with the square head and the screws used in conjunction with it are the brainchild of P.L. Robertson. At the time he came up with the idea, in 1906 in Milton, Ontario, the slot-head screwdriver was popular but it had a tendency to slip out of the screws as Robertson well knew. The story goes that Robertson once cut his hand using a slotted screwdriver and decided it was time to come up with an improvement. His screwdriver, which he began making in 1908, gripped the square-holed screws better and averted damage to work surfaces and fingers in the process.

One of Robertson's competitors, the Steel Company of Canada, tried to invalidate his patents, and a scathing story about him appeared in a 1910 issue of *Saturday Night* magazine. He responded with a one thousand-word letter to the editor.

Robertson, who was born in 1879, initially had trouble receiving financing to manufacture his invention, but still turned down an offer from Henry Ford. Instead, he founded Recess Screws Ltd. in England and set up a manufacturing plant in Milton, west of Toronto. By the end of World War II, he had five hundred employees and was a well-known philanthropist. Robertson died in 1951 a millionaire, secure in the knowledge that his screws and screwdrivers were popular worldwide.

Aris Alexanian

Alexanian Carpet and Flooring

Aris Alexanian had little sympathy for people who purchased poor quality rugs.

"To install fine furniture over something like a wall-to-wall tossmat is like putting Louis XIV pieces into a backwoods cabin," he once told an interviewer. Buying a cheap rug would never contribute to personal satisfaction and self-confidence, which buying a good quality rug would certainly do, he said in another interview.

As the president of Alexanian Carpet from 1925 until his death in June 1961, Alexanian was widely known as one of Canada's leading rug importers. Newspaper headlines referred to him as the Connoisseur of Carpets.

Alexanian was born in Agin, Turkey in 1901, where he learned rug weaving at the elbow of family members whose Armenian ancestors had been making rugs for four generations. At the age of nineteen, he fled to New York after spending six months hiding out from the Turks, who were at war with the Armenian population as part of a plan to build a Pan-Turkic empire.

After working at odd jobs for about a year in the Big Apple, he moved to Canada, settling west of Toronto in Georgetown, Ontario in 1922, where he became the superintendent of a home for Armenian boys he helped bring to Canada. For four years he supervised their education and helped place them with families. In the 1920s,

Aris Alexanian

Courtesy of the Hamilton Spectator

he founded the magazine *Ararat*, which provided the children in Georgetown with their first opportunity to write.

During the same period, he began working in the carpet and rug industry, in 1925 moving to Hamilton, Ontario, where he opened his first store under the name Alexanian's Oriental Rug Company. The store, which specialized in imported handknotted oriental rugs from around the world, earned a profit of only $60 in its first year.

Alexanian was an intrepid world traveller who was handy with a movie camera and went on numerous carpet-buying trips to the rug-manufacturing regions of the Middle East and India. One of his favorite pastimes was sharing the political, religious, social, and economic observations picked up during his many trips. His informal presentations were one of the most popular attractions in the social life of church groups in Hamilton. Between 1945 and 1958, his travels outside Canada covered more than three hundred thousand miles.

He was a warm and personable man but also a practical joker with a flair for the dramatic. Once on a visit to Ottawa and on the way to a costume party, he arrived at the airport dressed in Arabic garb, and convinced many around him that he actually was from Saudi Arabia. He even managed to dupe some of his close relatives.

Rarely did he turn down an opportunity. During the Depression, he was returning home from a customer visit and came across a dying lamb that likely was struck by a car. He brought it home, put it out of its misery, prepared it, and served it for dinner. He loved to cook, and always looked forward to any opportunities to practise his culinary skills, mostly away from home because the kitchen at his house was his wife Mary's domain.

Alexanian was an early member of the Kiwanis Club in Hamilton and supported the first Armenian church in Canada in St. Catharines, Ontario, and later the first Armenian church in Toronto. The Aris L. Alexanian Hall at St. Mary Armenian Church in Hamilton, Ontario was dedicated to his memory in 1986.

In his store, top-notch service was Alexanian's forté: During World War II, when quality Oriental carpets were hard to come by, he was forced to sell lower quality rugs. He kept track of all his customers and offered to replace their carpet with one of better quality following the war.

When broadloom appeared in the 1950s, Alexanian's added it to its line of products. More recently the store's selection was expanded to include vinyl, wood, laminates, and ceramics.

Alexanian remained active in the carpet business until his death at age sixty in Hamilton, when his company ran retail stores in Hamilton, Ottawa, and Kitchener, plus a rug cleaning and repair centre in Hamilton. Three of his sons became involved in the company and later a third generation became active. In 2002, Alexanian Carpet and Flooring had fourteen locations in ten cities throughout Ontario, as well as a national presence on the Internet.

Elizabeth Arden

Elizabeth Arden Inc.

"I want to keep people well and young and beautiful," Florence Nightingale Graham declared when she dropped out of school while living near Woodbridge, Ontario.

When keeping people healthy by following the path of her famous English nurse namesake didn't work, she turned her attention to keeping them beautiful. After moving to New York City and changing her name to Elizabeth Arden, the diminutive, blue-eyed Canadian became an innovator of renown in the world of beauty and one of America's wealthiest businesswomen as owner of the world-famous Elizabeth Arden cosmetics empire.

Early in life Graham made it known that celebrity status was on her radar screen. As a child growing up near Toronto in the late 1800s, Graham used to tell friends and family that her goal was to be "the richest little girl in the world."

One of five children of Susan and William Graham, she was raised on a tenant farm where she helped her father tend horses and sell produce at local markets. After a career in nursing fizzled, largely because the indignity of illness offended her, a brief working relationship with a hospital chemist who was experimenting with skin-healing creams led her to begin cooking up beautifying potions in the family kitchen.

When her father urged her to get a paying job, Graham worked as a clerk, stenographer, and dental assistant in Toronto, before moving to New York in 1908. She landed a job as a bookkeeper with the E.R. Squibb Pharmaceutical Company but soon moved to the laboratory where she spent long hours learning about skin care. Eventually, she left Squibb for a position with a beauty parlour where she learned how to gently rub creams into the sagging skin of many a wealthy New York woman. Before long clients were asking for "that nice Canadian girl." Soon after, she went into business with Elizabeth Hubbard, who had developed skin creams, tonics, and oils.

The pair opened a salon on Fifth Avenue but the partnership soured and Graham went solo. After borrowing $6,000 from her brother to pay the rent, she changed her name to Elizabeth Arden, keeping her former partner's first name and choosing Arden from Tennyson's famous poem "Enoch Arden." She also called herself Mrs. to gain respectability and came up with the idea of the brilliant red door which became the Elizabeth Arden signature.

As manager of a salon, the aggressive and confident Arden concocted a series of rouges and tinted powders that reflected her genius for shades of colour and enhanced her growing reputation with an ever-increasing number of clients, including wealthy socialites who dubbed her "the little Canadian woman with the magic hands."

Following a trip to Paris during which she met Thomas Lewis, a banker whom she would marry in 1915, Arden and a chemical company developed Venetian Cream Amoretta, her signature product. They also introduced a lotion to go with it, known as Ardena Skin Tonic. Throughout the 1920s and 1930s, Arden competed furiously with competitors such as Helena Rubenstein and Dorothy Gray by opening salons in Rome, Cannes, and Berlin, and marketing her wares worldwide. In 1944, it was reported that Arden was marketing about one thousand different products, although some accounts put the number at three hundred.

Over the years, she became known as a woman who couldn't accept criticism and railed against anyone who infringed on her right to run her own show. Her stiff backbone probably led to the failure of her first marriage after nineteen years, and the demise of her marriage to a Russian crown prince after just thirteen months.

For three decades, the little girl from Woodbridge lived on Fifth Avenue in a ten-room apartment decorated almost entirely in pink, her favourite colour. In her eighties, she continued to approve advertisements, check every new product, and visit salons unannounced.

Never one to look her age, the five-foot-two impeccably coiffed and attired Arden was on the leading edge of the cosmetics industry throughout her career. She inspired new ideas and breakthroughs such as full-service salons, exercise classes, and makeup to match skin colour. She was also an active supporter of many charities.

In 1954 she was honoured by the Canadian Women's Press Club of Toronto, and in the same year, she attended the opening ceremonies of Dalziel Pioneer Park (now Black Creek Pioneer Village) where she planted a tree on the land where she was born, lived, and played.

Arden died of a heart attack in 1966, at age eighty-two, although some observers pegged her age at eighty-four and others at eighty-nine. At the time, her company's annual sales were $60 million and the fortune she left behind was estimated at between $30 million and $40 million.

Name Dropper

In the late 1920s, Arden renewed her love of horses and began raising thoroughbreds on a farm in Lakeside, Maine. In 1946, when her stable won more races than any other in the United States, she made the cover of *Time* magazine. A year later, she became the first woman owner in history to win the Kentucky Derby with her thoroughbred Jet Pilot.

William G. Ballard

Dr. Ballard's Animal Food Products Limited

Remember that TV commercial several years ago in which an actor portraying Dr. Ballard helped a dog get healthier? Ever wonder if there really was such a person, or whether the good doctor was the figment of an ad writer's imagination?

There really was a Dr. Ballard, and he did improve the lives of many pets with his veterinary skills and the food he concocted. William George Ballard was born in Toronto and graduated as a veterinary surgeon in 1918. He practised in Grenfell, Saskatchewan for a few years before heading further west to Vancouver to set up a small animal practice.

In addition to performing surgery, Ballard researched animal dietetics. He had no specific plan to create a dog food company, but he certainly wasn't barking up the wrong tree by pursuing this interest. Many of his customers began to notice their pets were healthier than ever after they'd spent some time in Ballard's care. He had come up with a formula that stressed solid meat, and people flocked to his home to buy his food in bulk.

Ballard, his wife Mary, their three daughters, Olive, Isobel, and Emily, and son Bob worked weekends in the basement of their home, mixing, labelling, and packaging the popular pet food. The formula consisted of variations of red meat, vegetables, and cereal.

It wasn't just the food itself that proved popular; the innovative packaging helped, too. Dr. Ballard's was the first canned dog food in Canada. In 1931, Ballard set up in a small plant on Victoria Drive in Vancouver and within a year had so many orders that he decided to devote all his time to the manufacture and sale of pet food under the name Dr. Ballard's Animal Food Products Limited.

In 1933, at the height of the Depression, son Bob moved to Toronto to supervise sales and distribution there. Dr. Ballard's pet food soon grew popular in Ontario, Quebec, and the Maritimes, and by 1937 there was a manufacturing plant on Liberty Street in Toronto.

Ballard retired in 1948, and his son bought the business from him. Under Bob Ballard's direction, the company introduced flavoured pet food and thrived, although he once said in an interview that "my dad started this business and any success we have had is entirely due to his efforts." A new $500,000 plant was built on Lulu Island near Vancouver that was able to fill 240 cans a minute. The plant opening in 1950 attracted more than twenty thousand people and caused one of the worst traffic jams in area history.

Throughout his life, Ballard was also well known for the jumping horses he owned, and the many wins he had in the show ring. He purchased a former U.S. navy minesweeper in 1948 and had it retrofitted as a yacht, the *Marabell*. He was also on the board of directors at radio station CKNW and was a member of the Shaughnessy Masonic Lodge.

The company was purchased by Standard Brands (Canada) Ltd. in 1955 and despite other ownership during its long history, including Nestle Canada, the Dr. Ballard name was seen on store shelves until 2001, when Friskies, a division of Nestle, halted production. Ballard died in Vancouver in 1968 at the age of eighty-two.

Thomas Bata

Bata Shoe Organization

Thomas Bata was a young entrepreneur with a head for shoes.

Bata and his son Thomas are behind an Ontario-based company that has put footwear onto the feet of millions of people and provided jobs for thousands more.

The Bata Shoe Organization dates back to 1894 when Thomas (sometimes spelled Tomas) Bata was an apprentice in his father's shoe-making shop in the small community of Zlin in the former Austria-Hungary Empire (now the Czech Republic).

He persuaded his elder brother and sister to use $350 bequeathed by their mother to launch their own shoemaking company in Zlin, and despite a brush with bankruptcy in the first year, the business was soon thriving under Bata's leadership. Six years later it had a staff of 120.

As a youthful shoemaker, Bata's business concept was to use assembly line technology and innovative human resources in footwear manufacturing. He was driven by a desire to provide shoes to people around the world and the business goals of selling shoes where they were not available, reducing production time, and supplying stylish footwear at affordable prices.

In 1904, Bata spent six months working at a mechanized New England shoe factory. When he returned to Czechoslovakia, he introduced the assembly line to his company, and soon the firm grew so large that Zlin resembled a company town. In 1905, Bata was making twenty-two hundred pairs of shoes per day. Eventually, factories were established in Poland, Yugoslavia, Holland, Denmark, the United Kingdom, Switzerland, and the United States.

Bata's moral testament was that his business was not to be considered as simply a source of personal profit but rather as a vehicle of public trust: "We were motivated by the knowledge that our enterprise was providing an entire region with new previously unknown advantages, that its growth was contributing to the wealth and the education of the nation."

Unfortunately, Bata would not live to see his vision come to fruition in its entirety. In July 1932, he was killed in a plane crash while flying to Switzerland, leaving behind his son Thomas Jr. and his wife Marie. "Every nation has its heroes," read the eulogy at Bata's funeral. "The Czech nation's hero was a shoemaker." The company was left in the hands of his half brother Jan and was later taken over by Thomas Jr.

The Canadian connection to Bata Shoes was made in 1939, as the Nazis steamrollered their way across central Europe at a time when the company was making ten million pairs of shoes annually. Recognizing that the family empire was in danger, the young Bata, then in his mid-20s, smuggled the company's equipment to Canada where a new company town called Batawa was built near Trenton, Ontario, on land purchased from farmers.

In his book *Bata Shoemaker to the World*, Bata said he picked Canada because it was "the best of two worlds, a blend of British traditions with the progressiveness and dynamism of the United States."

From its new base 160 kilometres east of Toronto, Bata began building the empire he and his Swiss-born wife Sonja would later run for years from the company's headquarters in Don Mills, Ontario. Bata, who like his father began his working life as an apprentice, rebuilt the business by tapping into a huge global market for practical, sturdy shoes. One story says he once fired a salesman who returned from Africa with the gloomy view that the shoe market there was minimal because everyone walked around barefoot.

The company grew rapidly in the 1940s and 1950s by setting up fully integrated shoe industries, from tanneries to shoe shops, across Asia, Africa, and Latin America. Many of the factories were located in company towns in rural areas.

The company prospered despite its share of troubles, including slow times that forced the closure of the Batawa factory in 1999. In 2002, Bata had forty-eight manufacturing operations and was selling shoes out of more than forty-seven hundred company-owned retail stores employing fifty thousand people around the world. Annual sales topped $3 billion.

The Bata name is also found on the popular and world-renowned shoe museum set up in downtown Toronto by Sonja Bata.

Name Dropper

Batawa, the eastern Ontario community where Bata Shoes set up shop, is a combination of the Bata name and the last syllable of Ottawa. A buyer from the Eaton's department store chain suggested the name.

Bruce Becker

Becker's

Becker's is the name on hundreds of variety stores, but it could just as easily have been called Bazos.

Though the stores across Canada took their name from Bruce Becker, he played only a small role in establishing the company that bears his name. To understand how Becker's was formed, you first have to examine the life of Frank Bazos, a Greek immigrant who came to Toronto some eighty years ago.

According to the book *When Milk Came in Bottles* by Dave Thomas and Bob Marchant, Bazos was born in 1901 in Kerastary, a village in Greece, the eighth of nine children. He began working in Athens at age nine, and when his father died, Bazos got work as a tinsmith.

Two of his older brothers had immigrated to Chicago and then moved to Toronto where they opened up the Colonial Lunch, which later became Steeles Tavern on Yonge Street. Bazos couldn't get a passport but smuggled on board a steamship to New York City. By 1926 he had joined his brothers in Toronto, and though an adult, he attended grade school to learn English. He was soon making a living selling cigarettes and working at a macaroni factory. Bazos even spent time as a union organizer, according to one account, but gave it up after a worker shot at him with a gun.

Bazos bought Superior Ice Cream with a partner in 1932 and promptly renamed it Devon Ice Cream. The dairy business was successful for him, with his various brands being sold across Ontario. In 1955, he was bought out by food magnate Garfield Weston for about $1 million.

Around that same time, Bazos had read an article in *Reader's Digest* about an Ohio dairy, owned by Jim Lawson, that was selling milk in returnable jugs. He visited Lawson to see how the company worked, and it was there he met Bruce Becker, Lawson's son-in-law. Bazos persuaded Becker and Bob Lowe, a dairy engineer, to come to Toronto to start up a similar retail-based dairy distribution business. Bazos put up $100,000 to start it while Becker contributed $15,000.

They agreed to use Becker's name in the new enterprise because Bazos was still president of Devon Ice Cream at the time and thought using his own name might cause legal problems. Becker's started with five stores in Toronto and opened up seven days a week, no mean feat in the days when Sunday shopping was looked upon with abhorrence. They had to curtain off the canned good section of the store because the Lord's Day Act prevented most retail sales.

The firm was a success from the start. Sales reached about $800,000 in the first year, and six more stores were added the following year. But Becker didn't remain on the scene very long, according to Geoffrey Pottow, Bazos's son-in-law. One day, Becker stopped to help someone on Highway 401 near Toronto and was involved in a car accident. He suffered a multiple fracture of his leg, and while lying in hospital, he grew disenchanted with Canada. The feeling was apparently mutual at the company, and the two parted ways. Becker returned to Ohio and possibly opened his own convenience store, but no one from the company seems to have heard from him again. Even the old Lawson dairy in Ohio, which has since been renamed, has no records in its archives of Becker. Meanwhile, he left his name on a growing company in Canada, and his wife, Jean, had her name on bread products the firm sold.

By 1976, there were five hundred Becker's stores, and that number grew to more than seven hundred by the early 1990s. Bazos died in September 1994, and two years later Becker's was taken over by Silcorp Limited (formerly Silverwood Industries), which owned Mac's Milk and Mike's Milk stores. Silcorp and its stores were purchased in 1999 by Alimentation Couche-Tard, but the Becker's name remains on corner stores.

Alexander Graham Bell &
Alexander Melville Bell

Bell Canada

With the exception of Thomas Edison, there is probably no more famous inventor in the past 150 years than Alexander Graham Bell. Because his last name became synonymous with his primary invention, the telephone, the Bell name has had a familiar ring for decades.

Bell's story is generally well known. The son of Scottish immigrants who came to Canada in 1870, Bell later travelled from his home in Brantford, Ontario to Boston, Massachusetts, where he taught at a school for the deaf and experimented with his idea of how to send the human voice over a wire. He would discuss his idea at length with his father during visits to Brantford. In 1870, the U.S. Patent Office dropped a requirement that a working model accompany a patent application. Bell filed his patent application for the telephone without having such a model, and fortunately for him, completed it just a few hours before Elisha Gray, another inventor, filed his notice for the same idea. On March 10, 1876, while working in Boston, Bell uttered the famous words to his assistant "Mr. Watson, come here, I want you," that are considered to be the first ever spoken on a telephone.

Bell spent most of his life engaged in scientific research. He worked on the photoelectric cell, the iron lung, and the phonograph. In the early 1900s, he turned his attention to developing aircraft. His wife, Mabel Hubbard, who was deaf, shared his interest in science and philanthropic causes. The telephone made Bell a wealthy man, and his estate near

Alexander Graham Bell

Courtesy of the National Archives of Canada/C8355

Baddeck, Nova Scotia is one of the most popular tourist spots in the Maritimes. He died there in August 1922.

But an argument could be made that it was his father, Alexander Melville Bell, who gave his name to the Canadian phone company. In fact, he's considered to be the founder of the telephone industry in Canada. Alexander Graham Bell transferred the Canadian patent rights to his father, who then hired agents to solicit telephone rentals. It was Alexander Melville who established the first telephone networks in this country by leasing telephones in pairs.

Born in Edinburgh, Scotland in 1819, he became a professor of elocution and invented "visible speech," a written code which indicates how humans make vocal sounds. This was especially beneficial to the deaf.

It's important to remember that while the telephone today is ubiquitous and still a technological marvel, it was initially seen by many as no better a way to communicate than the telegraph. In fact, Bell Sr. tried to sell his patent rights in 1879 for $100,000, and no one bought them. Eventually National Bell of Boston bought the rights from him, and in 1880 Bell Telephone Company of Canada was incorporated. By the end of the first year, there were telephone exchanges in fourteen major cities.

Alexander Melville Bell was also a professor at Queen's University in Kingston, Ontario and moved to Washington, D.C. in 1881. He died there in 1905.

Though Bell is a famous name and company throughout North America, it generally concentrated its efforts in Canada in Ontario, Quebec, and the Eastern Arctic. As for the controversy sometimes raised about whether Canada can lay claim to being the home of the invention of the telephone, we leave it to Alexander Graham Bell himself. In a speech given in 1909 in Ottawa he said: "Of this you may be sure, the telephone was invented in Canada. It was made in the United States."

Name Dropper

Though most people say "hello" when they pick up the phone, that wasn't the word Bell would have chosen. He suggested telephone users say "ahoy" when answering a call, but the idea never caught on.

Walter and Jeanny Bick

Bick's Pickles

Walter and Jeanny Bick never intended to get into the pickle business. But when warm and humid weather in the summer of 1944 produced a glut of cucumbers, the couple was desperate to salvage tons of cukes before they rotted in their fields.

The Bicks dug out a family recipe from their native Holland and began producing dill pickles in a barn at Knollview, their 116-acre farm in the former suburb of Scarborough, now part of the Greater Toronto Area. "We got into pickles by sheer accident," said Walter.

The rest, as they say, is condiment history.

The family sold the cattle, chicken, and pigs they'd been raising since Walter's parents George and Lena Bick bought the farm in 1939 after coming to Canada from Amsterdam. Instead of selling their cucumbers to stores and markets, they turned them into pickles, said Walter, who apprenticed in the Dutch banking industry before coming to Canada at age twenty-two.

During the first few years, the Bicks packed their cucumber crop in fifty-gallon barrels of brine that were sold to restaurants, butcher shops, and army camps in the Toronto area. In 1952, they entered the retail trade when they packaged whole dills in twenty-four-ounce jars under the Bick's name, with the now-familiar cucumber in place of the letter *i* on the labels.

Soon after, the business expanded into a renovated barn on their farm and

BICK'S...THE PICK OF PICKLES

Bick's Pickles brochure.

Courtesy of Walter Bick

Canada's fastest-growing manufacturer of pickles and relishes was on its way to leadership in the Canadian pickle business.

As their business prospered, the Bicks saw many changes: Their product line expanded to include sweet mixed pickles, gherkins, cocktail onions, hot peppers, pickled beets, relishes, and sauerkraut; in 1958 their barn burnt in a fire and was replaced with a modern building. Gradually, sales of their products spread from Ontario to Western and Eastern Canada and around the world.

In 1966, with a staff that ranged between 125 in the summer and 65 in the winter, the Bicks made their biggest change when they sold their company, their farm, and their home to Robin Hood Flour Mills. Today, the company, known in Canada as Robin Hood Multifoods, operates a hundred-thousand-square-foot production facility and office on the property where the Bicks barrelled their first dills. Robin Hood also runs a Bick's plant in Dunnville, on the Niagara Peninsula.

"We sold because the company was bigger than we could handle," said Walter. "I was never a great delegator. In the beginning, I never realized we needed a sales manager, a purchasing agent but as business increased we had to hire these people ... however, the family run business way did not disappear."

The company's current owner is a wholly owned subsidiary of International Multifoods of Wayzata, Minneapolis. In addition to fifty different varieties of Bick's pickles and relishes, its consumer products lineup includes Habitant Pickles, Gattuso Olives, Woodman's Horseradish, Robin Hood Flour, Monarch Cake & Pastry Flour, and Red River Cereals.

Name Dropper

Like a cucumber on a cutting board, the Bicks' farm in the former Toronto borough of Scarborough was sliced in two when Highway 401 was built in the mid-1950s.

Henry Birks
Henry Birks & Sons

Henry Birks was a jewel of a craftsman in a long line of skilled family members.

The Birks had been making cutlery for British royalty and the upper classes since the sixteenth century, but it was Henry's business acumen in addition to his skills as a jeweller that helped build a retail empire across Canada and beyond. And no doubt, the blue boxes the company uses to package its goods are among the most recognizable containers in Canadian retail.

Birks was the son of John and Anne Birks, who immigrated to Montreal from Yorkshire, England in 1832. When Henry was born on November 30, 1840, Montreal was a city of about forty thousand people, the most prominent municipality in what is now Canada. Henry attended Montreal High School and after graduating in 1856, he went to work at Savage & Lyman, a Montreal clockmaker and jewelry firm considered to be the best in the colonies. Henry soon became a buyer,

The famous Birks blue box, a symbol of the company's reputation for quality.

Photo by Mark Kearney

travelling to Europe on behalf of the firm, and by 1868 he was store manager and partner earning about $1,000 a year. That year he married Harriet Walker, who would later bring a common-sense approach to life and a frugal attitude toward balanced budgets for the company that would bear the Birks name.

Though Henry's career at Savage & Lyman seemed secure, Canada underwent tough economic times in the 1870s, including repercussions from the collapse of the New York Stock Exchange in 1873, which caused the firm to suffer. By 1878 it was forced into liquidation, which set the stage for Birks's next and best move.

With $3,000 of his own money and $1,000 from his wife's uncle, Henry opened his own jewelry shop in March 1879 at 222 St. James St. in downtown Montreal. He had three staff: a watchmaker, a book-keeper/salesman, and a messenger boy.

At that time most businesses in Canada accepted credit and haggling between merchant and customer was the norm. But Birks decided he would take cash only and have a set price for everyone. Working out of a fifteen-by-fifty-foot space, he generated sales of $30,000 in his first year. His success continued and by 1887 he opened a jewelry factory in Montreal. His sons, William, John Henry, and Gerald, became partners in 1893 and the firm's name was changed to Henry Birks & Sons. They moved to a new office uptown on Phillips Square and as the company grew so did the area around it.

Birks's successes may be attributed to a blend of caution and foresight when it came to business. He'd take his time weighing certain moves, but once he'd made up his mind he acted quickly. He was generous in giving his sons increasing responsibility and stood aside when it came time to turn the business over to them.

Henry and Harriet didn't put on airs once they started making money, but saved their pennies and put earnings back into the business. Their life was centered around the store, their family, and the Presbyterian church. Henry, in fact, taught Sunday school for more than twenty years.

By the late 1890s, he was enjoying life. His staff referred to him as "the old gentleman" and he delighted in walking around the store aisles, dressed in formal attire, greeting customers. At about this time, the company began specializing in silver, a move that would make it famous across the country. By 1904, Birks & Sons had more than two hundred employees.

His sons, especially William, were keen to expand, and although Henry disagreed, Birks opened its first store outside of Montreal in Ottawa in 1901. According to a history of the company, *The First Century* by Kenneth MacLeod, Henry felt they were "making all the money that is good for us." But the sons' dreams of expansion won out, and through a series of acquisitions and growth, Birks spread across Canada and even opened an office in England.

Birks & Sons was a thriving enterprise in the late 1920s when Henry became ill in Florida and was brought back to Montreal General Hospital. He died on April 16, 1928. His son William continued to bring innovation to the firm, which continued to prosper in the twentieth century, particularly under William's son Henry, who oversaw the firm from the 1940s to the 1970s. Though the company went through turbulent times in the 1990s, the name Birks continues to be associated with the words "high quality" to this day.

Name Dropper

The Schenley Award, presented annually to outstanding players in the Canadian Football League, was made by Birks. Craftsmen worked more than 250 hours to create the sterling silver trophy. They have also created trophies for curling, the Calgary Stampede, and the Ontario Jockey Club over the years.

Eddie Black

Black Photo Corporation

Black's is Radio.

It doesn't quite roll off the tongue the same way "Black's is Photography" does, but if things had gone differently for Eddie Black, that's the slogan we might all know.

Edward Frederick Black, the son of a Toronto grocery merchant, was always keen on new ideas and fads. When radio was still relatively new, Black joined forces with a Kentucky entrepreneur to work at the Toronto Radio Company. He decided to set up shop himself in 1930, borrowed $500 from his father, and leased a store at 1440 Yonge St. This first Eddie Black's store sold radios and major appliances, but because of the Depression, business was difficult at first.

According to company history, Black got the idea of including cameras in his retail mix when King George and Queen Elizabeth visited the city as part of their 1939 Royal Tour. Black said of this event that "everyone all of a sudden became photographic conscious. We added a few cameras to a showcase in the store."

It was a good decision. Black also brought in movie cameras, and according to his son, Bob, had friends in the film business and was able to show feature movies at his house sometimes before the public got

to see them. He remembers a showing of *King Kong* at his sister's birthday party one year.

Retail suffered during World War II, and Black had to work at the Wartime Prices and Trade Board to earn enough to support his family. Son Bob recalls that within his first week of work

Eddie Black

Courtesy of Black Photo Corporation

there, the flamboyant Eddie asked if he could have the next week off to go duck hunting.

Black enjoyed hunting and fishing, and wasn't really a camera buff, says Bob. "Photography was just another part of his life." Bob and brother Bill, who joined the company at the end of the war, had more enthusiasm for cameras and began devoting more space for them and other products such as movie projectors. Bob admits "working with your father isn't the easiest thing," but in 1948, they opened up an Eddie Black's store in a nearby location that sold only photographic equipment, while Black continued to sell appliances and sporting goods in his shop.

Canadians became more interested in photography in the 1950s as colour became more commonplace and good quality Japanese equipment appeared on the market. In 1955, Black's expanded to four camera stores. The same couldn't be said for appliances by the late 1950s, however, as the market was flooded by several retailers. Black saw the writing on the wall and switched over to photography exclusively by the end of the decade.

Bob, who with Bill took over the business from Eddie in 1961, recalls his father's gregarious nature and enthusiasm for life. Black had a farm in Caledon East, north of Toronto, that seemed to be always filled with guests. He describes his father as "a big, handsome guy who loved to party" and enjoyed the company of others. Though the sons (two others, Barry and Bruce, also joined the firm) were in charge by the 1960s, Black still had an office in the main store and was consulted on major company decisions.

Black's began to thrive in the 1960s, partly because of the boom in photography and the brothers' business acumen of ploughing profits back into the business. While Eddie was a go-getter, the four brothers "were super conservative" when it came to running the company, Bob told us from his winter home in Florida. By 1966, there were sixteen Black's stores, and they had branched into colour processing.

The four brothers had "a phenomenal relationship" with their staff, everyone was on a first name basis, and employees benefited from profit-sharing plans, Bob recalls. Eddie Black died in August 1971, but the family ran the business until 1985, when it was purchased by George Gardiner, then chairman of Scott's Hospitality. When the four brothers retired in 1988, there were more than two hundred Black's stores across Canada. Fuji Photo Canada Inc. bought the firm in 1993, and the Black's name continues to be a familiar one throughout the country.

Name Dropper

"Black's is photography" is one of the best-known slogans in Canada. Bob Black says he got the idea while reading a brochure about Nikon cameras. There was a sentence that said Nikon is photography. "I thought, we can say that better than they can because we have all aspects of photography. It fitted us better than it did them." He has since been told by Kodak officials how much they wish they had that slogan for their company.

Mark Blumes

Mark's Work Wearhouse

After being fired by the Bay in the mid-1970s, Mark Blumes combined his love of business with $27,000 in severance pay to create one of Canada's best-known clothing companies. But the "larger than life, cigar smoking persona," as Blumes was once called, no longer pays much attention to the multi-million-dollar firm that still bears his name

Blumes parted ways with Mark's Work Wearhouse in 1995 when he wanted to take the company in a different direction from what the board of directors had in mind. "I was very wounded" by that, he said in an interview from Calgary in 2002 as he recalled some highlights from his Mark's Work Wearhouse days.

Blumes, who grew up in Calgary, was interested in business "from the time I was a wee snapper." This son of a doctor got a part-time job in high school selling furniture and discovered he was good at it. As a young man, he went to Winnipeg to take part in the Bay's management training program. He got there too late to start that year's program and in the meantime sold men's clothing. "That's how I got into apparel. I can still look at a man and tell him what size suit he needs."

Though Mark Blumes has long since left the company, Mark's Work Wearhouse stores are still a familiar part of Canada's retail landscape.

Photo by Mark Kearney

Blumes worked at the Bay for thirteen years, ultimately heading the men's fashion division for the Calgary store. However, during his last years there he was in dire need of a corneal transplant and ended up missing several months of work while hospitalized. When he returned, he discovered the store had "a boatload of inventory" that needed to be sold, and he disagreed with the boss on how it should be handled. He sent a letter to management, and then decided to share his thoughts with others in the company. About two years later he was fired for what he calls insubordination.

But before he was fired, Blumes was devising a plan to sell work clothes. He believed there was a niche in that market because department stores had narrow selection and few clothes that could meet workers' needs. He hatched the idea for his own business while trying to find good parkas for men heading to work on oil rigs.

His first store in Calgary was simply called Work Wearhouse, and he had no intention of putting his name on it until the company expanded to Ontario. There was another corporation already there with a similar name so lawyers suggested he put "Mark's" in front of it. "I hated it, but I went along with it reluctantly," he says. "The company's bigger than one person."

Regardless of his feelings, Mark's Work Wearhouse thrived and in just over two years Blumes had more than thirty stores and was ready to take the firm public. That period was one of his highlights in the business. "Getting a certified cheque made out to me personally for $1 million when we went public was kind of neat."

Mark's Work Wearhouse stores became familiar sights across Canada over the next decade or so, with brand names such as WindRiver and Denver Hayes proving to be popular sellers. But Blumes didn't like the way the company was developing, and was ousted in 1995. As part of the agreement, he wasn't allowed to work in the apparel business for the three years following. Blumes, who says "mostly I find my pleasure at looking at various business opportunities," has since started up two companies, both of which didn't succeed.

His latest venture, however, which sees him developing new products and brands from coffee shop franchises to the wedding business, is starting to gel, he says. Despite bad eyesight, Blumes still likes to golf occasionally and watch hockey in his spare time. He laments the direction his old company has gone, moving somewhat away from its work clothes roots, but Blumes says he doesn't think about the firm much these days.

Mark's Work Wearhouse has grown into some three hundred stores across Canada, posts steady profits, and carries a range of clothing for both men and women. In December 2001, Canadian Tire announced it was buying the firm for $114 million.

Joseph-Armand Bombardier
Bombardier Inc.

As a young lad of fourteen, Joseph-Armand Bombardier had a decision to make: Would he forge ahead with his religious studies and become a priest, or pursue his passionate interest in mechanics?

People whose world is covered with snow most of the time should be glad Bombardier chose mechanics.

In 1922, the boy who for years had amazed his family and friends by building toy tractors and locomotives out of old clocks, sewing machines, motors, and cigar boxes built his first snowmobile.

The prototype, tested with his brother Leopold, consisted of a four-passenger sleigh frame supporting a rear-mounted Model T engine with a spinning wooden propeller sticking out the back. As dogs barked and onlookers demanded they shut it down, the noisy and extremely dangerous contraption made its way along the streets of Valcourt in Quebec's Eastern Townships, where Bombardier had been born on April 16, 1907.

He was only fifteen, but Armand had begun his lifelong infatuation with the concept of a vehicle that would travel on snow and offer relief for country folks isolated during Quebec's harsh and snowy winters.

Two years later Bombardier dropped out of the St. Charles Baromée seminary in Sherbrooke, Quebec, and started working on engines, eventually moving to Montreal where he registered for evening courses in mechanics and electricity. He soon landed a job in a large auto repair garage as a first-class mechanic.

Joseph-Armand Bombardier

Courtesy of Musée J.-Armand Bombardier

In 1926, with a wealth of theoretical and practical training under his belt, the nineteen-year-old Bombardier returned to the Valcourt area, where he opened Garage Bombardier. He was a dealer for Imperial Oil and fixed cars, as well as threshers, ice saws, and pumps. His reputation as a mechanic who could diagnose and resolve most mechanical problems quickly helped the business flourish, so much so that he hired several friends and family members to help out.

His strength was his inventiveness: He built equipment with his own hands, once forging a drill and hydraulic press for producing steel and cast iron cylinders, gas tanks, and heaters. He also built his own dam and turbine to harness energy for his own use, long before the town of Valcourt introduced electricity.

After marrying Yvonne in 1929, Bombardier turned to the development of a motorized snow vehicle to replace the horse-drawn sled, which was a slow and inefficient mode of winter travel when snow made roads impassable in Quebec. For years, he wrestled with three key challenges — even distribution of the vehicle's weight to keep it level on snow, a safe and reliable propulsion engine, and suspension that would afford passengers a comfortable ride.

A tragedy in his own family played a role in the invention of his first commercial product. In January 1934, his two-year-old son Yvon needed immediate hospital treatment for appendicitis and peritonitis. But with roads snowed in, there was no way he could get the boy to the nearest hospital, fifty kilometres away in Sherbrooke, Quebec. His son's death made Armand all the more determined to create a snow machine that would help Quebeckers avoid similar tragedies.

Two years later Bombardier invented the B7, which stood for Bombardier and the seven passengers it could carry. With its lightweight plywood cabin, many said it resembled a futuristic tank on skis. He received a patent in June 1937 for his invention of a sprocket device that made the vehicle travel over snow, and production began under the business name L'Auto-Neige Bombardier Limitée.

The B7 sold for slightly more than $1,000, "about the same price as low-end automobiles of the time," writes Larry MacDonald in his book *The Bombardier Story*.

During World War II, a variety of models were built and the company erected new factories and added staff. After the war, production soared to one thousand units a year. In 1947–48, multiple-passenger vehicles were the company's mainstay and had boosted sales to $2.3 million when two events hit the company hard: The winter of that year was virtually snowless in Quebec, and the provincial government committed to keep all major roads clear of snow every winter. As a result, L'Auto-Neige Bombardier's sales dropped by 40 percent to $1.4 million in 1948–49.

These events convinced Bombardier of the need for smaller snowmobiles for people who travelled alone, such as doctors, trappers, and prospectors. He began working on prototypes and meanwhile, the company diversified into all-terrain vehicles for the mining, oil, and forestry industries, eventually developing the Muskeg Tractor, which was unveiled in 1953 to transport supplies over snow and swamps.

Bombardier's greatest breakthrough came in 1959, when after a long struggle to overcome financing issues and design problems, the company unveiled a small, lightweight snowmobile powered by a reliable two-cycle engine and utilizing a seamless, wide caterpillar track invented by his eldest son Germain. It was an instant hit.

In the February 1963 issue of *Imperial Oil Review* the machine was described as a "kind of scooter mounted on toy tracks and which growls like a runaway dishwasher." Bombardier's invention opened up communities across northern Canada in winter and introduced Canadians to a new winter sport — snowmobiling.

Bombardier died of cancer on February 18, 1964 at the age of fifty-six, but not before being granted more than forty patents and developing a robust business with sales of $10 million. Today, many of his inventions can be seen in the J.-Armand Bombardier Museum in Valcourt, Quebec.

Following his death, the company — now known as Bombardier Inc. — diversified further to become Canada's most important transportation conglomerate under the guidance of Germain Bombardier, and later Laurent Beaudoin, Joseph-Armand Bombardier's son-in-law. By the 1990s, more than two million snowmobiles had been sold and the Montreal-based company was also producing the Sea-Doo recreational watercraft, boats, and all-terrain vehicles. The firm had worldwide manufacturing interests in airplanes, trains, military vehicles, and public transportation systems. Its sales in 2001 were more than $16 billion.

Name Dropper

Bombardier's first snowmobile was called the Ski-Dog but when the literature was printed, a typographical error changed the name to Ski-Doo and the name stuck.

Benjamin and Charlotte Bowring

Bowring Canada

Watch- and clockmaker Benjamin Bowring was full of hope and enthusiasm when he set up shop in the booming frontier port of St. John's,
Newfoundland in 1811. But a year later he abandoned his enterprise.

Happily for the native of Exeter, England, his business closed because
of the success of a dry goods outlet operated next door by his wife,
Charlotte. Instead of working on timepieces, Bowring decided to help her
develop a retail and importing business that dealt in soaps, fabrics, china,
and a host of other goods the townspeople had taken a shine to.

For Bowring, who was in his 30s at the time, the decision to focus
on a single enterprise proved to be astute. With the community's retail
trade thriving, the shop evolved into a prosperous family-operated general department store business. Nearly two centuries later, Bowring is a
successful chain of upscale gift stores with more than sixty locations
across Canada. The company also runs a smaller chain of home furnishings outlets.

Despite uncertain economic conditions in St. John's in the early
1800s, Bowring managed to establish the company because of his family's business connections in England, which came in handy when he
bought dry goods and manufactured goods. He was also known as an
adventurous merchant who was willing to take risks. He and his wife
were helped by their five sons who were employed in the business; over
the years, five generations of Bowrings built the enterprise into a vast
global empire.

In 1823, Benjamin purchased two schooners to transport goods from
England, and over the next half-century the company acquired a fleet of
ships that travelled around the globe. After rebuilding following a fire in
1833, Bowring gave control of the firm to his son Charles and returned
to England with the rest of his family to set up a trading company.

From 1885 to 1940, Bowring family companies were known for
their oil tankers, cargo fleet, Red Cross trans-Atlantic passenger line,
marine insurance, coastal mail service down the east coast of North
America, seal fishing, and shipping dried salt cod fish to Europe and
South America.

After Benjamin died in Liverpool, England on June 1, 1846, the company expanded its insurance business and obtained substantial interests in metals, coffee, fertilizers, foodstuffs, petroleum products, chemicals, and many other commodities.

Two world wars wiped out a large share of the Bowring shipping fleet, and following World War II the main activity of the Newfoundland company was retailing. The business operated its landmark department store on Water Street in St John's, which was later expanded into a chain of smaller shops that became the basis for the current national chain of Bowring stores in Canada.

In 1984, the original Canadian arm of the global company was sold to outside interests. Though no longer connected to the founding family, Bowring remains a privately held, family owned and operated Canadian company. Its product line includes tableware, crystal and glass stemware, table linens, vases, patio accessories, lighting, garden accessories, soaps, bathroom accessories, decorative accents, furniture, music CDs and cassette tapes, and art.

Name Dropper

The company logo is the *Terra Nova*, a Bowring ship chartered by the British Navy for Admiral Robert Scott's famous journey to the Antarctic in 1911.

Jim Brickman

Brick Brewing Co. Ltd.

Though he grew up and still lives in the heart of Canada's Oktoberfest, it was Europe that inspired Jim Brickman to form his own brewery.

Brickman, whose nickname is "Brick," was born and raised in Waterloo, Ontario but went to school in Switzerland. While living in the shadow of the Alps, "my tastebud profile started leaning towards something with more character to it," he said in an interview. Though his initial career was in marketing and advertising, Brickman dreamed of having his own brewery.

Brickman liked Canadian beers, but found that imports here didn't have the same taste and freshness he remembered from his days touring Europe. Around 1980, at a time when microbreweries in Canada were virtually unheard of, Brickman began pouring the foundation for his dream. He visited sixty-eight breweries in twenty-nine countries to get a sense of what he wanted to brew and the size of brewery that would best fit the market. While it sounds glamorous, starting a microbrewery from scratch and securing funding wasn't easy. "It was excruciating to get this thing off the ground," Brickman says.

Eventually he settled on a combination of two beers, one from Germany and one from Czechoslovakia, and launched Brick Premium Lager in December 1984. He had no intention of naming the beer or brewery after himself: "I had to be convinced of that." Brickman wanted a local name such as Waterloo or K-W (Kitchener-Waterloo), but while using focus groups to help pick a name, someone suggested testing out his nickname. That's the one respondents liked the best.

Brick Premium Lager was an immediate success, indicating that there was a strong market for a different-tasting beer. Brickman spent most of his time in those early days just trying to meet demand and didn't really do any serious marketing for about five years. In its first year, Brick Brewery sold about thirty-five thousand cases, while these days it sells about 1.5 million, almost exclusively in southern Ontario.

The brewery has won about thirty gold medals for its beers, which include Red Baron and Waterloo Dark. And in a nod to nostalgia, the brewery announced in spring 2002 that it would start selling its Red

Cap Ale in the old stubby beer bottles that were popular from the 1960s to the 1980s. Although the company now competes with several microbreweries, there is still a lot of room to grow.

"Beer drinkers are more sophisticated than they've ever been, and they're more apt to experiment. That's the exciting thing."

William Knapp Buckley

W.K. Buckley Ltd.

For nearly sixty years, William Buckley earned a living by leaving a bad
taste in his customers' mouths.

After moving to Toronto in the summer of 1914, the native of
Wallace, Nova Scotia graduated from the Ontario College of Pharmacy
in 1915 and landed a job as a pharmacist at the T. Eaton Company's
downtown Toronto store. In 1918, he bought his own drugstore, and
when a worldwide flu epidemic broke out, "Doc," as he was nicknamed,
developed a medicine that suppressed the coughs of his clientele.

The syrup, known as Buckley's Mixture, was mixed in a butter
churn and sold for seventy-five cents a bottle. Its ingredients, including ammonium carbonate, menthol, oil of pine, and extract of Irish
moss, tasted awful. But it worked, and Buckley sold two thousand bottles in the first year. In his words, the mixture tasted "brisk."

Frank Buckley (left) and William Knapp Buckley (right).

Seeing tremendous potential, Buckley in 1920 founded W.K. Buckley Ltd., and converted a nearby house into a manufacturing facility where he made larger quantities of his cough medicine. In 1935, he sold his drug store to concentrate on the production and marketing of Buckley's Mixture.

In the 1930s and 1940s, his elixir was found in medicine cabinets in the United States, the Caribbean, New Zealand, Australia, and Holland. Along the way, Buckley, who had developed a reputation as a born salesman, also developed other products, including Buckley's White Rub and Jack and Jill children's cough syrup.

After Buckley died in January 1978, his son Frank assumed the presidency and became the spokesman in Buckley's "bad taste" ad campaign, which helped increase the company's market share in the cough and cold category by more than 10 percent. In radio, television, and print ads, Frank Buckley declared: "It tastes awful. And it works." In other advertisements, he quipped: "I came by my bad taste honestly; I inherited it from my father."

In 1920, the cough syrup people loved to hate rang up $40,000 worth of sales. These days, the privately owned Mississauga, Ontario company sells more than six million bottles of Buckley's Mixture annually and its entire product line reaps sales of more than $15 million a year.

Frank Buckley is often asked why he doesn't improve the taste of the mixture invented by his father. "We can't get rid of the taste," he replies. "If we do, we will be just another 'me too' cough medicine."

Name Dropper

Thanks to his interest in thoroughbreds, William Buckley developed Buckley's Zev, a remedy for respiratory ailments in horses. Named after an early winner of the Kentucky Derby, Zev is found in most Canadian racing stables.

Carlo Onerato Catelli

Catelli's

Pasta lovers in Canada should pause between bites to thank Carlo Onerato Catelli for making the dish popular in this country.

Born in February 1849 in Vedano, Italy, Catelli was the third son of Martino and Maria Catelli. As a young man still in school, Catelli came to Canada in 1866 and one year later, during the birth of this country in 1867, he started The Catelli Macaroni Company in a rundown Montreal warehouse. It was the first of its kind in Canada.

Many Italians had been immigrating to North America around this time, and Catelli got into the business to meet the demand for macaroni. Like many entrepreneurs, however, his business had humble beginnings. He only needed about three bags of flour a day to satisfy his customers' palates.

But the business began to grow and prosper, and Catelli soon became a well-known figure in Montreal business circles. He married Angelina Armand in 1879, and by the end of the nineteenth century was an acknowledged and respected leader of the Italian-Canadian community in Montreal and beyond.

Catelli was a founder of the Chamber of Commerce in Montreal and was its president from 1906 to 1908. He was also created a chevalier of the Crown of Italy in 1904 for his work in building Italian-Canadian relations. Once described as "a respectable gentleman who has achieved commercial success," Catelli was chosen the Honorary Canadian Representative to the International Exposition in Milan in 1906.

He retired from the business in 1910, but continued to be a key figure in the city. At the outbreak of World War I, the firm was controlled by Tancredi Bienvenu, and by World War II, the company not only dominated the pasta and tomato paste market in Canada but had a tremendous presence in Britain, too. In fact, after World War II, Catelli and other companies were exporting macaroni to Italy!

During his life, Catelli also helped found an orphanage in the city. The prosperous pasta pioneer died on October 3, 1937 at his home in Montreal on City Hall Avenue and was survived by a son, Leon, and a daughter, Marguerite. He was an important enough business figure beyond Canada to have received a brief obituary in the *New York Times.*

In the mid-1950s the company, now named Catelli-Habitant, became a subsidiary of Ogilvie Flour Mills Company Limited, Canada's largest flour-milling company. In 1968, Catelli-Habitant became a subsidiary of John Labatt Limited, and four years later, the famous sunshine/rainbow Catelli logo was created. The firm continued to expand in the 1980s and employed more than twelve hundred people throughout Canada and the northeastern United States, creating such products as pasta, pickles, sauces, soups, puddings, jams, and flour. In June 1989, Borden Inc., an American multi-food manufacturer, purchased Catelli, and two years later spent $20 million to renovate the Montreal plant and double its production capacity.

Jack and Carl Cole
Coles The Book People

If a maverick is defined as an unorthodox or independent-minded person, then Jack Cole probably fit that definition better than anyone in the bookstore business.

He and his older brother Carl not only created one of the most renowned bookstore chains in the country, they did it with a style that often rattled their fellow entrepreneurs as well as some in the publishing business.

Carl and Jack, whose real last name was Colofsky, were both born in Detroit, where their father, a Russian cabinetmaker, had moved. They later moved to Toronto and had difficult and poor childhoods. When Carl was twenty-two and Jack was fifteen, they opened their first bookstore in Toronto in 1935, not for any real love of books but because they saw a good opportunity, Jack's son David told us in an interview. The Book Exchange near the corner of Bloor and Spadina was a second hand bookstore that helped Carl pay his way through university. They changed the store's name to Coles in 1938.

Their second bookstore opened in 1939 at the corner of Yonge and Charles streets, and it did well enough that in 1956 the brothers opened

Jack Cole

Courtesy of David Cole

another store at Yonge and Dundas streets. Other stores in the Toronto area followed before the company expanded first to Richmond Hill and then to St. Catharines. The stores were not typical of what existed in Canada at the time. They had bright lights, lots of signs, specials, and remainder bins full of books at incredibly low prices.

According to David Cole,

Jack was the one who ran the business while Carl handled the financing. "My dad was a real innovator," he says. "My dad was fond of books, but was he a book lover? No. He was a retailer."

That might explain why Coles also sold sporting goods in the 1950s and 1960s in the same stores that carried books. That's why Coles stores of all places were the first in Canada to sell the Hula Hoop, the Slinky, and the Mechano set, according to David. The brothers, however, abandoned sporting goods by the late 1960s.

Jack Cole was often at odds with publishers because he didn't think they catered to public tastes and raised their ire by trying such marketing stunts as selling books by the pound. He was once described as "a schlock merchant, a hard-nosed hustler in a genteel world."

Cole also didn't endear himself to teachers with the introduction of Coles Notes in 1948. To the delight of many Canadian students and later those in more than seventy countries, Coles Notes offered a quick reference guide to a variety of subjects from English literature to math and chemistry. He sold the American rights to the guides, where they became the popular Cliff's Notes found south of the border.

Coles also opened stores in the United States in the early 1970s, but they proved unsuccessful and the idea was later abandoned. On June 7, 1972, Coles was the first bookseller to go public, but Jack and Carl still retained control of the company, which by now had more than two hundred stores. They sold their interest to Southam Inc. in 1978 for $34 million. Shortly thereafter, in 1980, the company opened one of the original book superstores, the 67,000-square-foot World's Biggest Bookstore, in downtown Toronto.

"They were proud of what they built," David says. "My father was always a step ahead when it came to merchandising."

David remembers Jack as a great family man who coached hockey and took his children fishing. He was an avid stamp collector and doted on his sixteen grandchildren until his death in January 1997. Carl Cole, who tended to shun the limelight, had died in 1994.

In 1994, Southam sold Coles to Pathfinder Capital and in April 1995, Coles and SmithBooks merged to form Chapters Inc. About six years later, Chapters had merged with Indigo Books to dominate the bookstore industry in Canada. Larry Stevenson, former CEO of Chapters, once said Jack Cole "was a guy who was always willing to try innovative things and often go against the grain."

Name Dropper

The first Coles Notes written in 1948 was for the French novella *Colomba* by Prosper Mérimée. The notes for *Merchant of Venice* followed shortly thereafter.

Samuel Cunard

Cunard Line Ltd.

By the time Samuel Cunard died in London at age seventy-eight, he had transformed the way ships navigated the world's oceans.

The Halifax-born son of a master carpenter and timber merchant, Cunard created a shipping line that operated the finest passenger liners in the world and dominated Atlantic shipping in the nineteenth century. Among its ships were the *Lusitania* and the *Queen Elizabeth.*

The hallmarks of the company were safety over profits, the best ships, officers and crew, and a handful of shipping innovations that contributed to the improvement of international navigation.

As a youngster, Cunard demonstrated remarkable business acumen. At age seventeen, he began managing his own general store and after joining his father in the timber business, he gradually expanded the family interests into coal, iron, shipping, and whaling. A. Cunard and Son opened for business in July 1813, and a year later its ships were carrying mail between Newfoundland, Bermuda, and Boston. Soon, the fleet numbered forty ships.

Early in his career, Samuel Cunard recognized the economic disadvantages of ships entirely dependent on wind. He dreamed of a

steam-powered "ocean railway" with passengers and cargo arriving by ship as punctually and as regularly as by train.

Although his idea was greeted with scorn, in 1833, the *Royal William* became the first ship to cross the Atlantic Ocean entirely by steam. Cunard was one of the vessel's principal shareholders.

Samuel Cunard

In 1839 Cunard won a contract to undertake regular mail service by steamship from Liverpool to Halifax, Quebec City, and Boston. With associates in Glasgow and Liverpool, he established the British and North American Royal Mail Steam Packet Company, the direct ancestor of the Cunard Line. Four steamships were built, and in July 1840, paddle steamer *Britannia* crossed the Atlantic from Liverpool to Halifax, and steamed on to Boston in fourteen days and eight hours, a feat that would lead to the decline and eventual disappearance of transatlantic commercial sailing ships.

In addition to an unparalleled safety record, Cunard's company was on the leading edge of shipping innovation, initiating the system of sailing with green lights to starboard, red to port, and white on the masthead, which became the standard for the entire maritime world. Its ships were also the first to enjoy the marvels of electric lights and wireless.

Cunard's enlightened views as an employer were far ahead of his time. It was always his view that if he picked employees well, paid them well, and treated them well, they would return the favour with loyalty and pride — and they did.

In 1859, Cunard was honoured by Queen Victoria with a knighthood. He died in 1865. The Cunard group became a public company in 1878, adopting the name Cunard Steamship Limited, and eventually absorbed Canadian Northern Steamships Limited and its principal competitor, the White Star Line.

The company is now known as the Cunard Line and is operated by Miami-based Cunard Line Limited. Its flagship is the luxury cruise ship *Queen Elizabeth 2*, which the company touts as "the world's most famous ship and the greatest liner of her time."

Name Dropper

Not a single life was lost on a Cunard ship in the first sixty-five years of the company's history until May 7, 1915, when a German submarine torpedoed the *Lusitania*, killing twelve hundred people. The disaster occurred fifty years after Cunard's death. Writer Mark Twain once remarked that "he felt himself rather safer on board a Cunard steamer than he did upon land."

Charles H. Doerr

Dare Foods

In 1892, Charles Doerr sold everything from soup to nuts at his grocery store in Berlin, Ontario (now Kitchener). But after meeting Ted Egan, a baker from nearby Guelph, Doerr and his associate focussed on making biscuits and candies.

With the opening of C.H. Doerr and Company, the seeds were sown for what would become Dare Foods, a Canadian company with a worldwide reputation for innovation and quality.

Egan eventually left the company and Doerr worked tirelessly to take advantage of the expanding Canadian market from the turn of the century until World War I. Numerous expansions enlarged the original store on the corner of Weber and Breithaupt streets.

In the early years, Doerr did everything but bake the products. Because there were no supermarket chains or centralized buying groups, biscuits and candies were sold in bulk to individual neighbourhood stores, each visited personally by Doerr. Twice a year he embarked on sales trips to allow local grocers to sample his products.

Popular items were traditional English drop cookies and stamped biscuits; sugar, molasses, and shortbread cookies; and soda crackers.

Customers also loved Doerr's individually hand-stencilled sandwich creams and his marshmallow cookies. The company's candy line included humbugs, toffees, gum drops, and seasonal specialties such as chocolate-coated marshmallow Easter eggs and Christmas cut rock candy. Many were handmade.

Charles H. Doerr

Courtesy of Dare Foods

Dare truck, circa 1955

Courtesy of Dare Foods

As word of Doerr quality spread, salespersons were hired and sales multiplied across Ontario. Soon, major national retail chains such as Woolworth and Kresge were distributing Doerr products across Canada. In 1919, the company landed a major contract with Hamblin Metcalf (later Smiles and Chuckles) to produce chocolate candies for export to England, added forty thousand square feet of space, and soon after bought modern chocolate-making equipment.

During his life, Doerr was known as responsible and sensible with few extravagances, other than ownership of two cars. He was cheerful and had a pleasant personality and lots of friends, many of whom were also businessmen. He was a commissioner of the Kitchener Public Utilities Commission for seventeen years, liked dancing, and was generous to his nine siblings, employing a number of them in his business and supporting the distant ones with annual gifts of money.

Doerr had three wives. The first died at age fifty-eight; he then married a long-time family friend who passed away two years later.

Doerr's third wife worked for him in the company office and lived for many years after his death.

The period 1920 to 1945 was among the company's toughest. The Great Depression caused sales to stagnate; in June 1941, Doerr died at age seventy-two, leaving his firm to his twenty-four-year-old grandson Carl, who had been raised by Doerr and his wife Susannah after his parents died in the great influenza epidemic. In February 1943, Carl watched helplessly as fire destroyed the company factory in the largest blaze in Kitchener's history.

Using facilities at the Howe Candy Company in Hamilton, Ontario, which had been acquired prior to the fire, Carl Doerr was able to continue production and finance a new plant on Kitchener's southern outskirts.

In 1945, the company and family names were legally changed to Dare because it was easier to pronounce and was an approximate equal of Doerr in sound.

Since then, the company has been responsible for several innovations in the biscuit and cookie industry, including cellophane packaging; assorted cookie packs, which contain several Dare favourites in the same package; and cookie bags sealed with a wire tie, which enables customers to reseal the bag to retain freshness. Such bags became the standard for biscuit packaging.

Also unique was the way Dare salespersons were trained to be merchandisers. To help retailers improve sales, they regularly arranged Dare products on store shelves and set up in-store product displays, the first in the industry to take such a hands-on approach.

In 1982, Dare introduced its Breton line of crackers; in 2001, the company completed an acquisition which added Wagon Wheels, Viva Puffs cookies, Grissol Melba Toast, Whippet chocolate-coated mallow cookies, and Loney dried soups and boullion to its lineup.

Today, the company that Charles Doerr founded is run by fourth generation members of the Dare family, led by president Carl Dare and his sons Graham, executive vice-president, and Bryan, senior vice-president. It operates bakeries in Kitchener, Ontario; Montreal, St-Lambert, and Ste-Martine, Quebec; Denver, Colorado; and Spartanburg, South Carolina, and candy factories in Toronto and Milton, Ontario. Its products are sold in more than twenty-five countries.

Name Dropper

In the tough Depression years, newly hired sixteen-year-old workers at Dare's Kitchener factory were paid seventeen cents an hour. At the time, Ontario's minimum wage for adults was twenty-two cents an hour.

William Mellis Christie

Christie, Brown & Company

Mr. Christie, the man who has filled millions of tummies with cookies, crackers, and snacks, is a Canadian who changed the course of the baking industry in North America. In 1848, at age nineteen, William Mellis Christie came to Canada from Huntley, Aberdeenshire, Scotland where he had apprenticed as a baker. He soon formed a partnership with James Mathers and Alexander Brown, working as an assistant baker and travelling salesman. When Mathers retired in 1850, Brown took Christie into the partnership, and twenty-eight years later, Christie became the sole owner of Christie, Brown & Company.

Around that time, Christie attended the Philadelphia Centennial Exhibition with samples of his biscuits and returned with silver and bronze medals. He became known throughout Canada for his high quality biscuits that today are found in kitchen pantries from St. John's to Victoria. In 1900, Christie died of cancer in Toronto and his son Robert took over the business, which at the time employed 375 people and had offices in Montreal and Toronto. In 1928, Christie, Brown & Company was sold to the National Biscuit Company (Nabisco) of the U.S. and has been in American hands ever since.

The company William Mellis Christie founded is now owned by Kraft Foods North America. It operates five biscuit bakeries in Toronto and Montreal, producing such well-known products as OREO and Chips Ahoy! Cookies, Premium Plus and Ritz crackers, PEEK FREANS and DAD'S Biscuits and David Strawberry Tarts.

Herbert Henry Dow

Dow Chemical Company

The connection may be tenuous, but Canadians can claim the founder of the world-famous Dow Chemical Company as one of their own.

Herbert Henry Dow wouldn't remember his early life here, but he was born in a brick house at Dundas and Pinnacle streets in Belleville, Ontario on February 26, 1866, the son of Joseph and Sarah Jane Dow. His father had been living in the eastern Ontario town since 1863, trying to drum up business for Irwin & White, a sewing machine company.

Just six weeks after Herbert was born, Joseph moved his family to Derby, Connecticut in an effort to find new customers for his company. Unfortunately, the sewing machine enterprise folded soon after.

Joseph had been a born tinkerer, and as a young boy Herbert picked up these skills working alongside his dad trying to solve mechanical problems. Young Herbert invented an incubator for chicken eggs at age twelve and later helped his father develop a steam engine that the U.S. Navy used for many years for torpedo propulsion. The Dows would eventually settle in Cleveland, and it was at the

Case School of Applied Science that Herbert Dow would graduate with a science degree in 1888. His interest in chemistry, being taught by some of the great minds of the time, and the ability to tinker and invent new products would help launch the successful company that bears his name.

Herbert Henry Dow, 1897

Courtesy of Post Street Archives

Herbert Henry Dow

As a young man, Dow had fallen in love with a schoolteacher named Mabelle Ross, but whether the chemistry wasn't right or she seemed unwilling to move to Midland, Michigan, where Dow was working, he married another teacher, Grace Anna Ball, instead.

Dow is considered by many to be one of the great inventors of the late nineteenth and early twentieth centuries. Dow's development of a new method to extract bromine, a dark red liquid chemical, from the brine trapped underground in Midland was key to establishing his career.

Dow was fired from the Midland Chemical Company in 1893 because he believed in open competition in the marketplace rather than large cartels. He then went off on his own to develop and research more products and techniques, including the production of bleach. He formed the Dow Process Company in 1896, but changed the name to the Dow Chemical Company in May 1897. Ironically, his new firm would absorb Midland Chemical Company three years later.

Dow Chemical would create many products in those first years, including Epsom salts, and during World War I it produced chemicals for explosives, medicines, dyes, and smokescreens. The early years weren't always easy as Dow had to battle monopolies and international cartels to open up the marketplace. Through the 1920s, Dow concentrated on other products, especially in the automobile industry. His Dowmetal pistons were used in the Indianapolis 500, for example.

Employees remembered Dow as a man full of ideas with a mind constantly at work. He enjoyed jokes and stories, but didn't tell them well himself and seemed to have little sense of play with his children or others. He was a notoriously bad driver, enjoyed travelling, was frugal with his money, and loved solving jigsaw puzzles. He was a great believer in education and his favourite saying was "if we can't do it better than others, why do it?" He held some ninety patents by the time he died on October 15, 1930 of cirrhosis of the liver.

His son Willard took over the company, which continued to blossom through to today. It would return to its Canadian roots when it opened a branch in Sarnia, Ontario in 1942 to help with the war effort.

Though the company has created products that are found in households and industries throughout the world, Dow Chemical has also had its share of controversy over the years. For example, it and other chemical companies' production of Agent Orange, used to defoliate forests in Vietnam, led to a massive lawsuit from veterans of the Vietnam War.

Today, Dow Chemical has annual sales of about $30 billion, more than one hundred manufacturing sites in thirty-three countries, and makes and sells more than two thousand chemicals and other products worldwide, including Ziploc bags and Styrofoam insulation.

William Dow

Dow Brewery Limited

A century after Montreal brewer William Dow passed away, the company that continued bottling beer with his name on the label adopted the slogan "Wouldn't a Dow go good now?"

Years earlier, it seems Dow already knew the answer to the catchy 1960s marketing phrase.

In the early 1830s, the popularity of Dow's brew made him one of the principal competitors in Montreal to Molson's, the largest brewery in the city at the time, and still a powerhouse in Canadian brewing circles. Beer making, as well as distilling, would make Dow a wealthy man, much to the delight of his father, a brewmaster in Scotland.

Dow received his early brewing experience in Scotland, where he was born on March 27, 1800. After working in the brewing business for several years, he immigrated to Canada in 1818 with a wealth of experience under his belt. He was hired as a foreman at Thomas Dunn's brewery, one of the few in Montreal at the time, and by November 1829, was a partner in the company known as Dunn and Dow. The firm employed Dow's younger brother, Andrew, also a brewer.

When Dunn died in 1834, the brothers carried on the company as William Dow and Company and it soon became one of the city's major brewer/distillers. A memorable year was 1863, when Dow's enterprise produced 700,000 gallons of beer, compared to Molson's 142,000 gallons.

After his brother died, Dow took on a number of partners, including a group of associates headed by Gilbert Scott. In 1864, Scott purchased the brewery and kept the Dow name on its products.

After leaving the brewing business, Dow, who never married, lived in an immense mansion at the top of Beaver Hall Hill in Montreal and played an active role in the banking, railway, shipping, canal building, steamship, and insurance industries. He was a member of the group that formed the Sun Life Insurance Company in 1865. He died in Montreal on December 7, 1868.

In the early 1900s, Dow Breweries became part of National Breweries in Montreal and later became a subsidiary of Canadian Breweries Limited. In the mid-1960s, Dow Ale was the number one brand in Quebec but its fame wouldn't last. In 1966, a tainted beer scandal linked to the death of more than a dozen Quebec City beer drinkers caused Dow to lose much of its market share to Labatt and Molson. The Dow brand name disappeared by 1973.

Name Dropper

Dow's Quebec City brewery was built on the site of La Braisserie du Roy, built by Governor of New France Jean Talon in 1668 as the site of Canada's first commercial brewery. In addition to brewing beer, Talon conducted Canada's first census in 1666.

Name Dropper

Although a determined rival of the Molson family in the beer and whisky business, William Dow was their associate in 1854 in the formation of Molsons Bank in Montreal.

Sam Dvorchak

Dickie Dee Ice Cream

The jingling bells of an ice cream bicycle conjure up images of hot summer days and the cool taste of frozen treats. And chances are that image conjures up the Dickie Dee name as well.

So how does someone whose name is Sam Dvorchak get linked with Dickie Dee?

Dvorchak, who had served overseas in the army, returned to Sherbrooke, Quebec in 1949 looking for work and before long started selling ice cream. In the process, he got the nickname "Mr. D."

It all started when a friend in Vancouver offered him a chance to head west to try out an ice cream vending bicycle. Dvorchak turned it into a success, loading up with ice cream from Crescent Creameries and selling his wares at such locations as freight yards and ball games. He acquired more bicycles from other locations in North America, began hiring staff, and produced more ice cream. Using his nickname, Dvorchak and his employees decided their little company needed a first name to go with "Dee." They chose Dickie, and Dickie Dee Ice Cream was born.

In 1951, Dvorchak met Syd Glow from Winnipeg, and they brought Dickie Dee Ice Cream to that city. Two teenagers, Sid and Earl Barish, worked for Glow, and in 1959, they convinced their father, Jack Barish, to buy the company from Dvorchak. Over the next thirty-three years, the Barish family expanded the business to other cities, gave young people a chance to earn good money, especially in the summer, and turned Dickie Dee into the largest ice cream bicycle business in the world. The bicycles were a familiar sight across Canadian streets and at various events, with people pouring out of their houses or lining up to buy the wide range of cool products.

Unilever Canada Inc., the world leader in ice cream sales, bought Dickie Dee Ice Cream in 1992. The brand still exists but the name is no longer seen on bicycle vendors. Treasure the memories.

Name Dropper

The Barishes created several other ice cream items during their tenures as owners of Dickie Dee. They launched the Richard D's line of ice cream products, choosing the name Richard to show that Dickie had grown up.

Timothy Eaton

Eaton's

The name Timothy Eaton evokes treasured memories of gaily decorated store windows, a parade that delighted generations of children every November, and the company's famous mail-order catalogue.

And it's no exaggeration to say Eaton is Canada's version of retailing superstars Rowland Macy in the United States and Charles Harrod in the United Kingdom. All founded tremendously successful department stores that became central to the lives of those who love to shop.

Eaton's climb to department store stardom began in 1854, when he arrived in Canada and took a job as a junior clerk in a general store near Georgetown, Ontario. Two years later he and his brother James, sons of an Irish tenant farmer, started the J. and T. Eaton General Store in a log building in Kirkton, a small community near Stratford, Ontario. In 1860, they moved to nearby St. Marys to sell dry goods, boots, farm tools, and kitchenware. Timothy married Margaret Wilson Beattie in 1861.

Eight years after tying the knot, Timothy decided to try his luck in the big city. When his business partnership with brother James dissolved in 1868, Timothy took his store-keeping experience and his wife to

Toronto and in 1869 purchased a dry goods store at 178 Yonge St. for $6,500 in cash.

Before long, the shop was taking advantage of a growing market brought on by increasing urbanization and industrialization in Toronto, not to mention rising living standards.

In 1883, Eaton moved to larger quarters on Yonge Street and three

Timothy Eaton

Courtesy of the National Archives of Canada/ C14088

years later the store doubled in size. To meet the product needs of his rapidly expanding business, Eaton in the 1880s and 1890s set up his own companies to manufacture clothing, paint, and chemicals and purchased farms to supply dairy products to his store and feed for his delivery horses.

In the years that followed, Eaton and his company were an integral facet of daily Canadian life as a full-line department store with a broad selection of goods, including jewelry, carpets, sporting goods, clothing, and appliances. A visit to an Eaton's store was a major happening for generations of Canadians, especially around Christmas when the stores' windows were filled with lights and holiday scenes.

Known as a pious, teetotalling Methodist who could be abrupt, gruff, and outspoken, Eaton was an innovator from the start: he was the first merchant in Toronto to sell goods for cash only and at one price; he coined and stood by the motto "Money refunded if goods not satisfactory" and he shortened store hours to ease his employees' long work week. He manufactured products under various house brand names; introduced the Santa Claus parade; and in 1884, launched the Eaton's catalogue, which came to hold a position second only to the family Bible in many Canadian households.

Originally called The Wishing Book, the catalogue carried just about everything, from farm tools, wedding rings, and lace to prefabricated homes, home remedies, and clothing. The 1896 version included a hand-powered washing machine for $3.75 and a year's supply of food for a man going on the Klondike gold rush for $68.69.

As Eaton's business prospered, his wife and five children (three other children died in infancy) adopted the comfortable lifestyle of other well-off Torontonians. They lived in a large home at the corner of Spadina Road and Lowther Avenue and spent summers at a lakefront property in Muskoka, north of Toronto, where they owned several steam yachts. Despite its wealth, the family never gave up its simple ways, which meant social vices such as cards, dancing, drinking, and smoking were no-nos.

In January 1907, about two years after opening a second store in Winnipeg, Eaton died of pneumonia. He left behind an estate worth $5.3 million and an empire that author Rod McQueen wrote in his book The Eatons: The Rise and Fall of Canada's Royal Family, "would weave itself into the very fabric of the land and the vital fibre of its people."

The company was taken over by Timothy's son John Craig and later by several of Timothy's relatives, who until the 1980s kept Eaton's at the forefront of Canadian department stores. In the 1950s, Eaton's laid claim to more than half of all department-store spending in Canada; in the 1990s, the company had eighty-five stores; and at one point, sales hit $2.1 billion.

But like its renowned catalogue, which disappeared in 1976, the business Timothy Eaton founded was erased from Canada's retail landscape, the victim of years of mismanagement, stiff competition from aggressive American retailers such as Wal-Mart, and an economic downturn in the late 1980s and early 1990s.

On February 27, 1997, the department store chain announced that after 128 years as a Canadian institution, it could no longer pay its bills. Twenty-one stores were closed, and on May 18, 1999, Eaton's hung a for sale sign on its remaining assets, including its flagship store in Toronto's Eaton Centre. As McQueen noted in his book, the family's Irish luck had run out.

"If Timothy Eaton were alive and saw this he'd be a pretty sad man," one bargain hunter said during an auction where cash registers, desks, and well-worn chairs from Eaton's better times were up for grabs.

Despite the company's downfall, the Eaton name survived, though only briefly. When Sears Canada Inc. acquired sixteen Eaton's stores in 1999, it kept the Eaton banner on upscale department stores reopened a year later in Toronto, Ottawa, Winnipeg, Calgary, Vancouver, and Victoria. But early in 2002, Sears dropped the Eaton name.

Name Dropper

When Timothy Eaton's private rail car the Eatonia was destroyed by fire a new car was built in 1916. The Eatonia II was seventy-eight feet long, had four staterooms panelled in Cuban mahogany, an observation area, a dining room with seating for ten on leather chairs, a full kitchen, and servants' quarters. The car was eventually sold to Canadian National Railways for use by VIPs such as royals and cabinet ministers. In 1972 Eaton's repurchased and restored the car, before donating it to Calgary's Heritage Park.

Ezra Butler Eddy

Eddy Match Company / E.B. Eddy Ltd.

Ezra Eddy has often been referred to as the king of Canada's match market. But this son of a Vermont farmer left a legacy that goes far beyond the manufacture of the friction matches used by generations of Canadians to light cigarettes, wood stoves, and campfires.

During a packed life that spanned the better part of seventy-nine years, Eddy gained a reputation as a politician committed to local interests, a philanthropist, and a far-sighted and canny industrialist who was the epitome of the self-made man.

Born in 1827 near Bristol, Vermont, he began his working career as a store clerk in New York City, and in the late 1840s was involved in various enterprises, including the dairy produce business and the manufacture of sulphur matches.

Lack of profits convinced him to move to Hull, Quebec in 1851, where he launched a family business making ten cases of matches a day, all packaged by his wife Zaida and local women and children. The matches were sold in a store near the factory; Eddy distributed them by horse and buggy.

Eventually, he diversified into wooden buckets, washboards, and clothespins and increased his match production to thirty cases a day. In the early 1860s he installed several generators at the Chaudiere Falls on the Ottawa River to power his growing enterprises.

In 1866, Eddy ventured into the lumber business when he rented a sawmill to meet a heavy demand for wood of all kinds. Soon after, he purchased his own mill near his match factory, and from then on, his rise was meteorical. With an annual output ranging from fifty to seventy-five million board feet of lumber, and a handful of sawmills under his control, he was one of the largest producers in the Ottawa Valley.

In 1871, Eddy entered politics as a Conservative member in the Quebec Legislative Assembly, a seat he held for four years. He also served as an alderman and mayor of Hull, during which time he introduced a bill creating the City of Hull.

Corporate life was not always rosy for Eddy. Between 1873 to 1882, his business interests were in dire straits as the result of the depressed lumber sector and a fire that severely damaged his plant. Eddy rebuilt, and in 1886 incorporated his enterprise as E.B. Eddy Manufacturing Company, with himself as president. Shortly after, he further diversified into the pulp and paper business, eventually producing tissue paper, printing paper, brown paper, and newsprint. He also expanded his match business.

Despite his busy career as an industrialist, Eddy found time to donate to many philanthropic causes in the Ottawa area, including churches, orphanages, and hospitals. Someone must have been smiling on him for his efforts, because in April 1900, he was one of the few businessmen located on the Chaudiere Falls to recover from a massive fire that destroyed much of the industrial part of Hull and Ottawa. His losses were estimated at $3 million.

By 1902 the company had rebuilt and was providing jobs for more than two thousand people who made paper, pulp, matches, paper bags, buckets, and tubs.

Eddy died in Hull on February 10, 1906 at the age of seventy-eight, leaving behind a thriving company and a fortune estimated at $2.5 million.

The match-making business was sold in 1928 to a Pembroke, Ontario company that continued to produce matches under the Eddy Match Company name until 1999 when it was closed and all production moved to Dallas, Texas.

In 1943, Eddy's company was purchased by George Weston Limited of Toronto, a national and international business powerhouse with holdings that over the years have included the Loblaws grocery chain, luxury apparel retailer Holt Renfrew, candymaker William Neilson Ltd., the Tamblyn Drugstore chain, and Connors Brothers Ltd. fish processors of New Brunswick.

In addition to a range of lumber and paper products, this version of the Eddy company manufactured a host of consumer products, including White Swan paper towels and toilet paper, Babies Only Please absorbent tissues, and Appleford waxed paper.

In 1998, Ezra Eddy's name disappeared for good when Domtar Inc. of Montreal acquired E.B. Eddy Ltd. and its U.S. affiliate. At the time, the company operated paper mills in Ottawa/Hull and Espanola, Ontario; Vancouver, British Columbia; and Port Huron, Michigan, which produced packaging and various kinds of papers.

Name Dropper

Ezra Eddy was known as one of the most progressive industrialists of his day. In 1883, he was among the first to use electricity in his factories, and in 1905 he was first to transport goods by truck.

Jack Fraser

Jack Fraser Stores Limited

According to a legend known to some company employees, the boss of one of Canada's most famous men's clothing stores originally came to Canada to be a Mountie.

But Jack Fraser got his men in another way, by offering quality clothes at affordable prices at stores that eventually spread across Canada.

Fraser's story begins in County Cavan, Ireland where he was born. He grew up on a farm and worked as a clerk at a general store. Longtime Jack Fraser employee Jim Walker says Fraser had some background in men's clothing before he set his sights on Canada. Whether he ever seriously followed up on his dreams of employment with the RCMP is now forgotten. Fraser found employment with a clothing wholesaler in Toronto. The job gave him a chance to travel across Canada, but the young Irishman soon had the urge to have his own shop.

He opened his first Jack Fraser store in 1926 at Danforth and Main streets in Toronto. Though Canada found itself in the Depression shortly thereafter, Fraser bought another business nearby as part of an expansion plan. "Everyone thought he was crazy to do this," Walker recalls. It was a struggle through those years and into World War II, but eventually Fraser's venture began to thrive. By the time Walker joined in 1948, there were five stores, located in Toronto, Oakville, and Newmarket.

Jack Fraser

Courtesy of Jim Walker

Fraser was a hands-on entrepreneur. He liked to keep an eye on his sales force and was keen to know why someone left the store without making a purchase. Fraser had both a tough and soft side to him, according to Walker. He believed he was a good judge of character and could be hard on those employees whom he didn't believe were doing a good job. To those he liked, he was friendly.

The 1950s was a good time for Jack Fraser stores. Fraser kept expanding his empire, often by purchasing rival stores in Ontario. The advent of shopping centres in that decade provided new market opportunities, though Fraser viewed them with skepticism at first. The first Jack Fraser store in such a centre was at Eglinton Square in Toronto's east end.

Though Walker remembers Fraser as a good dresser, he was by no means a fashion innovator. He'd keep an eye on his competitors to see what they were selling and at what price and had a knack for providing customers with good value.

"His life was basically around the business," says Walker, noting that Fraser liked to vacation in Arizona and Florida but would rarely stay away too long. Fraser also had a long association with the Royal Winter Fair, was its president at one time, and became a leading breeder of Guernsey cattle in Canada. Fraser owned a farm north of Toronto which he sold about a year before he died for more than $1 million.

He was a heavy smoker with a history of heart trouble. At the age of sixty-seven, Fraser died of a heart attack in August 1960 at the opening ceremonies of the Canadian National Exhibition. "It was a big shock to everybody," says Walker, who retired from the company in 1992. "He was more of a father figure to employees."

Neither Fraser's son nor daughter was interested in keeping the business in the family. Jack Fraser changed hands a few times, but each owner kept the name. The company made an arrangement with Woolco in 1962 to have its name and products in the men's clothing section of those department stores, and it proved to be a profitable venture. In July 1967, the Grafton Company, a clothing retailer with a long history in Canada, purchased the retail assets of Jack Fraser Stores Limited and changed the corporate name to Grafton-Fraser Limited.

With the arrival of enclosed shopping malls in Canada, more Jack Fraser stores opened up across the country. When the eightieth store opened in 1976, Jack Fraser's could be found in every province.

Like many retail operations, Grafton-Fraser went through tough times during an economic recession in the early 1990s. It divested itself of all non-core activities, but emerged leaner and stronger. Today there are more than one hundred Jack Fraser stores in Canada. Walker believes Fraser would be delighted that his name lives on more than forty years after his death, but perhaps disappointed that it didn't remain in family hands.

James Beatty Grafton

Grafton & Co.

The Grafton-Fraser company also operates several Grafton & Co. stores, and both the store and corporate names can be traced to a son of Irish immigrants who settled in Ontario in the nineteenth century.

In 1853, James Beatty Grafton, then sixteen, became an apprentice in the dry goods industry before going into partnership with Anthony Gregson. The two dealt in dry goods, millinery, and clothing. Five years later, Gregson retired, and Grafton's brother John became the new partner.

The company became a success through the latter half of the nineteenth century and in 1884, when Grafton's son, James John, became a partner, the company's named was changed to Grafton & Co. The firm expanded across Ontario, and one of its innovations, long before the days of Canadian Tire money, was "Grafton Dollars." Customers who made purchases received tickets that could be accumulated and traded in for merchandise or promotional gifts. Grafton & Co. purchased Jack Fraser in 1967.

Charles Edward Frosst

Charles E. Frosst and Co.

If you've ever awakened in the morning with a pounding head or assorted other aches, Charles Frosst has probably come to your rescue.

The pharmaceutical company Frosst founded in Montreal in 1899 introduced Canadians to a trio of numbered painkillers known as 217s, 222s, and 282s, which have been easing hurts and pains since World War I.

Though he was born in Richmond, Virginia, Frosst came to Canada in 1892 as a twenty-five-year-old salesman for Henry Wampole & Company. Wampole sent him all over Canada, and his soft accent and straight thinking helped him develop a reputation as an accomplished and knowledgeable pharmaceutical salesperson. He also cultivated contacts with a network of people in the medical establishment.

In 1899, at a time when the Canadian pharmaceutical industry was in its infancy, Frosst struck out on his own by setting up a drug company in Montreal, where he had an excellent relationship with McGill University's Department of Medicine. From the start, Frosst made it clear that Charles E. Frosst & Co. would introduce innovative new products.

Working from a modest two-thousand-square-foot laboratory, Frosst researched and developed his own formulas, built some of his own machinery, and initially handled the sale of his products. At the start of the Great War, he introduced Frosst 217s and Frosst 222s, numbers being a common way of identifying product lines at the time. With millions of pain sufferers around the globe using the pills, the company soon became a household name.

After the war, his son Eliot joined and the firm grew rapidly. By 1927, Frosst's lab had moved into a forty-thousand-square-foot building on Montreal's St. Antoine St. and sons John and Charles Jr. also came on board. Frosst family members teamed up to develop drugs to fight bacterial infections and in the early 1940s the company was licensed to produce Vitamin B_2 and develop veterinary drugs to treat small animals.

Although Charles Frosst Sr. appeared to be stern, he knew all his employees by name, how many children they had, and whether they liked playing bridge or watching the Montreal Canadiens. He encouraged staff to take pride in their work and approach him with their problems. His sense of humour was evidenced by the company's sponsorship of calendars and cartoons that facetiously caricatured the medical and pharmaceutical professions.

On the drug development side, Frosst was committed to thorough research and extensive testing before products went to market, according to a profile of the company by writer Mel James. He was also a major supporter of hospital research and provided numerous scholarships to medical and health care students.

In 1943, at age seventy-six, Frosst gave up his day-to-day work, leaving his sons in charge of the company. When he died in 1948, he was still making occasional visits to the company's Montreal headquarters, where his staff was developing the country's first radioactive pharmaceutical products, which later were sold in Canada and abroad.

In 1959 Charles Frosst and Co. went public and six years later it was acquired by Merck & Co. Inc., of New Jersey. In 2001, the company was known as Merck Frosst Canada Ltd. and its main activities — the discovery, development, manufacturing, and distribution of medicines — were much the same as those carried on by Charles Frosst a century earlier.

The company is still manufacturing 222s and 282s, but 217s were dropped some time ago.

Name Dropper

For nearly half a century, Charles E. Frosst and Co. produced annual Dingbat calendars, which featured humorous cartoons that hung in the waiting rooms of most doctors and dentists in Canada.

Alfred C. Fuller

Fuller Brush Company

Alfred Carl Fuller described himself as a bit of a "country bumpkin, unsophisticated and virtually unschooled" when he went into business almost one hundred years ago. And given that he grew up on a Nova Scotia farm, could barely read, and was once fired by his brother, the description was apt.

Despite these shortcomings, he managed to build a company that today does millions of dollars in annual sales.

Fuller was born on January 13, 1885 in Welsford, Nova Scotia, in the Annapolis Valley, where the Fullers lived on a seventy-five-acre farm. Alfred, one of twelve children, was called "Uppie" as a child because his friends couldn't pronounce "Alfie" properly. He worked on the farm until he left home at eighteen, and the only advice from his father was to be thrifty, save money, and live cleanly. He first moved to the Boston area in 1903, where three of his brothers and two sisters lived.

Fuller got a job as a trolley conductor, got fired after he derailed a car, and then held a few other jobs from which he was also fired, including a stint driving an express wagon for his brother Robert. Fuller left packages at wrong addresses and forgot important pickups, and Robert fired him. Alfred then went to work selling household brushes for a company door to door, and after about a year decided he could do better on his own.

Like so many successful businesses of the time, Fuller started his company in a home, in this case in the basement of his sister Annie's house. He had a few ideas for brushes that his previous employer had rejected. Four months later, in April 1906, he moved his operations to Hartford, Connecticut and decided to call his enterprise the Capitol Brush Company after seeing the state capitol building there.

The company grew as Fuller listened to his customers' needs and then created brushes to solve their cleaning problems. "My customers were my designers," he said. In his first nine months, Fuller grossed $5,000; it was good money for the time, but Fuller dealers would generate that much about every ten minutes some fifty years later. Fuller began expanding to other states and eventually into Canada. In 1913, he realized he hadn't registered the Capitol company name, so he took the opportunity to rename the firm The Fuller Brush Company. By 1919, the company recorded its first $1 million in annual sales.

Fuller's company prospered through the twentieth century. The phrase "The Fuller Brush Man" became famous enough to inspire a 1948 movie of that name starring Red Skelton. Two years later Lucille Ball starred in *The Fuller Brush Girl*.

Today, the company's large manufacturing plant in Great Bend, Kansas offers more than two thousand different home and personal care products. Fuller, who divorced his first wife in 1930 and remarried in 1932, died in December 1973.

Name Dropper

Fuller wasn't the first one in his family to own a brush business. His older brother Dwight had been a brush salesman who branched out on his own. But the brush manufacturing process in those days created a lot of dust, and the bad air he breathed is thought to be the reason Dwight died in 1901. No wonder Fuller's parents weren't initially supportive of Alfred's move to the brush-making business.

Gilbert and James Ganong

Ganong Brothers Limited

In the early 1870s, Gilbert Ganong's career plans suddenly shifted Though he'd saved $400 to attend medical school, he was persuaded by his brother James to invest his savings in the grocery business instead.

So, rather than delivering babies, stitching minor wounds, and writing prescriptions, Gilbert would eventually manufacture and sell lollipops, candies, chocolates, candy bars, and the Chicken Bone, a cinnamon-flavoured pink hard candy that would become an East Coast favourite.

Gilbert's foray into entrepreneurship began in 1872, when he and James, a former jockey, bought into a wholesale and retail grocery business in St. Stephen, New Brunswick, about thirty-five kilometres from the Atlantic Ocean.

In 1876, the brothers opened a bakery and confectionery factory and in 1879 they and a partner started the St. Croix Soap Factory. Much of their early business activity took place in the period when legendary confectioners Henri Nestle of Switzerland and Walter Lowney and Milton Hershey of the United States were launching their businesses.

Gilbert Ganong   *James Ganong*

Photos courtesy of Ganong Brothers Limited

Gilbert and James Ganong

In 1884, the Ganongs split their enterprise in two, with James taking the soap business and Gilbert the food enterprises, under the name Ganong Brothers. In 1886, Gilbert built a new three-storey confectionery factory on St. Stephen's main street. Though the factory was levelled several times by fires, Ganong Brothers rebuilt and became a major force in Canada's candy industry. In 1891, the company captured 7 percent of the nation's confectionery business.

Three years later, Gilbert gave up his bakery to specialize in confectionery manufacturing and by the early 1900s had opened a cross-Canada network of sales offices. Shortly after, Ganong's popular Pal-o-Mine chocolate bar was introduced.

Although he was a busy candymaker, Gilbert also had a sweet tooth for politics. A staunch Conservative, he represented the St. Stephen area in Parliament for three terms between 1896 and 1908, always as a member of the opposition. One of his pet issues was support for the temperance movement. In 1917, G.W., as he was known around St. Stephen, was appointed New Brunswick's lieutenant-governor. He died that year, twenty-nine years after his brother James passed away.

During the years Gilbert Ganong headed the company, Ganong's was responsible for a handful of innovations in the confectionery industry: It installed the first lozenge machine in Canada, was first to imprint chocolates on the bottom, and it invented and introduced the first five-cent chocolate nut bar in North America. The company's record of innovation continued after Gilbert's death. In 1920, Ganong Brothers was the first confectioner in Canada to use Cellophane packaging, and in 1932 it was the first in the country to sell heart-shaped boxes of Valentine chocolates.

Despite several takeover bids, the company has remained in the hands of the Ganong family, largely because of its commitment to the community. Family members who have operated the business since the 1920s include Arthur Ganong, Whidden Ganong, and David Ganong.

The modern version of Ganong Brothers Limited operates a manufacturing facility in St. Stephen, where it makes fruit snacks, lozenges, jelly beans, the Pal-o-Mine chocolate bar, gums, bagged candy, and its flagship product, Delecto chocolates. The company's original plant, on Milltown Boulevard in St. Stephen, is now a retail outlet and chocolate museum.

Name Dropper

In 1933, Ganong's introduced the Sea Sun chocolate bar, which contained a tablespoon of cod liver oil as a palatable way of giving children a dose of the vile-tasting oil. Despite its initial success, the bar was discontinued when the company, at the request of the federal Health Department, was unable to prove how much cod liver oil was in each bar.

Louis Garneau

Louis Garneau Sports Inc.

Wherever there are cyclists and cross-country skiers, you're likely to see Louis Garneau's name.

After racing for Canada in the 1984 Los Angeles Olympics and winning 150 races worldwide, the Quebec-based cyclist bought a sewing machine and started making bicycle shorts for his friends on the Canadian cycling team. The company, now known as Louis Garneau Sports Inc., was launched in his father's garage in Ste. Foy, Quebec.

These days, the company is run by Garneau and his wife Monique Arsenault in St-Augustin-de-Desmaures, Quebec, and is a major manufacturer of clothing, helmets, and accessories for cycling; cross-country ski wear; swim suits; children's apparel; bicycles; and fitness equipment. The firm has a manufacturing plant in the United States and a warehouse in France.

As a racer, Garneau gained the experience to lead a company and the will to succeed. He beat legendary Canadian cyclist Steve Bauer in an individual race at Montreal's Velodrome, was a member of the Canadian cycling team for seven years, and at his peak in 1982 was ranked eleventh in the world in the one-hundred-kilometre team time trial event.

Garneau drives his business the way he would cycle a race, by focussing on goals and working with his team. From 1984 to 1990, his vision ran like a well-tuned racing bike: sales doubled every year and by 1985, he was in a 5,000-square-foot factory with 16 employees. By 1989, there were 118 employees in a

Louis Garneau

Courtesy of Louis Garneau Sports Inc.

32,000-square-foot facility, and he was also running a plant in Newport, Vermont.

The recession of 1990–91 showed Garneau the need for innovation. After studying all bike helmets on the market, he designed his own helmet line, which retails in the $30 to $140 range and is among the top three best-sellers in the world. In 2002, helmets made up nearly 40 percent of his business.

The firm has about 50 percent of the market in cycling and cross-country accessories in Canada and is the only company making bicycle helmets and sunglasses in Canada.

Louis Garneau Sports Inc. has twenty distributors in the world and twenty-five hundred accounts in the U.S. and Canada alone. Its lines sell in Canada, the U.S., Europe, South America, Japan, and Australia. Olympic and world champions such as Myriam Bedard, Lance Armstrong, and Curt Harnett wear Garneau products.

Garneau was able to make the leap to international sales because of the helmets and his passion. "I was not a world champion in cycling and some of my friends were, so I decided to be a world champion in business," he told the *Financial Post* in 1996.

Pasquale Gattuso

Gattuso Food Corporation

When a teenaged Pasquale Gattuso tried to borrow $2,000 to start a grocery business in the mid-1930s, his family and friends thought he was nuts. According to family lore, even Gattuso thought his chance of securing a loan was zero because he had no collateral.

But when he strolled into the head office of the National Bank of Canada in Montreal he was so persuasive that a manager lent him the cash — an enormous risk during the Depression. Ironically, Gattuso later became one of the bank's major stockholders.

The son of Calabrian immigrants, Gattuso was born in Montreal on April 30, 1918. His father worked in the Canadian Pacific Railway yards and Gattuso grew up near Molson's Brewery. At age thirteen, he was already showing his entrepreneurial flair by peddling newspapers and dealing in scrap metal. At seventeen, with the blessing of his bank manager and borrowed money in hand, he and brothers Francesco and Matteo opened the Corona Grocery.

The core of their business was importing olives and olive oil in bulk, and Pasquale could often be found in the store's basement stuffing olives to sell to other neighbourhood grocers. Along the way he took night courses at the Université de Montreal, and during World War II served with Les Fusiliers Mont-Royal. He was discharged after a year because of ill health, according to his obituary in the *Montreal Gazette*.

In 1945, Gattuso married Lina Pierpaoli and the couple had a son and two daughters.

The family's food business prospered thanks to the increasing demand by post-war immigrants for Italian specialty items. By 1948, the Gattusos had opened a corporate headquarters and their pasta and tomato products were staples in most North American supermarkets. In the 1950s, gross sales were $1 million a year; by the time Gattuso sold the company in 1967, annual sales were close to $10 million. Over the years, its product line had expanded to include pickles and instant "snacks in a cup."

Once out of the food business, Gattuso acquired the Buckingham Mills carpet company in Springhill, Nova Scotia, which he later sold.

He continued to run an import-export business until the early 1990s, when he suffered the first in a series of strokes.

Gattuso, who died in October 2001, was a solitary man with a grave demeanour, given to lapses of silence. He was modest and low key, but always elegantly dressed. He seldom travelled or entertained. He owned a Cadillac but rarely drove it because he couldn't concentrate behind the wheel. In a 1965 profile in *Globe* magazine, writer Betty Lee described Gattuso as "up in the clouds, always lost in thought."

Gattuso was an enthusiastic booster of local boxing and wrestling matches, and in the 1960s owned an Italian soccer team in Montreal. After being invited to join the Young Men's Hebrew Association by supermarket executive Sam Steinberg, his largest client, Gattuso went on to become a governor of the association. He was also a generous contributor to Roman Catholic charities.

The Gattuso name continues to appear on food products marketed by a number of companies, including Robin Hood Multifoods and Campbell Soup Limited.

Ben Ginter

Uncle Ben's Brewery

Bulldozers and beer: An odd pairing to be sure, but one that would make millions for British Columbia entrepreneur Ben Ginter.

Ginter was born in Wolyn, Poland in 1923 and spent much of his early life near Swan River, Manitoba after his family immigrated to the Prairies in the midst of the Depression. After leaving school at age thirteen, he rode the rails to Ontario, where he worked as a labourer before returning to Winnipeg for a career in construction. Over time, he became a master mechanic, foreman, and supervisor.

In 1948, Ginter and a partner started a construction company that relied mainly on government contracts to pay the bills. A year later, Ginter and his wife Grace moved to British Columbia, and the company set up operations in Prince George. Its inventory consisted of eight bulldozers and a grader.

Then came Ginter's entry into brewing, more by chance than design. While looking for a storage yard and repair shed for his construction equipment in 1962, he bought the defunct Caribou Brewing Company plant in Prince George for $150,000. The building housed a large, still usable copper brewing kettle.

When the locals learned Ginter planned to turn the old brewery into a construction yard, the mayor and local businessmen convinced him to reopen the brewery. He was wary until Carling Brewery in Vancouver bought the brew kettle. It convinced him that a major brewery wanted him off its turf, so he hired a brewmaster and reopened the old brewery as Tartan Brewing, later changing the name to Uncle Ben's Brewery.

Ginter, a strapping 240-pound hulk of a man with a black beard, a crew cut, and thick upper arms, became well known for waging a running battle with large national breweries, and for his use of sales gimmicks such as borrowing names from big American breweries and deliberately misspelling them on his labels. Pabst became "Paaps" and "Budweiser" became "Budd" until Miller, Pabst, and Anheuser-Busch issued a cease and desist order. But he was also innovative, producing B.C.'s first canned beer and introducing the first refund for empty cans.

By 1965, his brewery-and-construction empire consisted of four-teen companies with $25 million in government and private contracts for construction of railways, roads, and factories. By 1974, he had handled $350 million worth of government work alone and used his fortune to build an impressive home on the outskirts of Prince George. He was also known for his beer, eventually becoming a "minor beer baron," according to the *Vancouver Province*, which said his Old Blue Lager and Uncle Ben's Malt Liquor, brewed at plants in Prince George, B.C.; Red Deer, Alberta; and Winnipeg, Manitoba, were rated as top-class beers by international authorities.

In the mid-1970s, however, Ginter's world came crashing down. Though he claimed his companies offered plenty of security to back his bank loans, his brewery and construction companies were put into receivership in 1976. It led to the demise of his construction companies and the beer with Ginter's bearded face on its labels.

Ginter died of a heart attack in Richmond, B.C. in July 1982.

Mike's Hard Lemonade

The man behind Mike's Hard Lemonade is actually named Don. When a British Columbia maker of alcoholic beverages jumped into the spiked lemonade drink market in the mid-1990s, marketing expert Don Chisholm was hired to create a brand and give it a personality and a name. About eight different concepts were developed, but the name that stood out with consumers was "Mike."

"We wanted a name to attach to a hard lemonade that was approachable, fun, and cheerful," Chisholm told *Marketing Magazine* in 1999. "So Mike's personification is a fun, party, happy-go-lucky guy who is infatuated with lemons."

William Gooderham and James Worts

Gooderham and Worts Distillery

Making spirits was a family affair for the Worts and Gooderham clans. In the early 1830s, brothers-in-law James Worts and William Gooderham founded a milling business in Toronto which eventually became the Gooderham and Worts Distillery. In later years, the founders' sons would play key roles in the company.

Worts, a mill owner in Suffolk, England, immigrated to Toronto with his son in 1831 and built a seventy-foot-tall wind-driven flour mill at the mouth of the Don River in what was then York. A year later he was joined by Gooderham, son of a Norfolk, England farmer, and they formed the partnership of Worts and Gooderham.

In 1834, two weeks after his wife Elizabeth died in childbirth, Worts drowned himself in the mill's well.

With his partner gone, Gooderham forged on, adding a distillery to the business in 1837 to process surplus grain. In 1845, he made Worts's eldest son James a partner in the enterprise, which they renamed Gooderham and Worts. In 1861 the pair built the largest distillery in Canada West, also at the mouth of the Don River.

Most of James Worts's time was spent managing the distillery, which experienced rapid growth. Eventually, Worts and Gooderham diversified their interests. Worts invested heavily in the Bank of Toronto, which Gooderham had helped found, and over the years both served as its president. Their other interests included railway building, livestock yards, retailing, and woolen mills.

Distilling, however, remained their mainstay. In the 1870s, the company's 150 workers were producing one of every three gallons of proof spirits manufactured in Canada. Gooderham was one of Toronto's most prominent businessmen when he died in August 1881, leaving the distillery he and James Worts had started to their sons, James Worts and George Gooderham.

The two men, and in later years other members of their families, ran the distillery until it was sold in 1923 to wealthy Torontonian Harry Hatch. In 1926, Gooderham & Worts purchased distiller Hiram Walker & Sons of Walkerville, Ontario.

Gooderham & Worts whisky is marketed today by Corby's Distilleries Ltd. Its historic Toronto distillery, which was closed in 1990, is being redeveloped. For years the site was a hot spot for movie producers, who used the 5.2-hectare property and its buildings to shoot more than seven hundred movies.

Henry Corby

Corby's Distilleries Ltd.

Henry Corby's name has been spotted in many a Canadian liquour cabinet over the years. Corby was a baker-turned-distiller who was born in Hanwell, England and came to the eastern Ontario community of Belleville in 1832.

He operated a small food shop and bakery and sold grain before buying a grist mill on the Moira River, six kilometres north of Belleville in 1857. Two years later he built a distillery, which soon overtook the mill in importance.

Known as "Honest Henry Corby," he was mayor of Belleville in 1867 and sat in the Ontario legislature, representing the people of East Hastings from 1867 to 1875. The father of fifteen children, Corby died in October 1881 but his named lived on; the town where his distillery was located was named Corbyville, and his son Harry ran the operation until 1905.

In 1914, Corby's joined forces in Corbyville with American J.P. Wiser, who had operated Wiser's Distillery in Prescott, Ontario since 1862. The Corbyville distillery closed in 1991, leaving Corby's Distilleries Ltd. with a small distillery in Montreal. Corby's is Canada's leading importer of wines, and markets products such as Beefeater Gin, Polar Ice Vodka, Tia Maria, and Wiser's De Luxe whisky, which are distilled by Hiram Walker & Sons Ltd. Both firms are controlled by Allied Domecq PLC of the U.K.

Name Dropper

Henry Corby suffered tragedy before he knew success. In 1838, his first wife and the couple's three children drowned in the Bay of Quinte at Belleville when the sleigh they were riding in broke through the ice.

Peter Goudas

Goudas Food Products and Investments Ltd.

He's been a construction manager, aircraft mechanic, and even a disk jockey known as Mr. Wu, but it's the name Mr. Goudas, found on dozens of multicultural food products, that Canadian shoppers recognize.

Peter Goudas, who was born in a suburb of Athens, Greece in 1942, was one of four children. According to information supplied by Goudas Foods, he started working part-time while still in school making and decorating plates and vases. An avid swimmer, Goudas studied drafting and engineering before starting his own construction business at age sixteen. Four years later he was drafted into the Greek air force, where he worked as a mechanic.

But air force life didn't soar for him, and with about $100 in his pocket he immigrated to Canada in 1967 with no real job prospects or plans for what he might do in his new home in Toronto. On top of that he not only couldn't speak English, he also wasn't familiar with the Roman alphabet used here.

But Goudas was anything but a quitter. Times were tough initially, and he even slept on the city's streets on occasion, but he managed to improve his language skills by watching television. Goudas later found work at Peabody Engineering, a firm that made air conditioners and boilers. Two years later, when he was ready to strike out on his own, he bought a food packaging plant. His background as a mechanic came in handy for repairing machines that needed fixing.

Though his name is synonymous with food today, Goudas really didn't have definite plans for what he was going to do with this plant. As he later told writer Okey Chigbo in an article in the *Metropolitan Toronto Business Journal*, "there was nobody packaging ethnic food at the time. I knew there was a demand for it. So I said why not?"

Starting with packages of rice, Goudas has since built a food empire that covers a wide range of products such as chickpeas, spices, more than thirty different kinds of beans, and a wide array of Chinese, Indian, and Caribbean specialties. A hard worker, Goudas started building a reputation as an expert in these foods. But food wasn't his only passion in those early days.

According to the *Business Journal* article, Goudas bought a night-club in 1970 that specialized in Latin and Caribbean music. He would spin records there occasionally and got the name "Mr. Wu" from patrons who thought he looked Oriental. "I never did it for the profit," he told the magazine. "I loved to go out and have a good time with my friends on the weekend; I also loved music. So, I thought, why not buy a club where we can all meet and have a party."

His food company thrived until 1979 when he had an accident and then had troubles keeping the business afloat while recuperating in hospital. But the ambitious entrepreneur bounced back with vigour. Using a temporary line of credit, Goudas rebuilt the business to the point where it's one of the most popular and successful in the country today. He has suppliers from around the world and services more than twenty food store chains and three thousand independent grocers.

James Grand and Samuel Toy

Grand & Toy

From the start James Grand was a stationer who wasn't stationary.

When he started his office supplies business in Toronto in 1882, he would gather orders, buy paper on credit, and deliver products by wagon door to door. In fact, Grand is believed to be the first person in Toronto to sell stationery to customers this way.

He was the eldest child of an officer of the Regiment of Royal Engineers who settled in Toronto from England. At age fourteen, Grand began working in the publishing business. By 1882, Grand had a wife and infant son to support and decided that going into business for himself was the solution.

When he started his stationery/office supplies business, Grand used his mother's kitchen table as a counter and set up shop on the second floor of a building at 4 Leader Lane. By August 1883, business was so hectic he realized he couldn't continue single-handedly. Enter Samuel Toy, Grand's brother-in-law. The two formed the partnership Grand & Toy and within three years, total annual sales cracked the $15,000 mark.

By 1895, Grand & Toy moved to better headquarters at Wellington and Jordan streets, and four years later they had about twelve employees, including Grand's son Percy. The company expanded their delivery area beyond Toronto's downtown. Then what was a catastrophe for the city in 1904 turned into a bonus for Grand & Toy.

In April that year, a fire raged through the city's core, destroying buildings and causing $10 million in damage. Thanks to Percy's vigilance in dousing any flaming debris from the Grand & Toy roof, the company's store was not damaged. That left Grand & Toy as the only office supplier in the downtown area, and customers flocked there to replenish their supplies. They were handed wastebaskets to hold their supplies as they moved around the store, likely making it the first time self-serve shopping occurred at a stationery store.

Toy was the brains behind introducing the company's catalogue that same year, which also helped boost sales. Despite Toy's death two years later, the firm continued to flourish. James Grand's health began to fail in 1913, and Percy took over more responsibilities. In

1922, when James died, Percy became president, with his brothers, Arthur and Ernest, placed in senior roles. Grand & Toy opened its first branch store in Toronto in 1926, and as skyscrapers became popular in the following years, the company began landing contracts to furnish these new office centres.

When Percy died in 1954, his son, James R. Grand, succeeded him as head of the firm, and a year later the company opened a store in Hamilton, the first one outside of Toronto. Grand & Toy continued to blossom and expand through the next couple of decades, especially in Western Canada. In 1996, it was purchased by the U.S.-based company Boise Cascade Office Products, and today there are thirty-four Grand & Toy locations in Canada employing fifteen hundred people. Sales are in excess of $120 million. From its humble beginnings on the second floor of a Toronto building, it is now North America's leading office products dealer.

Name Dropper

The next time you use a pencil think of Percy Grand. In 1927, he was looking for a pencil that wouldn't roll off his desk, like the hexagonal ones that were popular at that time. But he wanted one that was more comfortable to use. He filed down the sharp edges of a hexagonal pencil to create the Roundedge Pencil, which was smoother to hold but still didn't roll. It's the prototype for virtually all pencils today and is still sold in vast quantities by Grand & Toy.

Harvey _____?

Harvey's

The man who inspired the name of one of Canada's leading hamburger and fast food chains likely didn't know about his claim to fame. And we'll never be sure if this mysterious Harvey, whoever he was, even bit into one of the juicy burgers that bear his name.

Harvey's was the brainchild of Toronto-area restaurateur Rick Mauran, who brought charbroiled burgers to Canada in 1959. Although there is something of an urban myth that the chain was named after the title character in the famous Jimmy Stewart movie *Harvey*, the real story is simpler. Mauran chose the Harvey name after seeing it in a newspaper story. Company history doesn't provide the context of what the story was even about, but Mauran thought the name had personality, was easy to spell, and memorable. And it was short. Mauran had hired a sign painter for his first restaurant who charged by the letter.

The first Harvey's opened at 9741 Yonge Street in Richmond Hill, Ontario, where burgers, fries, and onion rings are still hot sellers. Since

Harvey's sign

Photo by Randy Ray

A typical Harvey's restaurant.

Photo by Mark Kearney

then, the chain has grown enormously across Canada. Its first franchised restaurant opened in 1962 in Sarnia, Ontario, and by the time CARA Operations Ltd. bought the company in 1979, there were more than eighty Harvey's restaurants. In 1980, Harvey's opened Canada's first drive-thru restaurant in Pembroke, Ontario, and today there are 375 outlets nationwide. More than nine thousand employees serve up over one million burgers each week, and CARA Restaurant Group has total sales of more than $1.2 billion.

A few other Harvey's tidbits to chew on:

- Harvey's has served up more than one billion burgers since 1959.
- Four out of five guests order pickles on their burger.
- The most frequently requested Harvey's topping is mustard.
- The northernmost Harvey's is in Edmonton.
- In 1999, Harvey's became the first national chain to introduce a veggieburger to its permanent menu.

Kelsey's

A road in Barrington, Illinois is the source for the name of one of Canada's most popular restaurant chains. Back in the 1970s, when Paul Jeffery and his brother were visiting a friend in Barrington, Illinois, they frequented a bar on Kelsey's Road. Jeffery liked the name "Kelsey's" enough to slap it onto the front of the first road-house-style eatery he opened in Oakville, Ontario in 1978. These days there are some ninety-five Kelsey's, stretching from Quebec to British Columbia.

The familiar Kelsey's sign.

Photo by Randy Ray

Kenneth Harvey and James Woods

Harvey Woods Ltd.

The average person may not ponder his or her underwear labels, but in case you do — Harvey Woods wasn't the name of some guy with a passion for panties.

In fact, the name comes from the amalgamation of the names of a Woodstock, Ontario industry pioneer, K.W. Harvey, and the owner of a Toronto knitting mill, James W. Woods.

Textile companies were important and large employers in Woodstock during the twentieth century. Harvey started out with the Oxford Knitting Co. in 1906, sold it three years later, and then left town. He came back to Woodstock in 1912 and opened Ken Knit, specializing in ladies' and children's underwear. Within a couple of years he had renamed it Harvey Knitting Co. He expanded it in the 1920s and 1930s, making hosiery and underwear, until his factories were taken over by York Knitting Co.

Back in 1904, Woods had started Puritan Knitting Mills in Toronto to supply a leading wholesaler. It was renamed York Knitting Mills in 1911, and by the 1920s, it too was producing underwear under the name Woods Underwear Company.

York Knitting Co. bought out Harvey in 1937. Woods, who had been knighted, died in 1941, but his sons and grandsons were prominent figures in the amalgamated company for many years after. The Harvey Woods logo became prominent after World War II, and by 1964, all of York's manufacturing and its head office had been moved from Toronto to Woodstock.

Though it had used the retail name Harvey Woods for many years, it wasn't until 1966 that the company officially became Harvey Woods Ltd. By the early 1970s, Harvey Woods employed almost one thousand people making and selling underwear and socks. The 1980s weren't kind to the business, however, and in 1985, Harvey Woods was purchased by T.A.G. Apparel Group for about $9 million. The Harvey Woods name remained on the labels.

Five years later, T.A.G. went into receivership and closed its Harvey Woods division, putting six hundred people out of work. The

MacLean Group Inc. bought the Harvey Woods factory in 1992 and started manufacturing hosiery on a small scale. As of 2002, Stanfield's owned the Harvey Woods name with respect to underwear, and there are many shops that still sell that brand.

Theodor Heintzman

Heintzman Pianos

Optician, machinist, and locomotive maker. Theodor Heintzman tried on all those hats before tuning in to piano making as his true occupation. In time, his musical instruments would become famous around the world.

Born in Berlin, Germany in 1817, Heintzman (at birth his name was given as Theodore August Heintzmann) dabbled in several careers, at one point receiving credit for producing the draft for the first locomotive built in Berlin.

But from his teens onward, there was always a strong connection to the craft of making musical instruments. His father and father-in-law were piano makers who specialized in manufacturing high-quality instruments that could be crafted by a single skilled artisan. As a young boy, Heintzman apprenticed as a cabinetmaker and later learned key making.

After he was married in 1844, he worked for his wife's uncle as a piano and instrument maker, quickly learning the business of both building and selling pianos.

When Heintzman died, he was at the helm of an internationally renowned Canadian piano manufacturing company that would become one of the oldest music firms in North America. Some say the Heintzman name was better known throughout the British Empire prior to World War I than the name of any other trademarked Canadian product.

Heintzman's journey toward Canada began in 1849, when he moved his family from Berlin to New York to flee military and political unrest in revolutionary Germany. While in New York, he perfected his craft by working with a piano company that also employed Heinrich Engelhardt Steinweg, founder of the Steinway piano firm. He later moved to Buffalo to form a partnership in the Western Piano Company.

Heintzman sold his interest during a financial panic in 1857 and resettled in Toronto in 1860 where he is said to have assembled his first Canadian piano single-handedly in his kitchen. The instrument sold quickly because of the superior detail of its cabinet and its brilliant tone, and Heintzman used his profits to build more pianos.

In a matter of years, Heintzman was known as a craftsman who, unlike some of his competitors, aimed at high quality rather than low price. In 1866, with financial backing from his son-in-law Karl Bender, he set up Heintzman and Company in downtown Toronto, that year making twelve pianos and employing twelve people. In subsequent years the company moved to various larger premises.

As a devotee to the technical side of his instruments, Heintzman, father of eleven children, patented the agraffe bridge, which extended across the cast-iron frame of the piano to keep its strings from slipping. The bridge also improved clarity and tone.

By 1890, the firm was one of Toronto's largest manufacturing firms and was producing one thousand pianos annually. Outside of his work as a piano maker, Heintzman was a member of the German Reform Club, a Freemason, and a benefactor of First Lutheran Church.

When his wife Matilda died suddenly in 1890, his health began to deteriorate and control of the company gradually fell into the hands of George and Herman, two of his six sons. George, who was known as an aggressive salesman, built the company his father founded into a national and international success story.

By the time the elder Heintzman passed away in July 1899 at age eighty-two, his pianos had won at least eleven awards in the United States and throughout the British Empire, including the prestigious William Prince of Wales Medal in London (1886).

Heintzman and Company remained in Toronto until 1978, when operations were moved to Hanover, Ontario, where production at times reached fifteen hundred upright and grand pianos a year. After a number of mergers and ownership changes (the firm was once owned by furniture maker Sklar-Pepplar), the company closed in the mid-1980s.

Name Dropper

In 1888, a Heintzman piano was played at the Royal Albert Hall in London, England before Queen Victoria, who was heard to remark, "I didn't realize that such beautiful instruments could be made in the colonies."

Irene Hill

Irene Hill Women's Wear

Like many Ottawa merchants, Irene Hill counted on the purchasing power of thousands of federal government employees to keep her cash registers ringing. Over the years, they came through for her.

The Ottawa native grew up a short drive east of Ottawa in the communities of Vars and Carlsbad Springs. She started Irene Hill's women's wear in 1952 with a single outlet on Bank Street in downtown Ottawa, and during most lunch hours a steady stream of civil servants flowed into her small two-storey shop.

By the mid-1970s, when she was married to John Johnston-Berresford and going by the name Irene Johnston-Berresford, she was operating a handful of stores under the Irene Hill banner in Ottawa and neighbouring Hull, Quebec. She helped start another store in Atlanta before selling the Ottawa-area stores in 1970 or 1971 to businessmen John St. Onge and David King, said cousin and former employee Debra Crowe. She remained as general manager until 1975.

Several years later, the chain was sold again, this time to Comark Services Inc. of Mississauga, Ontario, which is controlled by a wealthy family based in the Netherlands. Under Comark the chain expanded to approximately three hundred stores by the mid-1980s; eventually the Irene Hill name was changed to Cleo.

Mrs. Berresford-Johnston died in Ottawa on May 1, 1995 at age seventy-nine. She had no children.

In an obituary in the *Ottawa Citizen*, she was remembered by her husband John as a shrewd businesswoman who learned the tricks of her trade while working at the Reitmans clothing chain. He attributes her success to government workers who "finally got to know that Irene Hill's was the only place they could get a real bargain — and good clothes."

Johnston-Berresford developed a reputation as a clothier who sold quality classic styles at reasonable prices. She knew her customers and what they wanted, Crowe told the *Citizen*. "She expected a lot from her staff," and at the same time she was very fair and professional. In return, her employees were very loyal, said Crowe.

Roy Hill

Hilroy Envelopes and Stationery Ltd.

Anyone who was ever a student probably remembers shopping for Hilroy notebooks, binders, and loose-leaf paper every August when it was time to return to school. Students have been scribbling in Hilroy products for more than half a century.

But who the heck is Roy Hill?

Put his last name in front of his first, remove one of the letter *l*'s and you have the answer: Hill, a native of the village of King north of Toronto, is the founder of a Canadian paper products company who, in the late 1950s, rearranged his name to christen his business Hilroy Envelopes and Stationery Ltd.

Born in 1892, Hill took his first job at age twelve, working for $3 a week as an office boy. Eager to get ahead, he began taking commerce courses at night school and seven years later landed a $7-a-week job in the warehouse of a textbook publisher. By age twenty-four, he had more than quadrupled his earnings as a travelling salesman for a stationery firm covering the territory from Winnipeg to Montreal.

By this time, his knowledge of the stationery business was outstanding, and in 1918, he disregarded the pessimism of skeptical business associates and made a decision that eventually put the Hilroy name in front of Canadians from coast to coast. He borrowed $432 on a life insurance policy, added a $1,500 loan from his parents, and formed Canadian Pad and Paper Co. Limited.

"While working for another company he began asking all kinds of questions, such as 'who did this job? What's that machine for? Where is this made?'" recalls his great-nephew, Doug Hill. "Someone said to him 'Why don't you go and mind your own business?' So he did. He started his own company."

Canadian Pad and Paper opened for business on the second floor of a remodelled home in downtown Toronto, where Hill had five employees and was the manager, salesman, shipper, receiver, and paper cutter. He often worked from 7 a.m. to 11 p.m., cutting and trimming pads or books manufactured during the day. In the evenings, his wife,

Elsie, with baby in tow, would come to the factory by streetcar to wrap and label the day's production.

Expansions took the firm to new quarters on King Street and in 1929 to Madison Avenue in Toronto, where Hill built a new factory. The company prospered, based on his business philosophy of honesty, integrity, quality, and treating his employees with dignity and respect.

In 1932, Hill purchased the entire stock of Eaton, Crane, and Pike. Thirteen years later he bought L.P. Bouvier Co. Limited, and formed a new company known as Bouvier Envelopes Limited. When bigger quarters were needed in the mid-1940s, he purchased eleven acres from the township of York and in 1947 built a 145,000-square-foot factory, which has since been expanded to 250,000 square feet.

The Hilroy name arrived on the scene in 1958, when Canadian Pad and Paper Co. Ltd., Eaton, Crane, and Pike Limited, and Bouvier Envelopes Limited merged to become Hilroy Envelopes and Stationery Limited.

In the late 1950s and 1960s, Hill made several shrewd moves to solidify his business, including the 1959 purchase of the Canadian Stationery Co. Limited in Joliette, Quebec and the founding of new branches of his existing firm, including Hilroy Envelopes (Western) Limited in Winnipeg; Hilroy Quebec Limitée in Montreal; and Hilroy Envelopes and Stationery in Calgary.

By then, Hilroy notebooks and loose-leaf paper with the three holes were being used by millions of Canadian students.

In 1968, Hill sold the business to Abitibi Paper to become part of what was known as Abitibi-Price Inc. He remained at Hilroy as chairman of the board and remained an Abitibi director until his death in 1978.

On December 1, 1994, Hilroy was purchased by The Mead Corporation of Dayton, Ohio and became Mead Scool & Office Products (Canada). Mead later continued to operate under the name Hilroy — A Mead Company. Mead later changed the name of its school and office products division to Mead Consumer & Office Products Division to reflect changes in its product line. On January 1, 2002, The Mead Corporation merged with U.S. envelope company Westvaco of Stanford, Connecticut. Today, Hilroy employs about 250 people at its Toronto factory and is a major manufacturer and importer of refills, binders, coil books, brief covers, file folders, pads, and envelopes. It is the exclusive marketer and distributor of The MeadWestvaco product line to Canadian consumers.

John Holt and G.R. Renfrew

Holt Renfrew

Sometimes the person who starts a company isn't part of its famous brand name. While the name Holt Renfrew today conjures up a sense of quality clothing, it was actually William Samuel Henderson who got the firm started. Messrs. Holt and Renfrew would show up later.

Henderson came from Londonderry, Ireland in 1834 to Quebec City to sell a variety of hats and caps. The first firm he worked for was Ashton and Company, but by 1837 he had taken control and set up shop on rue Buade.

Business was good, and twelve years later Henderson began expanding the company by getting into the fur business. Three years later, he sold the shop to his brother John. In 1860, G.R. Renfrew, an employee, became a partner to form Henderson, Renfrew & Co. After another change in partnership in 1867, John Holt joined the company, and he too, eventually took a controlling interest. The two bought Henderson out, and the name Holt Renfrew & Co. Ltd. would become official in 1908.

In the 1880s, the company was appointed Furrier-in-Ordinary to her Majesty Queen Victoria, and its association with the British royalty continued with three other monarchs. In fact, in 1948, Holt Renfrew was asked to create a Labrador wild mink coat as Canada's gift for then-Princess Elizabeth's wedding.

By 1889, Holt Renfrew had opened a second store in Toronto on Yonge and Adelaide streets. More stores in other cities followed and to meet their shoppers' sophisticated tastes the company became the exclusive representative of such haute couture lines as Christian Dior and Valentino. In fact, in the 1930s and 1940s Holt Renfrew secured the oldest existing contract with the house of Christian Dior. When Yves Saint Laurent opened his own maison in Paris, Holt Renfrew promptly procured the exclusive rights in Canada for Saint Laurent Haute.

Ownership of the firm changed hands a couple of times between American companies in the 1960s, but in 1986 Holt Renfrew returned to its Canadian roots when it was purchased by Wittington Investments Ltd., chaired by Galen Weston, whose company, George

Weston Ltd., of Toronto, has vast holdings, including Canadian companies Weston's Bakery, Loblaws, and Neilson Dairy. Several stores were renovated and different marketing styles were introduced to appeal to a broader range of shoppers.

Today, patrons can buy a wide selection of designer and private label women's and men's fashions, cosmetics, fragrances, jewellery, accessories, and home furnishings. In addition to several stores in Montreal and Toronto, there are others in Ottawa, Quebec City, Vancouver, Calgary, and Edmonton.

Tim Horton
Tim Hortons Donuts

To many hockey fans, Tim Horton was a legendary National Hockey League defenceman whose name is etched onto the Stanley Cup four times as a member of the Toronto Maple Leafs. To those who couldn't care less about hockey, he is a name on a sign and a synonym for a regular coffee and a Dutchie to go.

"Mr. Horton will be famous long after most Timbit dunkers have forgotten what he did for a living," *Globe and Mail* reporter John Saunders once wrote.

In fact, Horton supported himself and his family by playing professional hockey in the 1950s, '60s and '70s, not by peddling Timbits, donuts, and coffee. During his hockey career, the Tim Hortons donut chain was merely a sideline, but one that would earn millions of dollars for others long after he was killed in a 1974 car accident.

Miles Gilbert "Tim" Horton was born in the northern Ontario mining community of Cochrane on January 12, 1930, about eighteen months before Conn Smythe opened Maple Leaf Gardens. He was a quiet but muscular kid who played his early hockey in Copper Cliff near Sudbury before heading south to play for Toronto's St. Michael's Majors in 1947.

As a youngster, his dream was to be a fighter pilot. As a young hockey player, his focus changed to pro hockey and he

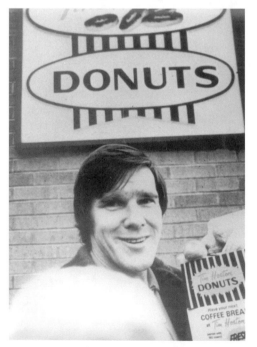

Tim Horton

Courtesy of Tim Hortons

developed into a tough but capable rushing defenceman. Shortly after joining the Majors his penchant for penalties earned him the nickname "Tim the Terrible."

After a promising junior career, Horton played for the Pittsburgh Hornets of the American Hockey League before he, with his trademark Marine Corps brushcut, joined Toronto as a regular rearguard in 1952.

Horton wore number 7 for the Leafs until the 1969–70 season when he was traded to the New York Rangers. In 1971–72 he joined the Pittsburgh Penguins before being acquired by Punch Imlach's Buffalo Sabres in 1972. He was in his second season with Buffalo when he died.

Despite being shortsighted and nearly blind in his left eye (he was also nicknamed "Mr. Magoo" and "Clark Kent" for the thick, dark-rimmed glasses he wore away from the rink), Horton was a rock-steady rearguard who left a legacy in the NHL. Playing for much of his career with fellow defensive stalwarts Allan Stanley, Bobby Baun, and Carl Brewer, Horton's Leafs won the Stanley Cup in 1962, 1963, 1964, and 1967. He was voted to the NHL's first all-star team three times and in 1977 was inducted into the Hockey Hall of Fame.

"He was one of those steady defencemen who never set many fires but was always around to put them out," sports columnist Dick Beddoes once wrote about Horton, who was known for his powerful slapshot, extraordinary strength, and his love for donuts, fast cars, and booze. Teammates remember him as modestly confident about his abilities, approachable, generous, and considerate, although he had his share of off-ice temper tantrums.

The night of his death, the forty-four-year-old Horton was named third star after the Sabres fell 4-2 to the Leafs at Maple Leaf Gardens. He died at 4:30 a.m., when he was thrown from his high-performance Ford Pantera as it flipped several times after leaving the Queen Elizabeth Way in St. Catharines, Ontario. The car was a signing bonus when Horton inked his second contract with the Sabres.

During his NHL career, Horton logged 1,446 regular season games, scored 115 goals and 403 assists, and registered 1,611 minutes in penalties. Another impressive statistic was the success of his donut business, which in its first decade had grown from a single franchise to thirty-five outlets.

The business was launched in February 1964 when Horton and two partners formed Tim Donut Ltd., which licensed Horton's name for use in their proposed chain of donut shops. Two months later, they opened the first Tim Hortons franchise on Ottawa Street in Hamilton, Ontario, where a dozen donuts cost sixty-nine cents and a cup of coffee was a dime. As donuts filled with cream or jelly and coated with sugar and honey glaze flew off the shelves that spring, Horton was helping the Leafs capture their third successive Cup.

Why did Horton get into the donut business? As an investment and because he had a sweet tooth, according to *Open Ice: The Tim Horton Story* by Douglas Hunter. "I love eating donuts and that was one of the big reasons that I opened my first donut shop. Buying donuts was costing me too much money," Horton said in 1969.

Until the mid-1980s, the logo found on Tim Hortons signs, coffee cups, bags, and donut boxes was Horton's signature and an oval depicting a stack of four donuts, one for each of his daughters. Today, the donuts are gone from the company's advertising but his signature is still on the signs that dot neighbourhoods across Canada.

In the mid-1960s, Horton took over his partners' shares in the company and soon after met ex-police officer Ron Joyce, who became owner of two Hamilton franchises, including the first one opened by the company. In 1967, Joyce became Horton's business partner and eventually built the company into one of Canada's most popular and successful food chains. In 1975, he bought control of the company from Horton's wife Lori for $1 million and a Cadillac. Twenty years later, the company, then known as TDL Group Ltd., merged with Ohio-based Wendy's International Inc.

Today, the name that brought hockey fans to their feet in the 1950s, '60s and '70s is found on more than 2,000 donut shops in Canada and some 140 in the United States.

Name Dropper

Donuts were not Horton's first business venture. In the late 1950s, he ran a service station and car dealership in Toronto. In 1963, he was a partner in an unsuccessful chain of drive-in chicken and burger restaurants in the Toronto area. He also ran a burger outlet in North Bay in partnership with his brother Gerry.

Robin's Donuts

If you believe that the early bird catches the worm and maybe even a donut and a coffee, then you'll understand the story behind Robin's Donuts.

Despite the name on the chain's signs, there's no person named Robin. The company got its name in 1975 when cofounders of the company, Harvey Cardwell and George Spicer, were in Thunder Bay working on plans to launch a donut franchise. They planned to call the firm Superior Donuts, but when they saw a robin in the backyard they liked the early morning connotation and went with the name of the bird. There are about 240 Robin's Donuts stores from Victoria to Cape Breton, and you'll find a lot of early birds there every morning, many munching on Robin's eggs, tiny treats similar to the Timbits sold at rival Tim Hortons outlets.

The Robin's Donuts chain is operated by the Afton Food Group Ltd., which is based in Burlington, Ontario and also operates Donut Delite Café, among other franchises.

John Inglis

John Inglis and Sons

If you've done a load of laundry or cooked a meal, you've met John Inglis in a round-about way.

Since the end of World War II, his surname has been a fixture in Canadian kitchens and laundry rooms, where it can be found on washing machines, clothes dryers, stoves, refrigerators, and dishwashers built by the company he founded in 1859.

But Inglis is known for more than just household appliances. His name is connected to a diverse range of goods, including guns and fishing equipment, that have played a role in the lives of generations of Canadians since before Confederation.

In 1850, at age thirty-six, Inglis immigrated to Canada from England and worked in Hamilton, Oakville, and the Niagara Peninsula, where he honed the metalworker and patternmaker's skills he'd learned in England and Scotland. Nine years later, he moved to Guelph, Ontario, and with two partners founded Mair, Inglis & Evatt, which built machinery for grist and flour mills.

Within ten years, Inglis and his counterparts were also making pulleys, fly wheels, steam engines, and water wheels — the basic

Name Dropper

Inglis's Toronto plant on Strachan Avenue has been called "Canada's most important factory." Few Canadian factories ever manufactured the range of products this one did; few have seen as many generations of workers pass through the same factory gates; few have played such a major role in equipping other industries as this one; it was one of a small number of plants to have witnessed so many changes in manufacturing over the course of their existence. The plant was a snapshot of worker history over 108 years in the same location.

> ## Name Dropper
>
> Toronto's Central Prison was located next to John Inglis's early Toronto factory on Strachan Avenue. More than once, public hangings and lashings were conducted during factory hours. Prisoners made brooms in the prison.

technology of Canada's industrial revolution — as well as chains, window grates, and manhole covers. A decade later, Inglis, a native of Castleton, Roxboroughshire, Scotland, and a new partner, Daniel Hunter, were making engines and mill machinery under the name Inglis & Hunter.

Having outgrown its Guelph factory, the company moved to Strachan Avenue in Toronto in 1881 and soon took advantage of the city's growing manufacturing sector. Within a year, output was five times that of the Guelph enterprise; by 1885, a new factory had been built that eventually dwarfed everything in the neighbourhood but the churches.

Two years later, Hunter left and the company's name was changed to John Inglis and Sons, with William Inglis, one of John's five sons, playing a large role. At the time, John Inglis was a prominent member of the Canadian Manufacturers' Association.

In April 1899, with his company growing by leaps and bounds and in the midst of diversifying its products, John Inglis died. William took over and under his direction, John Inglis and Sons began manufacturing marine steam engines and waterworks pumping engines, at the same time discontinuing production of its other products. In 1904, the company was forced to rebuild after a major fire.

In 1935, when Inglis was a key manufacturer of equipment used by other industries, William Inglis died. Reeling from the effects of the Depression, and without an Inglis at the helm for the first time in seventy-five years, the company closed the doors of its Toronto factory, which over the years had provided jobs for thousands of Torontonians. Shortly after, American-born industrialist Major J.E. Hahn purchased the company and obtained the right to use the name John Inglis Co. Limited. In 1938, Inglis began manufacturing guns for Canada and other countries.

When World War II ended in 1945, Inglis continued to make heavy equipment such as boilers, pumps, and tanks for the mining, brewing, and steel industries. And for the first time, the company began manufacturing consumer products, such as fishing tackle, house trailers, lipstick holders, and home appliances.

In the late 1940s, John Inglis and Co. affiliated with the company that evolved into American-owned Whirlpool Corporation, eventual owners of Inglis. The product line changed to wringer washers, and later, automatic washers, electric and gas dryers, dishwashers, and refrigerators.

In 1972, Inglis produced its one-millionth automatic washer and began manufacturing appliances under the Whirlpool brand name. The next year, the company name became Inglis Limited. In the mid-1980s Whirlpool Corporation of Ohio assumed majority ownership and in 1989 closed the Toronto plant, which at the time made only washing machines.

Factories in the Ontario communities of Stoney Creek, Cambridge, and Mississauga were also closed.

Since 2001, Inglis has been known as Whirlpool Canada Ltd. Despite the new name, plants in Quebec and the U.S. continue to build and sell appliances which bear John Inglis's name.

Name Dropper

Among the guns made at the Inglis factory in Toronto was the Inglis Browning High Power pistol, Canada's first and only mass-produced handgun. It was produced only briefly, but has provided more than half a century of service in numerous armies and remains the official sidearm of the Canadian Forces.

Kenneth Colin Irving

Irving Group of Companies

Unlike a handful of other ambitious New Brunswickers, Kenneth Colin Irving found fame and fortune close to home.

Louis B. Mayer made his mark in Hollywood, where he became the most powerful figure in the American film business; Richard Bedford Bennett moved to Ottawa to become Canada's eleventh prime minister; Maxwell Aitken, later Lord Beaverbrook, found stardom as a financier, politician, and media baron based in London, England.

K.C. Irving, by contrast, had no taste for life on the world stage. He chose to sink his roots deep into New Brunswick soil, where he saw opportunities that weren't available elsewhere. Between the early 1930s and 1970, this stay-at-home vision helped him blossom from a small-time businessman in Saint John into one of Canada's richest men.

The empire Irving built has been described as a world-class operation with influence extending into virtually every corner of New Brunswick and beyond. Its power is based on one simple policy — own 100 percent, because total ownership means total control. Most Irving companies issue no stock publicly, publish no annual reports, and its head honchos rarely speak with the media.

"If there ever was a company town covering 28,000 square miles, with a population of 600,000, New Brunswick is it; and the company is K.C. Irving Ltd.," authors Russell Hunt and Robert Campbell write in their book K.C. *Irving: The Art of the Industrialist.* "There is hardly a pie in New Brunswick worth having a finger in, in which you won't find an Irving digit."

Visit a convenience store or a restaurant, walk into a lumberyard or hardware store, turn on the radio in New Brunswick "and chances are you make K.C. and his clan richer," John DeMont declared in his book *Citizens Irving: K.C. Irving and His Legacy,* which points out that the Irvings own a fleet of aircraft, more ships than the Canadian navy, and a security company that is thought to be larger than all but two police forces in New Brunswick, as well as companies that make prefabricated homes, office buildings, and frozen food. "They sell heavy equipment, tires, life insurance, personal computers and translation services. They run tugboats, and dredging outfits, apartment buildings, a restaurant chain and a string of home heating companies."

Irving was born in 1899, in Bouctouche, New Brunswick, where his father, J.D., owned vast tracts of land and operated mills and stores, which helped him become powerful and wealthy.

He started working in the family store and lumber mill after school. When World War I interrupted the calm life in Bouctouche, Irving enlisted in the Royal Flying Corps and headed to Britain for pilot training. The war ended before he finished his training.

Back home, he decided against university and instead worked at a smelt fishery and a sawmill, and later developed skills as an auto mechanic. He eventually returned to his father's store, where one of his first jobs was collecting delinquent accounts. Soon he was helping with purchasing, but he had bigger plans, all connected to the rising popularity of the automobiles that had begun chugging along the muddy roads of his hometown.

Irving began selling Model T Fords at a local dealership in 1922 and by all accounts was a top-notch salesman. Eventually he had his own dealership and began selling gasoline for Imperial Oil. When he parted company with Imperial Oil in 1924, Irving embarked on a number of ventures that led to a string of entrepreneurial successes that would make him a rich man.

Miffed that the petroleum giant had put him out of business, he launched his own oil company in 1924, the K.C. Irving Oil and Gas Company. Its signs soon became a familiar sight throughout the Atlantic provinces, as would Primrose, Irving Oil's first gasoline.

By 1927, he had Ford dealerships and service stations in four New Brunswick towns, and two years later, had incorporated the Irving Oil Company. Three years later, the big red, white, and blue Irving diamond adorned filling stations in more than twenty communities in New Brunswick and Nova Scotia.

Irving had also become a family man. He and his wife Harriet, who once worked at the Irving family store in Bouctouche, had three sons, James, Arthur, and John.

When his father died in 1933, Irving took over the family lumber business. By the end of 1934, he owned thirty service stations and sold his products at three thousand retail outlets. An Irving-controlled construction company built all of his gas stations.

When car sales slumped in the mid 1930s, Irving jumped into the bus and trucking business and his company S.M.T. (Eastern) soon became New Brunswick's largest passenger bus and freight truck operator. He had begun to take control over the province's roadways: He sold cars, fuelled and repaired them, and most freight and passengers used his trucks and buses, all of which were repaired and fuelled by Irving gas and oil. His company also built bus bodies.

In the late 1930s, Irving purchased the near-bankrupt Canada Veneers Ltd. of Saint John and began producing veneer that was used to build Mosquito aircraft bodies in Britain, Canada, and Australia. In the mid-1940s, Irving cemented his presence in New Brunswick by purchasing 1.5 million acres of prime timberland — an area equivalent to that of Prince Edward Island. It made him one of the province's largest landowners.

He purchased New Brunswick Publishing Co., publisher of the *Telegraph-Journal* and the *Evening-Time Globe*, Saint John's two dailies, in 1944, then bought and expanded a Saint John pulp mill to make paper for his newspapers.

Eight years later, Irving Oil controlled twenty-three companies and had assets of more than $30 million. More than four thousand people were on the payroll in New Brunswick and three thousand more worked in Quebec, Maine, and Ontario.

Irving "had an uncanny knack for buying beleaguered or bankrupt enterprises, turning them around and incorporating them into the rest of his empire while, at the same time, pressing for new markets," wrote DeMont. "His real genius was his ability to look ahead, to anticipate, to know where real opportunities lay. He was like a chess master planning his moves. Maybe the payoff didn't come right away but it came."

A prime example was his purchase of the Saint John Dry Dock Co. Ltd., the biggest shipyard in the British Commonwealth. When Irving sealed the deal in May 1959, business was slow and its workforce had dropped to three hundred workers, from fifteen hundred during World War II. Within days, Irving landed a $3 million contract, and several years later, he won a $3.5 billion contract to build frigates for the Canadian navy.

In 1960, Irving made his biggest move, building an oil refinery in Saint John with an initial capacity of forty thousand barrels a day. At the time, he owned 55 intermingled companies, ran 1,900 service station outlets, owned 150 cargo vessels, 4 New Brunswick daily newspapers, and radio and television outlets in Moncton and Saint John. His holdings were valued at about $300 million and about 8 percent of the province's workforce worked for Irving's companies.

In peace and war Irving was at his best as an integrator of companies. When he built his refinery, structural steel came from his steel company; his oil company provided fuel and service for his buses and trucks; and his construction companies built his gas stations. His ownership of all of New Brunswick's English language daily newspapers, as well as control of radio and television outlets, allowed him to manage what the media was saying about his operations, which were either loved or despised, depending on whom you talked to.

The 1970 Davey Commission, set up to probe ownership and control of Canada's media, estimated that Irving's TV stations reached 94.9 percent of New Brunswick's potential audience. Nevertheless, attempts by the federal government's Combines Investigations Branch to break up the Irving media monopoly failed.

With his media empire under scrutiny in 1971, Irving and his wife suddenly left Canada for the Bahamas and later Bermuda, for reasons never disclosed, though most speculate he fled to avoid paying taxes. The weekly *King's County Record* called Irving's departure "the darkest day in the history of the province."

Under the watchful eye of their father, his sons, who began expanding the Irving empire into Maine, assumed day-to-day operation of the companies. In the late 1980s the Irving family controlled three hundred companies in the eastern U.S. According to *Forbes* magazine, the family had a personal worth of $4.1 billion (U.S.) in 2002.

Before and after K.C.'s death, the Saint John-based Irving Group of Companies has been widely criticized for damaging the environment. However, its enterprises have won kudos from a variety of organizations, including the World Wildlife Fund of Canada, the Atlantic Salmon Federation, and the Canadian Council of Ministers of the Environment, for their environmental efforts.

In New Brunswick, company spokesperson Mary Keith says the Irvings are involved in the largest private tree improvement program in Canada.

Samuel and Beatrice Irwin

Irwin Toy Limited

He could sell just about anything while she had a knack for figures. What started out as a two-person operation in 1926 selling souvenirs and other small items eventually became the number one toy company in Canada.

Anyone growing up in the 1950s and beyond probably knows the Irwin name. Among the toys the company has sold over the years are the Slinky, the Yo-Yo, Pound Puppies, and Pro Star tabletop hockey games.

Samuel Irwin grew up on a farm near Orangeville, Ontario. He would visit future wife Beatrice Whiteside, who lived in Alliston, Ontario, by driving his jalopy over the rough roads of the time. As a young man, he worked as a clerk for Hill's General Store in Orangeville and then moved to Toronto, where he was an employee at Eaton's, Simpson's, and then a wholesale dry goods firm.

After serving overseas in World War I, Sam found work selling business courses. That led to a job selling specialty items such as souvenirs for Rumsay & Company, and Sam thought he could make more money with a similar business of his own. He and Beatrice married in 1924 and decided two years later to open their shop, Irwin Specialties, near Yonge Street and St. Clair Avenue in Toronto.

"My dad was really a salesman and good at it," Arnold Irwin told us from his winter residence in Florida. "My mother was more meticulous and kept the records."

Samuel and Beatrice Irwin

Courtesy of Arnold Irwin

By 1935, there were five salesmen employed to cover the country, and the firm was specializing in selling toys, games, and souvenirs. The company did well, due in part to Sam's penchant for taking chances and his love travel that took him around the world seeking business opportunities. In the late 1930s, while in England, he bought up old and unwanted souvenirs of King George VI's coronation ceremony at a cheap price. Employees back home were surprised at how much he shipped back, Arnold says, but by placing them in Christmas stockings that the firm sold to other companies, Sam managed to move all the merchandise.

The Irwin company, which was a wholesale firm, had other successes thanks to Sam's skill at spotting bargains. After World War II broke out, there was a lot of public pressure on stores not to sell German- and Japanese-made goods. Samuel saw this as an opportunity. He bought up the goods, mostly toys, at bargain prices, and within a year the shops realized they were low on stock and had to buy the merchandise back from him. "He made a fortune," Arnold says.

After the war, however, the company was running into financial difficulty and Sam suffered a nervous breakdown. A friend suggested Sam bring his two sons, Mac and Arnold, into the business. Both were still in university and managed to finish their studies even after they went to work for their father around 1950.

It was Mac and Arnold who started moving the company even more into the toy business. They allied themselves with several strong manufacturers and secured rights early on to sell products that became successes. As the company grew, both Sam and Bea continued to take an active role. Both worked hard and would often take work home with them on weekends and holidays, Arnold says.

But tragedy struck in 1968. Sam, who was always a "hesitant swimmer," drowned in the swimming pool at his north Toronto home. It was never clear what happened.

Arnold says his father, like many of his generation, quit school at an early age, but "he was very much in awe of people who had an education." When Samuel died, his sons set up a fund that would help pay for employees' children to attend university.

Irwin Toy went public in 1969 and had a long string of profitable years. Like their parents, Arnold and Mac, who were president and vice-president respectively in the company, believed in putting in an honest days' work. "We were really hard working. We spent a lot of time in the business. We thrived on it, and we enjoyed it. It didn't seem like work."

Arnold describes the company of that era as one big family, with low turnover and many long-term employees. His mother stayed on as a company director for several years, and when she got older they made her an honorary director. She died at age eighty-nine.

Irwin Toy, meanwhile, continued to expand, initiating direct sales of toys in the U.S. in 1991, and setting up in Australia in 1997. In April 2001, an affiliate of the Toronto-based Livgroup Investments Ltd. bought the company and turned it back into a private company. Its brands are sold in more than fifty countries around the world.

Name Dropper

The education fund set up by the Irwins proved to be a blessing many years later when Arnold's wife had to be rushed to the hospital. The doctor who treated her was an employee's son who had had his schooling paid for partially by the company.

Allan Jackson and Donald Triggs
Jackson-Triggs Vintners

It sounds like the kind of thesis any student or wine lover would toast.

But for Allan Jackson it was a scientific way to earn his undergraduate and doctoral degree. In doing so, it led him down a path to co-founding one of Canada's most popular wine companies.

Jackson, who grew up in Hamilton, Ontario, earned his PhD from McMaster University in 1977 by studying the taste characteristics of different grape and wine varietals. Though it conjures up images of late nights sipping from a beaker or a test tube, Jackson says his research was on the chemistry of why most Canadian wines "tasted like hell" in those days. What he learned was that the type of grapes being used here didn't make for the best-tasting wine.

About the same time he submitted his thesis, Jackson landed a job at Labatt, which was just beginning to branch out from its popular line of beers to researching ways to improve the quality of Canadian wines. The young scholar looked after research and quality control for the company's wine divisions.

Ironically for two men whose names are associated with wine, Donald Triggs was also working for a beer company, heading up Labatt's American wine group. It was here the two met, but it would be several years before they joined forces in their own winery.

Don Triggs and Allan Jackson, co-founders of Jackson-Triggs Vintners outside their new Niagara Estate Winery in July 2001.

Photo by Stephen Dominick

Allan Jackson and Donald Triggs

Triggs, who grew up in rural Manitoba, began acquiring his taste for wine while at the University of Manitoba. Though he was a Labatt employee for several years, "I had always had the idea of running my own business. It always appealed to me." In May 1989, he and Jackson got their chance. Labatt was looking to get out of the wine business, and the two men and two other colleagues saw this as an opportunity to buy out the division.

They established Cartier Wines and Beverages, and over the next five years acquired wineries and merged with other Canadian wine producers to create a parent company, Vincor International Inc. Jackson says they decided to create a series of products under the Jackson-Triggs name, because market research indicated that consumers liked the idea of winemakers having their names on bottles. Such labelling also stands for pride and craftsmanship, adds Triggs.

Their first wines were well received by the public, and they introduced several others which won awards and wowed critics. Their Sauvignon Blanc was so exceptional that one reviewer wrote "I tried calling Ripley's Believe it or Not, for here was a Canadian-made wine that knocked the socks off the imported Sauvignon Blancs."

Both Jackson and Triggs are pleased with the reception their wines have had, and they still personally test all their products. "You get a special thrill seeing your name on the wine when you see it in the store," says Jackson. "It's a great feeling." Adds Triggs: "When you have your name on the label, you care more. It's a sense of responsibility. You know the customers are going to call you so you wear the performance of your company on your sleeve."

When Jackson isn't involved with the business, he enjoys gardening, cycling, and reading at his home in Stoney Creek, Ontario. Triggs, who has houses in Toronto and Niagara-on-the-Lake, owns a vineyard with his wife Elaine, which is appropriately called Delaine Vineyard. He's also a serious art collector, loves music, and sits on a variety of boards, including the Richard Ivey School of Business in London, Ontario; Brock University in St. Catharines, Ontario; and AboutFace, an organization that assists those who are facially different. He loves wine, of course, and "if you asked me if there were only one kind of wine I could take with me to a deserted island, it would be Pinot Noir. It's the most diverse."

Vincor, which has been publicly traded since 1996, is the leading vintner in Canada and the fourth-largest wine producer in North America. The company also owns and operates a chain of more than 160 Wine Rack retail outlets in Ontario.

Name Dropper

Why Jackson-Triggs and not Triggs-Jackson? According to Triggs, the former simply tested better during initial market research. But Jackson says that Triggs-Jackson reminded focus groups too much of the lawn mower company Briggs & Stratton.

Alexander Keith

Alexander Keith Brewery

When Alexander Keith arrived in Halifax in 1817, he had all the tools necessary to run his own brewery. When it came to brewing, some said he was a perfectionist.

As a teenager in Halkirk, Caithness in northern Scotland, his father, a highly respected farmer, financed his business education to prepare him for the world of commerce. At age seventeen, he was sent to Sunderland in northern England to learn the basics of brewing and malting from an uncle. He later gained practical experience in London and Edinburgh.

By the time he landed in North America, Keith's recipe for beer-making had the ring of a modern-day television advertisement: Brew beer slowly and carefully and take the time to get it right, using only the finest pure barley malt and hops. At age twenty-two, he was practising what he preached as a brewmaster and business manager at a small Halifax brewery owned by Charles Boggs.

Three years later, he purchased the business and began brewing under the name Nova Scotia Brewery.

Legendary for his hospitality and known as a devoted husband and father to his eight children, Keith was confronted by his first major business challenge when the economy weakened in the years after the War of 1812. Although land and buildings were devalued and business stagnated, he decided to take a gamble by expanding his brewery in 1822. His hunch paid off: the economy improved and headed into a ten-year boom.

Keith made a name for himself as a brewer of strong ales and porter, as well as conventional ginger and spruce beers, which were milder brews with a distinctive taste that was popular in North America at the time. Prosperous times enabled him to move to larger quarters on Lower Water Street in Halifax.

When the boom ended and a cholera epidemic struck, the city was again in a slump. Keith again threw caution to the wind and enlarged his brewery; his instinct proved correct. In 1833, abolition of the slave trade in the sugar islands of the West Indies sent rum prices skyrocketing, making ale the most affordable and popular drink in Halifax, author Allen Winn Sneath writes in his book *Brewed in Canada*.

In 1853, Keith's only son Donald became a full partner in the firm and the brewery name was changed to Alex Keith & Son.

Although brewing his famous India Pale Ale was his first love, Keith always found time to play a leading role in Halifax's social and business communities. He held directorships with the Bank of Nova Scotia, the Halifax Fire Insurance Company, the Halifax Gas, Light and Water Company, the Provincial Permanent Building, and the Investment Society. He helped found the Halifax Marine Insurance Association.

He served as commissioner of the Court of Common Pleas for Halifax before its incorporation and was a member of the city's first council from 1843 to 1854. He served as mayor of Halifax three times. In the 1840 general election, he lost his bid to win a seat for the Conservative Party in Halifax. At the time of Confederation he was offered a Senate seat but declined. He was a leader of the Freemasons, and in 1869 became grandmaster of the Nova Scotia Freemasons. Keith was a respected philanthropist who was involved in several charitable and cultural societies. He died in Halifax in 1873, leaving an estate worth $271,000.

Following his death, Keith's son continued to run the brewery, which maintained its family ties until 1928, when his granddaughter sold it to the Oland & Sons brewery. Keith's and its India Pale Ale became part of the Labatt family in 1971, when the London, Ontario-based brewery acquired Oland.

Name Dropper

In 1867, Alexander Keith sent barrels of his ale to Prince Edward Island to help the Fathers of Confederation celebrate the creation of Canada.

Vickie Kerr

Miss Vickie's Potato Chips

Like most moms, Vickie Kerr wanted her young children to steer clear of junk food. And like most young farm couples, she and her husband Bill were often challenged to make ends meet.

So, in 1986, Kerr began making her own potato chips in the kitchen at the family's 165-acre potato farm near New Lowell, Ontario, northwest of Toronto.

After experimenting for more than a year with potatoes hand-picked on their farm, the couple came up with their own brand of homemade chips. Made with thick-sliced potatoes with the skins left on, cooked and stirred by hand in kettles of peanut oil, and lightly salted with sea salt, her chips were crisp and free of cholesterol and preservatives. They also contained plenty of the vitamin A and potassium that are lost when chips are commercially produced.

Miss Vickie's chips were a hit with her children, her neighbours, and, within a few months, several retail outlets in the New Lowell area.

"We had come up with a healthy snack food for the kids," says Kerr, a Montreal native who had worked as a hotel receptionist, pre-school teacher, and co-owner of a tavern before deep-frying her first potato chip. "But we also had the potential for a business, which is something I wanted from the start. Potato growing was a cutthroat business ... one farmer would think nothing of cutting another out of the business. Financially, we were always on the edge, so Miss Vickie's was a godsend."

After taking a third mortgage on their property, the Kerrs went into the potato chip business in earnest in 1989 on the farm they'd purchased nine years earlier, near the land on which her husband's family had grown potatoes for several generations. Ironically, potato chip maker Humpty Dumpty was among the buyers of the Kerrs' early crops.

After importing a cooking kettle from New Hampshire, Kerr developed a business plan, increased production, and took aim at the health food market. As she canvassed local retail outlets in her pickup truck, her first question to product buyers was always the same: "Are you willing to pay more for a snack food that is healthy and tastes better?"

Because money was needed to cover expenses, her second question was usually, "Are you willing to pay cash?"

On both counts, the answer was often "yes."

Kerr's first customer was a gas station/variety store in New Lowell, which purchased seventy-two bags of her chips. Within weeks, Miss Vickie's chips were being stocked by grocery stores, drug stores, and other businesses in the immediate area. She often received calls at home from retailers wondering how they could get her product, which sold to customers for more than $2 for a 180-gram bag, about double the price of other brands.

"We never had trouble keeping up with the demand," she says.

Soon, the operation had expanded from one kettle to six and the Kerrs had converted a potato storage building into a processing facility. Two dozen trucks were on the road, and within twelve months her chips were being sold in the Toronto area.

First-year sales were about $1 million and by the second year, when her products were being sold throughout southern and central Ontario and as far east as Montreal and Ottawa, sales had risen by 200 percent. The product line consisted of salted and non-salted varieties. Eventually, barbecue-flavoured chips were added under the name Mr. Vickie's, as a way of recognizing the work of husband Bill, who was the small company's production expert, while Vickie handled promotion, marketing, and quality control. In 1992, Miss Vickie's Salsa and Corn Chips were added.

By then, their chips — still hand-stirred in kettles and using peanut oil — were being made in plants in Coquitlam, British Columbia and Pointe Claire, Quebec, as well as on their farm.

A year later, as the couple was developing a salt and vinegar-flavoured chip and seeking a better distribution channel, they sold the company to Hostess Frito-Lay for an undisclosed sum. With daily production of eighty-five thousand bags of chips, the company held a little more than 1 percent of the Canadian potato chip market.

"The company was our baby, so selling out was tough," said Vickie, noting that the couple was putting in eighty-hour weeks and vacations were rare. "We had planned on keeping the company for a long time as a place where the kids would work. But we wanted a change, we wanted to slow down and spend more time with our growing family."

After visiting Phoenix, Arizona for several years because Bill wanted drier weather, the family moved there full-time in the mid-1990s.

Bill died in a car accident in 1997; Vickie remained in Pheonix, where she was working for a criminal attorney at the time.

In 2002, Miss Vickie's chips were being made in Canada in plants in Taber, Alberta and Pointe Claire, Quebec. Several new flavours have been added since Kerr ran the company.

Name Dropper

Victoria's was the initial name for Vickie Kerr's chips but that was later changed to Miss Vickie's. "After returning from a food convention in the U.S., Bill just seemed to think it sounded better," says Vickie.

James Lewis Kraft

Kraft Foods

In the world of food products, J.L. Kraft was certainly the big cheese.

His name has become synonymous in Canada and around the world with such famous products as Jell-O, Miracle Whip, and that staple of university students everywhere, Kraft Dinner.

Born in the Niagara region community of Stevensville, Ontario in the 1870s, Kraft was one of eleven children in a Mennonite family who grew up on a dairy farm. When he was eighteen, he landed a job at Ferguson's grocery store in Fort Erie, Ontario before investing in a cheese company in Buffalo. In 1903, Kraft moved to Chicago with $65 to his name and decided to rent a wagon and a horse named Paddy. According to company history, Kraft bought cheese every day from the city's warehouses and resold it to local merchants who didn't want to make the trip themselves. From this humble beginning, Kraft built up his business to the point that he decided to manufacture cheese and brought in four of his brothers to help him with his enterprise.

In 1909, JL Kraft and Brothers Co. began importing cheeses from Europe, but it was Kraft's dream to make cheese that would keep longer, cook better, and be packaged in convenient sizes. At the time, cheddar cheese, the most popular variety in the U.S., molded or dried quickly and was difficult to ship long distances. As Kraft continued to sell different cheeses, however, he experimented with ways of making cheese a more marketable commodity. Kraft sold $5,000 worth of pasteurized cheese in 1915, and the next year sales jumped to $150,000.

The year 1916 would be key in Kraft's life. He received a patent for what would become known as processed cheese, narrowly beating out another company that was working on a similar process. To his credit, Kraft would later share the patent rights with the company.

Four years later, Kraft entered the Canadian market selling processed cheese and bread on a national scale. The famous Kraft kitchens were also started in the 1920s, and some of the products resulting from this approach were Miracle Whip in 1933 and Kraft Dinner in 1937. It was said that by the 1930s, Kraft was selling three million pounds of cheese a day. Per capita cheese consumption in the

U.S. increased by 50 percent between 1918 and 1945, largely because of Kraft's efforts and innovations.

Kraft was also an innovator when it came to advertising. As early as 1911, he was advertising on Chicago's elevated trains, using billboards, and mailing circulars to retailers. He was among the first to use coloured ads in magazines, and in 1933 the company began using radio to advertise its products by sponsoring the Kraft Musical Review. Though he was in his 70s by the time television arrived, Kraft embraced the new medium and created the Kraft Television Theatre.

The company prospered throughout his life, and by the time Kraft died in 1953, the firm had become one of the most recognizable brand names in the world. The company merged with General Foods in 1989 and continues to produce an array of famous products including Minute Rice, Cool Whip, Maxwell House coffee, and Tang.

Not bad for a young man who started out with less than $100 in his pocket.

Name Dropper

One of Kraft's hobbies was to make rings with semi-precious stones and give them to employees as awards for their hard work. He had to abandon the idea as the number of workers began to grow.

John Kinder Labatt

John Labatt Ltd.

Feel free to pull a cold Labatt Blue or a Labatt 50 out of the fridge as you read about the man who was ultimately responsible for giving us those brews.

John Kinder Labatt, born in Ireland in 1803, was the eldest of seven children. It wasn't a spirit of adventure but instead a desire to pay off his father-in-law's debts that brought him to Upper Canada in 1833. Labatt was accompanied by his wife Eliza, her mother, younger sister, and brother. They settled near what is now London, Ontario because land was cheaper there than in more urban areas of the colony.

Labatt was a successful farmer and sent his children to the best boarding school in the area. He was said to be hard-working and had his first brush with a local brewery by supplying it with barley. Around 1846, he travelled to Great Britain but returned to Canada where the cost of living wasn't so high. At about the same time he wrote to his wife, saying "I fancy I should like brewing better than anything else."

John Kinder Labatt

Courtesy of Labatt Archives

In 1847, he joined forces with fellow farmer Samuel Eccles and invested £2,000 in a small brewery on London, Ontario's Thames River that had been started by John Balkwell in 1828. There were only six staff, and they managed to produce about one thousand bottles that first year. Several years later,

Labatt became the sole owner of the business and renamed it John Labatt Brewery.

The brewery grew, and Labatt's business acumen ensured that it was one of the best in the region. He teamed up with fellow brewer John Carling to build a road in London so that beer could be more easily shipped to rural areas, but it was the coming of the railway to London in the 1850s that helped secure his brewery's growth.

In addition to brewing, Labatt was a town councillor, a member of the local Board of Trade, and the founder of the London Permanent Building and Savings Society and Western Permanent Building Society. He was an active participant at St. Paul's Anglican Church and was known to have helped the needy during a depression in the 1850s.

Labatt suffered from heart disease in later life and died on October 26, 1866. His obituary noted that he was "remarkable for his energetic, shrewd business qualities" and that he was a friend to people of all classes.

Wife Eliza and son John Jr. took over the business upon Labatt's death. A fire destroyed the brewery in 1874, but nine months later a new one was completed that could produce thirty thousand barrels of beer annually. In 1878, the company's India Pale Ale won a gold medal at the Paris International Exposition.

Labatt's was one of the few breweries to survive Prohibition in Canada because it was able to export to the U.S. and it produced two "temperance ales" that had less than 2 percent alcohol. One of the more unusual happenings in the company's later history was the kidnapping of John Labatt III in 1934. He was returned unharmed after three days, and despite some arrests, the matter was never fully explained.

In 1945, John Labatt Limited became a publicly traded company and about twenty years later began diversifying into other food products. Labatt's was one of the original partners in the Toronto Blue Jays franchise and is now part of Interbrew S.A., a Belgium-based firm. Despite a long labour dispute in early 2002, the company still brews beer in London, notably Blue, Blue Light, and Budweiser, producing about 817.6 million bottles of beer annually. If lined up end to end they'd stretch about 198,000 kilometres; that's enough to cover the Trans-Canada Highway about twenty-five times or to stretch more than halfway to the moon.

And it's done on about the same spot where John Labatt first practised his craft.

Name Dropper

It's perhaps fitting that Canadians like to refer to the Victoria Day holiday as "the May 2-4 weekend." According to company history, John Labatt introduced the idea in 1850 as London councillor, and other cities began to follow suit until it became a national holiday.

Thomas Carling

Carling Brewery

John Labatt wasn't the only famous brewer to come from London, Ontario. Thomas Carling, originally from Yorkshire, England, also set up shop in the bustling southwestern Ontario town of the mid-nineteenth century.

Carling came to Canada in 1818 and eventually prospered as a farmer near London. He served as a volunteer in the 1837 Rebellion, and started his brewery in 1843 using a recipe from his native Yorkshire. By 1849, he was ready to retire and left the brewery to his sons William and John. Carling would live to be eighty-three and was described as "a man of character and influence."

His sons nurtured the business, built a new brewery in 1879, which burned down shortly thereafter, and then recovered to create a joint stock corporation in 1882 called The Carling Brewery & Malting Company of London Ltd. Ironically, John Carling, who achieved national fame as a federal and provincial politician, never drank beer because it disagreed with his system.

Though the Carling name is now owned by Molson Brewery, it can still be found on such brands as Carling Ice and Black Label.

Robert Laidlaw

Laidlaw Inc.

Like many a budding Canadian entrepreneur, Robert Laidlaw had a dream but lacked the cash to turn it into reality.

"He got into business in 1924 by going to the bank and asking for a loan for his first truck," his daughter Dorothy Butler recalled in an interview with the *Hamilton Spectator*. "The banker asked him what he had for collateral and dad, who had nothing, said, 'I've got these two hands.' And the banker said, 'Mister, you've also got a loan.'"

Thanks to the good faith of his bank manager, the twenty-four-year-old native of Hagersville, Ontario, bought a 1918 Reo stake truck, purchased an eighteen-can milk route, and began hauling milk and mixed freight, mostly to nearby Hamilton.

It was the beginning of a career that would see Laidlaw become one of Canada's most well-known trucking magnates. Although he sold the company in 1959, his name is still found on trucks and buses that ply highways and byways in Canada and the United States.

Laidlaw was born in 1900 just outside Hagersville, the youngest of John and Margaret Laidlaw's seven children. After leaving school at an early age, he farmed in Saskatchewan and worked on his father's farm and at his brother Tom's garage before deciding to try his hand at trucking.

Along the way, Laidlaw met and courted Edna Reynolds of Port Dover. They were married in 1925.

By 1929, Laidlaw had three trucks on the road and in 1930 purchased his first tractor and semi-trailer unit, "a truck which drew the admiration of the whole community," according to documents obtained from the Haldimand County Museum.

His big break came soon after when the Canadian Gypsum Company established a wallboard plant and hired Laidlaw to truck products from its Hagersville operation to a wide area of Ontario. "The (trucking) business expanded and prospered, even through the Depression Years," says the book *Down Memory Lane: A Glimpse of Hagersville's Past* by Don Brown.

In 1939, a modern warehouse was built just north of Hagersville and eleven years later, the building was expanded. As the business grew, the Laidlaw family built a large home and enjoyed flashy cars and fine antiques.

According to a profile in the *Hamilton Spectator*, Laidlaw loved cards, hunting, Camel cigarettes, and boats, but "most of all he liked being a trucker … he liked to hang out with the drivers, swapping stories, helping out financially when there was need and taking little credit."

At one point he picked up the tab for the funeral of one of his drivers' daughters who was killed in a car accident.

By the late 1950s, Laidlaw's trucking empire had grown to fifty trucks and eighteen staff and he was faced with a choice — expand or sell. In ill health and with none of his three daughters interested in running the business, he sold out. The buyer was trucker Michael DeGroote, who got his start in trucking by hauling manure in the area. The $325,000 sale was sealed with a handshake in January 1959.

DeGroote kept the Laidlaw name on the trucks as part of the sale and also, he said later, because "Laidlaw Transport sounds a hell of a lot better than DeGroote Transport."

His trucking company may have been gone but Laidlaw stayed behind the wheel, driving a garden tractor and the cars he loved. In summer, he'd cut his neighbours' grass and in winter, he'd clear their sidewalks. Eventually he grew ill and was forced to give up driving altogether. Laidlaw died in 1967 after a lengthy illness. All six of the pallbearers at his funeral, including DeGroote, were truckers.

Under DeGroote, the company went on to become Laidlaw Inc. based in Burlington, Ontario, with diversified holdings in trucking, solid waste management, and school busing. DeGroote sold the trucking business in 1984 to Contrans Corp. of Woodstock, Ontario, which continues to use the Laidlaw name on 625 rigs based in Woodstock, Guelph, and Hagersville, which serve Ontario, Eastern Canada, and the eastern United States.

DeGroote, one-time owner of the Hamilton Tiger-Cats, sold the rest of the company to Canadian Pacific Limited in 1988. In 2002, more than twenty thousand school buses across North America operated by Laidlaw Inc. still carried Laidlaw's name.

Ablan Leon

Leon's Furniture

Thanks to one mattress, Leon's is a household name in thousands of Canadian living rooms, bedrooms, and kitchens.

In the early 1900s, Ablan Leon left his native Lebanon and settled near Welland, Ontario on the Niagara Peninsula, where he worked in a factory. Soon after, he began selling clothing door to door out of a suitcase.

After squirrelling away some of his profits, he bought a small building in the working-class area of Welland, and in 1909, opened The A. Leon Company, a dry goods business with a product line that included pants, blankets, shoes, and linens.

He quickly established a reputation as a merchant who was honest and caring, and who always stood behind his goods. As immigration levels rose steadily early in the century, Leon noticed that many new Canadians were having difficulty obtaining credit. He responded by providing credit to people who were unable to find it elsewhere.

"Welland was a small town back then, where a good reputation was important to a business," says Terry Leon, Ablan's grandson. "For that reason he always did what was necessary to satisfy people, whether it meant refunding their money or offering to exchange a product."

Eventually, Ablan and his wife Lena started a family, which would grow to eleven children, most of whom worked in the store at one time or another.

Ablan Leon

Courtesy of Leon's Furniture

Their jobs ranged from dusting furniture and sweeping floors to washing windows and serving customers.

Which brings us to the mattress: There are two versions of the event that convinced Ablan to turn from dry goods to the retail furniture business. One has it that when one of his sons was to be married, Ablan purchased a mattress as a wedding gift; another has him buying a mattress for his wife's birthday. Whatever the case, the mattress was delivered and leaned against his store's outside wall where a passerby offered to buy it for more than Leon had paid.

"He asked a price he thought no one would pay, and it sold," says Terry Leon. "Now you have to know that Ablan believed in and always taught his children to ask only a fair price which represented good value for their customers. Following this philosophy he said to himself, 'If furniture is this easy and quick to sell, I should get into the furniture business.'"

The Leon's furniture business was launched in the same Welland store where Ablan sold dry goods. When he died in 1942, several of his children took the reigns of the company, which at that point was still a single-outlet business. Eventually three sons, Lewie, Tom, and Edward, and daughter Marjorie operated the enterprise. Over the years, both Lewie and Tom served as presidents.

On several occasions they increased the size of the Welland outlet to accommodate a bigger selection, and in the late 1940s and early 1950s the business expanded into the nearby communities of Fort Erie, Niagara Falls, and Port Colborne. Leon's broke into the Toronto market in the mid-1960s by purchasing the business Times Furniture, which ran four outlets in the Toronto area; it also ran two New Era furniture stores in Toronto. Both companies eventually took the Leon's name and by the late 1960s, Leon's Toronto stores had became synonymous with value and a gigantic selection of brand-name merchandise for every room in the house.

In 1969, Leon's Furniture went public on the Toronto Stock Exchange to raise capital for a new wave of expansion.

Four years later, Leon's opened a warehouse showroom in Canada, a massive 150,000-square-foot building in Toronto, which was believed to be the country's first "big box" retail outlet. When the public accepted this radical new approach enthusiastically, the company began erecting huge new showrooms across Canada.

Ablan Leon

Early in the 1980s, Leon's saw a need for showrooms in smaller towns across Canada and the idea of Leon's franchise stores was born. Today, with nearly fifty locations across Canada from Newfoundland to Alberta, the Leon's name is well represented by many independent entrepreneurs who carry the same selection of product as the corporate stores.

Leon's annual sales exceed half a billion dollars, it has two thousand associates, and its bright yellow trucks and humourous TV ads, often featuring promotions such as its "Don't Pay a Cent Event," are seen in most parts of Canada. In 2002, about ten members of the Leon family were heavily involved in the company, including grandsons Mark, who is company president; Terry, vice-president; and Eddie, director of merchandising.

Albert Edward LePage
Royal LePage Real Estate Ltd.

Selling real estate was regarded as the lowliest of Canada's professions — until Albert Edward LePage arrived on the scene in the early 1900s.

LePage, who often said "if you failed at everything else, you went into real estate," turned the industry on its ear when he began selling houses in Toronto in 1913.

In an era when real estate agents were viewed as highly unethical and disorganized and who did little selling in the summer and between November and early January, LePage demonstrated a brand of get-up-and-go that polished the tarnished image of his colleagues.

After leaving a job at his father's manufacturing company in Toronto at age twenty-six, the Charlottetown native began selling homes for a friend who had found considerable success on the Toronto real estate scene. Soon after, LePage started A.E. LePage Ltd., where one of his first innovations was the installation of his own office telephone at a time when most sales representatives shared phones. To set himself apart from other agents, he called himself a "bungalow specialist."

LePage, who often arrived for work outfitted in a bow tie and a straw hat, claimed to be the first agent to place descriptive advertisements in newspapers and he was among the first to take clients through the homes he had listed (previously buyers visited properties on

Albert Edward LePage

Courtesy of Royal LePage Real Estate Services, Ltd.

their own). In 1929, when he was building and selling homes, he accomplished the unbelievable by erecting a five-bedroom bungalow in one day and topped his achievement by selling the place within twenty-four hours.

At the end of World War I, his drive to end bad practices in real estate was instrumental in the formation of the Toronto Real Estate Board. He was its president in 1928. By 1940, LePage was subdividing prestigious estates and selling the lots as subdivisions. He is said to be the only real estate agent to have listed Casa Loma in Toronto.

When LePage retired and sold his company in 1953, A.E. LePage Ltd. was a residential real estate company based in Toronto and offering its services within a twenty-mile radius of the city. Eventually, it became the largest real estate firm in Canada, engaged in residential sales as well as land assembly. A.E. Lepage Ltd. did much of the appraisal work for the St. Lawrence Seaway and was responsible for assembling land in downtown Toronto where the Toronto-Dominion Centre now stands. LePage died on June 4, 1968.

In 1984, A.E. LePage and Royal Trust merged their real estate brokerages to become Royal LePage Real Estate Services Ltd. The company is a wholly owned subsidiary of Trilon Financial Corporation, with more than nine thousand employees, five hundred offices in Canada, and total sales of more than $8 billion (US).

Name Dropper

A.E. LePage's nephew, William Nelson Le Page of Prince Edward Island, founded the LePage glue business in the early 1870s.

William Nelson Le Page

LePage Glue

William Nelson Le Page is Canada's glue czar.

Born in 1849, near Charlottetown, Prince Edward Island, Le Page in the 1870s used the skins of codfish to invent an industrial glue that was extremely strong, had a long shelf life, and, unlike other adhesives of the day, was ready to use.

Soon after, he developed a home version of the glue, as well as inks, flower food, lubricating oil, metal polish, and the familiar white mucilage that for generations has been a standard issue for Canadian students, alongside pencils, pink erasers, and Hilroy notebooks.

The son of a P.E.I. farmer, Le Page moved to Massachusetts as a young man, where he worked as a tinsmith, merchant, and chemist. Eventually, he and partners started The Russia Cement Company in Rockport, Massachusetts, where Le Page discovered that fish skins discarded by the area's fishing industry could be processed using vinegar and other components to make an adhesive that was soft and pourable.

Le Page's invention was viewed as a breakthrough because most other glue consisted of a mixture of gelatin and cattle parts that required heating before use. Eventually, the company moved to Gloucester, Massachusetts, where the factory remains to this day.

Initially the fish glue was sold to manufacturers, who used it to cement together leather belts used in industry. In 1880, an award-winning mixture known as Le Page's Liquid Glue was marketed for home use. Two years later, Le Page took on two new partners and sold stock to raise money for expansion.

Between 1880 and 1887, the company sold fifty million bottles of the glue worldwide. Over the years, Le Page, the father of six children, also invented a pocket gun holster, an oarlock, and various preserving processes.

In the 1890s, Le Page sold his share of the company but kept the rights to the Le Page name, which later was stuck together as one word — LePage. A legal battle with his former partners over ownership of the name ensued, with Le Page eventually losing, in part because he had never given up his Canadian citizenship, says his great-great-granddaughter Vanessa Le Page.

With much of his fortune lost, Le Page, who enjoyed travelling, fishing, and being outdoors, moved to British Columbia in 1897, eventually settling in Vancouver, where he was unable to match his earlier entrepreneurial success. He died there in 1919. Following his death, Le Page's marketing prowess as a glue maker was noted in the *Vancouver Daily Province*.

"He placed upon the market a mucilage and glue that bore his name and is said to have spent a fortune advertising his products. In the pages of Harper's Magazine and in other popular journals he initiated advertising campaigns which startled the American public, and was among the forerunners of the great national advertisers of the present time."

LePage's Inc. set up a Canadian operation in Montreal in 1941 and moved to Toronto in 1951. In 1960, LePage's Ltd. in Canada was formed, separate from LePage's U.S.A. and LePage's U.K. Henkel Corporation of Germany, one of Europe's largest chemical companies, has owned the company since 1995. LePage continues to make glue and other adhesives in Brampton, Ontario.

Theodore Pringle Loblaw
Loblaws Companies Ltd.

As a youngster, Theodore Pringle Loblaw dreamed of becoming a locomotive engineer. Unfortunately, his career aspirations were derailed by the death of his father when he was less than a year old and the passing of his mother when he was fifteen.

Instead, Loblaw plunged headlong into the retail grocery trade in the late 1800s. It was a career move that would bear fruit. By the time he reached middle age, he was the millionaire co-owner of the Loblaw grocery chain.

After his mother died, Loblaw worked on farms for two years while growing up in the care of his grandparents near his birthplace in Alliston, Ontario, near Toronto. In 1889, he moved to Toronto with $20 in his pocket and a new dream dancing in his head — to follow in the footsteps of department store moguls Timothy Eaton and Robert Simpson, says a seventy-fifth anniversary booklet produced by Loblaws and *Canadian Grocer* magazine.

After a brief stint at Eaton's, he received his first taste of the grocery business working for $3 a week at a downtown grocery store where he met Milton Cork, son of the store's owner and his eventual partner in the

Loblaws chain. On his nights off, Loblaw took courses in accounting and bookkeeping, and before long, he showed signs of the promise that would propel him to the pinnacle of the grocery game.

Theodore Pringle Loblaw

Courtesy of Canadian Grocer *magazine*

Theodore Pringle Loblaw

One of his first innovations was a new, more efficient record-keeping system for his employer; he also learned the value of thriftiness.

"The longer I live, the more I am convinced that the difference between a clerk who saves part of his salary and the one that spends all of his is the difference in a few years between the owner of a business and the man out of a job," he once told an interviewer.

By the early 1900s, as chain department stores owned and operated by the same person or company made their appearance in Canada, Loblaw and Cork were experienced grocerymen with much in common. Both wanted to take a stab at running a foodstore chain and both believed it was time for a change in the way grocery stores were run.

To help stores become more competitive, they wanted to abandon the pre-World War I system whereby food processors and producers set retail prices; they also wanted stores to be self-serve and run on a cash-and-carry basis, a big change from the old, more labour-intensive way, which saw foodstuffs selected by store clerks, delivered weekly, and paid for once a month.

After operating a chain of nineteen traditional-style grocery stores in Toronto between 1910 and 1919, Loblaw sold out, formed a partnership with Cork, and the pair opened two self-serve Loblaws stores by 1920. Ten years later, the company had expanded to ninety-five outlets in Ontario, with annual sales of $18.4 million, under the name Loblaws Groceterias Co., with Loblaw as president.

Unlike stores Loblaw had owned previously, these outlets had about three thousand square feet of selling space, featured rotunda rest rooms, drinking fountains, artificial refrigeration, modern electric lighting, improved ventilation, the latest equipment in the packing departments, and in most cases, average sales of $250,000 a year.

Innovations introduced by Loblaw included a system which tracked sales, allowing the chain to eliminate slow-selling lines, and the practice of buying most products with cash direct from farmers or manufacturers to get the best discounts and reduce potential losses through bad debts. Loblaws also manufactured, packed, and distributed its own brands of butter, bacon, coffee, cake, cookies, and a handful of other products.

In 1933, with the company numbering more than one hundred stores and engaged in a rivalry with the much larger Dominion Stores chain, Loblaw died suddenly from an infection acquired after a minor sinus operation. He was sixty-one.

Cork took over as president and general manager of Loblaw Groceterias Co. and in 1947, at age seventy-seven, sold his share of the 113-store chain to George Weston Ltd. By 1955, Weston, the world's biggest and wealthiest baker, had gained voting control of Loblaws. Among the innovations of modern-day Loblaws management was the introduction in the mid-1980s of the President's Choice lineup of housebrand products, such as The Decadent Chocolate Chip Cookie, Green Products, and the Memories of and Too Good to Be True lines.

They were hawked on television and in a newspaper flyer known as the *Insider's Report* by Dave Nichol, president of Loblaw Supermarkets Ltd. at the time. In 1993, Nichol and his very recognizable mug left Loblaw and began marketing beer and other alcoholic beverages with his name on the label.

Today, the firm started by Theodore Pringle Loblaw and Milton Cork is known as Loblaws Companies Ltd. In addition to being Canada's largest food distributor, operating more than 1,100 stores under a variety of banners, including Loblaws, Fortinos, No Frills, Atlantic Superstore, Zehrs Markets, and Your Independent Grocer, Provigo, and Extra Foods, some of its outlets contain full line pharmacies and wine stores and offer a range of services including dry cleaning, banking, and flower sales.

Loblaws Store

Photo by Randy Ray

The company generates more than $20 billion in annual sales, and in 2002 announced plans to open, expand, or remodel more than 130 stores, expand into hardware products, and build gas stations.

Name Dropper

After Loblaw sold his original chain of nineteen stores they became the nucleus for Dominion Stores Ltd., Loblaws' main rival in the 1930s.

Name Dropper

In 2002, the smallest Loblaw store is about five times the size of a typical outlet operated by Theodore Pringle Loblaw in 1928.

Moses Loeb

M. Loeb Ltd.

For Ottawa's Moses Loeb, the road to big bucks was paved with penny candies.

After moving to the nation's capital in 1911, the former teacher sold jawbreakers and black balls from a tiny candy store not far from Parliament Hill. The sweet treats laid the foundation for M. Loeb Ltd., one of North America's largest food distribution companies in the 1970s.

When Moses Loeb's son Bertram sold out in a high-profile takeover in 1977, the company was a multi-million-dollar operation, selling and distributing groceries under the Loeb and IGA (Independent Alliance of Grocers) banners in Ontario, Quebec, Alberta, British Columbia, and the United States. It also ran supermarkets in Israel.

In a May 1962 article that credited Moses Loeb for laying the cornerstone of the company, trade publication *Supermarket Methods* described the firm as "one of the greatest success stories of the decade, and undoubtedly a major factor in the renaissance of food wholesaling in Canada."

Moses Loeb was a twenty-four-year-old Russian immigrant when he came to Ottawa from Cincinnati, Ohio in search of a cooler climate and a good place to start a family. In 1912, shortly after marrying Rose Cohen, he paid $200 for a small candy store in Ottawa's LeBreton Flats neighborhood.

Moses Loeb

Courtesy of the Ottawa Jewish Archives

The store was close to a railway station and was busy only when the trains arrived, so when sales were slow, Rose ran the show while her husband hitched up a horse and wagon and wholesaled candy to other merchants.

The tiny 160-square-foot enterprise's first warehouse was the living room of the family home. In 1916, the store was expanded to nine hundred square feet, and four years later, Loeb had a second team of horses and his first car, a Model T Ford. His family soon expanded to six sons.

About the time of the Depression, Loeb bought a candy factory, and despite tough times, the penny sweets he made continued to find a market. Eventually, his salespeople began travelling through western Quebec and the Ottawa and St. Lawrence valleys, peddling an expanded product line that included cigarettes and tobacco.

"They would take in armloads of penny candies — jawbreakers, blackballs, honeymoons, marshmallow prunes — the whole lot and they'd sell plenty," *Supermarket Methods* reported.

This "store-door mobile warehouse" was the first merchandising technique employed by M. Loeb Ltd., which until 1949 was mainly a wholesale tobacco and confectionery distributor. The candy sideline existed until the early 1950s, when annual sales topped the $5 million mark.

Moses Loeb remained the driving force until his son Henry, a doctor, passed away in 1949 at the age of twenty-eight. Shortly after, his health began to fail and he died of cancer in February 1951. His sons Norman, David, Jules, and Bertram took over the company.

In an interview with the *Ottawa Citizen*, Bertram described his father as a believer in honesty, hard work, good music, and literature. He would go to the synagogue on Saturday mornings but was always back at work in the afternoon. "He told us to treat people fairly, to protect the family reputation, and never to gamble."

Supermarket Methods referred to Moses Loeb as a philosophical man who believed that reputation was a greater gift than gold. "He is remembered as a man who had few signed contracts with anyone — the man's word was his bond. Some of the old-time customers remember Moses as a man whose word was unimpeachable."

With the founder gone, it became apparent that candy and tobacco couldn't support his sons and their growing families. And many of the small grocers that his company supplied were losing business to the new A&P and Loblaw supermarkets. Under the direction of his boys, led by Bertram, who was president and chief executive officer, the company bought the regional rights to the IGA franchise in 1951 and later acquired several other food businesses.

The business grew to more than forty supermarkets and in the mid-1970s had sales of more than $1 billion. The company also owned a national pharmaceutical products distributor and under the Loeb name distributed grocery products in the Chicago area; Washington, D.C.; California; and Western Canada. In the late 1950s, the company opened Supersol supermarkets in Israel, the first of which was officially opened in Tel Aviv by the wife of Ed Sullivan, host of a then-popular American TV variety show.

In the 1960s, with sales increasing by more than 40 percent a year, the company was the darling of U.S. and Canadian investors. But the made-in-Ottawa success story began to fall apart as a result of increased competition, infighting within the Loeb family, and over-ambitious growth.

In 1979, Provigo Distribution Inc. of Montreal, which later became a subsidiary of Loblaw Cos. Ltd., took full control of M. Loeb Ltd. In 1999, the company sold forty-one of ninety-two Loeb supermarkets to Metro-Richelieu Inc. of Montreal.

Although the Loebs no longer run the company, their name remains on supermarkets and various products such as hamburgers and pizzas sold at Loeb stores in Ontario and Quebec. It's also attached to various healthcare and educational institutions in Ottawa that Moses Loeb and later generations of his family have supported over the years, including the Moses and Rose Loeb Medical Research Centre.

Moses Loeb spent much of his life building his business but always found time to support and promote the local Jewish community and education. He was involved in the establishment of a Jewish school — known as a Talmud Torah — in downtown Ottawa in the 1920s and later was instrumental in helping develop plans for a Jewish school-synagogue-community centre complex.

In November 1938, while chairman of the Talmud Torah's board of directors, he revealed his commitment to Jewish education in a report to the board. "We are earnestly determined to give the children in our community, regardless of station or position, the best Hebrew education and Jewish training that is in our power," says a document obtained from the Ottawa Jewish Archives.

Jack Long and Jack McQuade
Long & McQuade

Jack Long enjoyed a career performing alongside such musicians as Moe Koffman, Gordon Lightfoot, and Nat King Cole, but it was in the musical instrument business where he made his name across Canada.

In the 1940s, Long started playing trumpet while in Grade 9 at Toronto's Humberside Collegiate. By Grade 13 he was a member of the musician's union and played regularly with adult bands. "The other kids didn't have money back then, but I was always loaded," he says of those long-ago lucrative gigs.

Prior to opening a musical instruments shop in Toronto, Long played at Toronto's King Edward Hotel, various lounges in Montreal, and went on the road in the U.S. with his pianist wife, Carol, whom he met at the University of Toronto while he was earning his Bachelor of Music degree. Long obtained a franchise to sell band instruments in the Toronto area in August 1956, working out of two rooms in a house at 100 Carlton Street, just a short walk from Maple Leaf Gardens. Long continued to play gigs six nights a week for several years to make ends meet.

Soon after starting the company, his friend Jack McQuade, a top studio drummer in Toronto, came looking for space to teach. With McQuade on the premises for a few hours each week, he began selling drums, and the new partnership, Long & McQuade, was formed.

Because this was the early days of rock and roll, the two started getting requests to supply guitars and basses, and they became distributors for Fender products from their first shop located just north of Bloor and Yonge streets where Toronto's main public library now stands.

Musical giants who purchased equipment at Long & McQuade included Gordon Lightfoot; David Clayton-Thomas of Blood, Sweat and Tears; Robbie Robertson of The Band; and Neil Young.

McQuade, who wasn't as keen as Long about the business side of music, eventually phased himself out of the company, selling half his shares to Long in 1963 and the rest about three years later. By then, the Long & McQuade name was firmly established. McQuade died in 1976 of cancer.

Long & McQuade expanded from its Toronto base in the 1970s, opening stores in Vancouver, Winnipeg, and Windsor. It later added outlets in such places as Calgary, Edmonton, Regina, and Oshawa, Ontario. These days there are about twenty Long & McQuade shops stretching from Victoria to Ottawa with Long's son Steve as president. "I love hanging around the music store and talking with musicians," says Jack. "I always considered myself more a musician than a businessman."

Name Dropper

Long recalls playing a gig many years ago with then unknown Gordon Lightfoot on drums. "He used to say he was going to be big once he got his folk act going." When the gig ended, Lightfoot, who later had such hits as "Sundown" and "The Wreck of the Edmund Fitzgerald," came by the store to buy a Martin acoustic guitar. "I couldn't understand why he wanted a guitar because to me he was a drummer."

William C. Macdonald

Macdonald Tobacco Co.

It's hard to imagine, but the man whose company introduced Canadians to Export "A" cigarettes and El Producto cigars once described smoking as a "wasteful habit" and the chewing of tobacco as "disgusting."

More than likely, that's why William Macdonald, the founder of what would become tobacco giant RJR Macdonald Inc., became one of Canada's pre-eminent humanitarians, donating millions of dollars to educate the country's youth.

Macdonald was born in Prince Edward Island in 1831, the sixth of seven children, and was educated at the General Academy of Charlottetown, now the University of Prince Edward Island. After a disagreement with his father, he ran away to Boston, where he started his business career as a clerk in a counting house. As a sideline, he exported goods to Halifax.

In 1852, he joined his older brother Augustine in Montreal where they set up as oil and commission merchants. In 1858, they began importing tobacco from Louisville, Kentucky and manufacturing tobacco plugs under the name of McDonald Brothers and Co., which, unlike their surname, for some reason was spelled "Mc."

By 1866 the name was altered to W.C. McDonald, Tobacco Merchants and Manufacturers with William as the sole proprietor. Because the corporate logo was a heart-shaped tin label, the product became known as the "tobacco with a heart," a trademark that lasted more than a century.

In 1876, William Macdonald expanded his manufacturing facilities to the Ontario Street East site in Montreal where the original building is still used for research and manufacturing.

As his tobacco business became successful, the shy and unpretentious Macdonald became an integral part of the financial establishment of Montreal and in Canada. Named a director of the Bank of Montreal, he established himself as a leading philanthropist, ultimately pouring millions of dollars into health and educational causes, particularly at McGill University in Montreal. He funded a student and science building and provided numerous scholarships.

For his generous support of various health and education causes, Queen Victoria knighted him in 1898. At that time he changed the spelling of the name of his thriving tobacco company from McDonald to Macdonald.

As Sir William, he continued to support rural education, providing funding for colleges in agriculture and household sciences in P.E.I., Nova Scotia, New Brunswick, Quebec, British Columbia, and Ontario. He also provided money for the consolidation of Vancouver and Victoria colleges into the McGill University College of British Columbia, which later became the University of British Columbia. In 1914, he was nominated president and chancellor of Montreal's McGill.

When he died in 1917, Macdonald, a bachelor, left his tobacco enterprise to the Stewart brothers, who had started their careers with the company as clerks. Walter Stewart became president, and under his management the company extended production to cut pipe tobacco and the first "roll your own" finecuts.

In 1922, cigarette production was added, with cigarettes being sold in packages of 10s, 20s, and 50s. In 1928 Export cigarettes were introduced. First known as British Consol Export, the cigarette package became distinctive in 1935 with the addition of a Scottish lassie wearing a Macdonald of Sleat tartan kilt. Created by Canadian artist Rex Woods, the lassie has remained a company symbol ever since.

During World War II, the company provided cigarettes to Canadian troops overseas. By 1945, 50 percent of the Canadian forces smoked Export cigarettes. This helped the company maintain a dominant share of the domestic market during the first post-war decade. The company diversified into cigar making during the 1960s.

The Stewarts retained ownership of Macdonald Tobacco until 1974 when R.J. Reynolds Industries of Winston-Salem, North Carolina bought it. Four years later the name was changed to RJR-Macdonald Inc. to take advantage of the growing recognition of R.J. Reynolds as a major multinational corporation.

In 1999, the company was purchased by Japan Tobacco Inc. and is now known as JTI-Macdonald Corp., which continues to manufacture and market a full range of Virginia tobacco type cigarette brands, fine cut tobaccos, cigars, cigarette papers, and tobacco sundries, including Export "A". The company is also the exclusive Canadian importer for various R.J. Reynolds brands manufactured in Winston-Salem, including Winston, Camel, and Salem. Its fine cut tobaccos include Export "A", Daily Mail, Zigzag, and British Consols, and its leading cigar brands are Tueros and El Producto. Its head office is in Toronto.

John B. Maclean
Maclean's *Magazine*/*Maclean-Hunter*

The man who launched one of the most successful magazine empires in Canada might never have done so if he'd had better marks in English.

John Bayne Maclean was tapped to become a principal at a high school in Port Hope, Ontario, but his low English marks prevented him from taking the post. Instead he turned to journalism. Within a few years, he began publishing his own trade magazines and would eventually found one of Canada's most notable periodicals, *Maclean's* magazine.

Maclean was born in Crieff, Ontario on September 26, 1862, the son of a minister, Andrew Maclean, and Christine Maclean, née Cameron. He attended school in Owen Sound before heading to Toronto to complete his education. When a career in education didn't pan out, Maclean got a reporting job in 1882 at the *Toronto World* newspaper for the grand salary of five dollars a week.

Toronto was a thriving city of eighty-six thousand then, with busy city streets full of bicycles and horse-drawn streetcars, the kind of place where a hard-working young man could succeed. Though Maclean was supplementing his income with some freelance pieces, he moved over to the *Toronto Daily Mail* within a couple of months at almost twice the salary. He soon became an editor handling business news, and despite his busy schedule, took up fencing and became the national junior champion.

Maclean, who would also spell his name McLean and MacLean at times, saved his money, and in 1887 started his own publication, the *Canadian Grocer*. In an era when few magazines thrived, Maclean was able to establish it on a firm foundation — so firm, in fact, that the magazine still exists today. The first issue was sixteen pages and carried a subscription price of two dollars a year.

The success of *Canadian Grocer* led Maclean to create other trade publications, such as *Hardware and Metal*, *The Dry Goods Review*, and *Druggist's Weekly*. If that wasn't enough, Maclean, a longtime admirer of Canada's first prime minister, Sir John A. Macdonald, also edited the financial pages of the *Empire*, a Toronto newspaper with a definite Conservative party slant.

John B. Maclean

Maclean's success also gave him a taste for the cosmopolitan life, and in the 1890s he moved to Montreal. With the help of his brother Hugh, he still managed the trade papers in Toronto but also pursued his lifelong interest in the militia. He would eventually carry the rank of colonel.

The editor/publisher liked moving in wealthy circles in both Canada and the U.S. On October 31, 1900 he married Anna Denison Slade, who had grown up well-to-do in Boston. The couple settled in Toronto and their son Hector Andrew was born in 1903. That same year Maclean hired Horace Talmadge Hunter as an ad salesman, and the young man immediately worked well with Maclean and eventually ran the day-to-day activities of the publishing company. Several years later, when he was made a full partner, the company name was changed to Maclean-Hunter.

Maclean continued to launch and acquire new magazines, notably *The Business Man's* magazine. He changed its title to *Busy Man's* magazine and then re-named it *Maclean's* in 1911. It was an era when several other magazines such as *McCall's* and *Collier's* bore the name of their publishers. He also started *The Financial Post* in January 1907 and *Chatelaine* in 1928.

Despite all this success, Maclean's life wasn't without tragedy, according to his biography, *A Gentleman of the Press* by Floyd Chalmers. Maclean's wife was struck with polio early in their marriage and their son Hector died in 1919. A perfectionist, frugal, and often hard-working man, Maclean nevertheless enjoyed riding and travelling. When he died on September 25, 1950, he left an estate of just over $1 million and his company was publishing more than thirty magazines.

Maclean-Hunter continues to publish a wealth of trade magazines as well as the ever-popular *Maclean's* and *Chatelaine*.

Name Dropper

Though trade magazines helped Maclean amass his fortune, their titles were not the most gripping. Among the magazines he owned during his lifetime were *The Sanitary Engineer*, *Men's Wear Review*, and *Bookseller and Stationer*.

Roland Macleod

Macleods True Value

For decades, Macleods stores have been as common a sight throughout the prairies as gophers, grain elevators, and tractors.

Back in 1917, as the prairies began to grow with an influx of new immigrants and prosperous farms, Roland Macleod decided it was a promising time to start selling agricultural supplies using mail order catalogues. He had owned a hardware store in Saskatchewan, and he believed that farmers were paying too much for supplies.

He teamed up with his brother-in-law Athol McBean, a grain broker, and a few other associates and formed Macleods Limited, located on Notre Dame Avenue East in Winnipeg. Using a variety of business connections, Macleod was able to get great deals from suppliers on such products as harnesses, saddles, plows, gasoline engines, and other farm implements. Using the slogan "Factory to Farm," operating on a cash only basis, and offering a satisfaction guaranteed policy, Macleod established a profitable business in its first year.

By 1926, the company had total sales of more than $1 million. By putting more emphasis on replacement parts, Macleods was able to weather the Depression of the 1930s, and he began expanding beyond Manitoba to open retail stores not only in larger western cities but also in small towns such as Melfort, Saskatchewan and Lloydminster, Alberta. According to a company history, Macleod once said, "It was not surprising to any of us that Macleods could open a store and operate it at an immediate profit. We had built up goodwill in every area of Western Canada through selling by mail on a thoroughly acceptable basis to the farmer."

Macleods continued to grow and expand its variety of merchandise after being purchased by Gamble-Skogmo Inc. (the same company that would later buy Stedmans) in 1945. Macleod retired the following year. Macleods would join forces with Stedmans in 1964 and is known by the True Value name today. There are still many Macleods True Value stores in Canada, particularly in the western provinces, which, like Stedmans, are owned by Tru*Serv Canada Co-operative Inc. of Winnipeg.

Harvey Reginald MacMillan
MacMillan Bloedel Ltd.

For a guy who grew up in poverty in rural Ontario, Harvey Reginald MacMillan did more than all right for himself.

Born in 1885 in a Quaker community near Newmarket, Ontario, H.R., as he was known later in life, was raised on a farm by his Scottish grandfather. He was only two years old when his father died and he rarely saw his mother, who worked as a housekeeper to make ends meet.

Nevertheless, he managed to graduate with honours in biology from the Ontario Agricultural College in Guelph and receive a Masters degree in forestry from Yale University before moving to Western Canada, where from the tall timber of British Columbia he carved out one of the biggest lumber empires in North America.

When he retired in 1970, MacMillan left behind a dynamic career as a civil servant and entrepreneur, which saw him build MacMillan Bloedel Ltd. into one of the most powerful forestry companies on the globe.

After completing his degree at Yale in 1908, he was hired by the federal government's Dominion Survey Branch but almost had his

Harvey Reginald MacMillan

forestry career cut short when a cold caught while surveying in the Rocky Mountains developed into tuberculosis. After a two-year battle with the disease, he returned to the forestry department in 1911, and that year married his high-school sweetheart, Edna Mulloy, with whom he had two daughters.

A year later he was hired as chief forester by the B.C. government and over the years held various civil service posts, including that of special trade commissioner for the federal government to seek world markets for Canadian lumber and as a member of the Imperial Munitions Board to obtain Sitka spruce, the best wood for aircraft manufacturing. Later in life he was the federal government's lumber commissioner, and during World War II he served as president of the Canadian Chamber of Commerce.

MacMillan's entrepreneurial career began in 1919 when he established H.R. MacMillan Export Co. Ltd., with the financial backing of a London lumber buyer. The firm evolved into the biggest export company in B.C. and by the mid-1930s held a near monopoly position in the province. In 1951, MacMillan merged his forest products empire with Bloedel, Stewart & Welch, one of B.C.'s largest logging and sawmilling outfits and MacMillan's primary competitor.

The merger was B.C.'s largest, producing a company with combined assets of $100 million, making MacMillan & Bloedel Ltd., as it was then known, one of the largest forestry firms in the world. MacMillan was its chairman.

Five years later, at age seventy-one, he stepped down as chairman to head the company's powerful finance and policy committee. A stroke in 1966 slowed him down but he did not retire from active participation in the business until 1970, at age eighty-four, when he was made a Companion of the Order of Canada. Over the years he donated nearly $10 million to the University of British Columbia, supporting faculties concerned with forestry, fish biology, and conservation.

MacMillan died in 1976 at the age of ninety-one. MacMillan Bloedel was later purchased by U.S.-based Weyerhauser.

During MacMillan's time at the helm, the company's attitudes toward labour relations, community responsibility, and the forests it owned were, with rare exception, applauded, but "this has not always been the case since he left," Ken Drushka wrote in his book *HR: A Biography of H.R. MacMillan.*

After MacMillan departed, MacMillan Bloedel, along with other forestry companies, was widely criticized for damaging forests by clear cutting, closing mills, and disrupting communities. "MacMillan Bloedel Ltd., the largest forest company in the country, became a symbol of everything the public disliked about large forest corporations," wrote Drushka.

In more recent times, however, the company has changed direction, largely because its executives are more committed to forest management. In 1995, said Drushka, "MacMillan would be much more likely to identify with the company that bears his name."

Name Dropper

The other half of the MacMillan-Bloedel partnership was lumberman Prentice "Bing" Bloedel, who was born in Bellingham, Washington in 1900. He wanted to become a schoolteacher but instead joined his father's logging business, Bloedel, Stewart & Welch, one of the largest logging and sawmilling companies on the British Columbia coast, and was its president when it merged with MacMillan's company. Bloedel, who made possible the construction of the Bloedel Conservatory in Vancouver, retired in 1972 and moved to Seattle, where he died in 1996.

Daniel Massey

Massey-Harris Company Ltd./
Massey-Ferguson Ltd.

In the years leading up to Confederation, farmer Daniel Massey was distressed by the long hours and backbreaking work involved in tilling fields and raising crops. So he took matters into his own hands.

"The tools on farms all over the world are the same as those used in the days of the Pharoahs," he wrote in a 1840 letter to a newspaper in Cobourg, Ontario, near where he lived and farmed. "There has been a small metal share added to the plough and some smart Scot has put a long handle on the sicle a few years ago ... but the backbreaking chores of sowing, reaping, threshing and cultivating are still nightmares to most farmers."

Not content to wait for others to embrace mechanization, Massey, then forty-two, began manufacturing and importing implements that eased the workload for farmers and simplified the process of moving produce from field to kitchen table.

From this modest beginning sprang one of the largest and most important firms in Canada's history, the Massey Company, which under a new name more than a century later would be described as being as widespread and all-enveloping as Coca-Cola.

Massey was born in Windsor, Vermont in 1798 and spent his early years near Watertown, New York, before moving across Lake Ontario with his family to Grafton, about 125 kilometres east of Toronto. After working on the family's one-hundred-acre farm until he was nineteen, he rented his own land nearby, but instead of farming, he began working as a contractor clearing land.

Business was good as newcomers flocked to fertile areas on the north side of the lake. By 1830, Massey and his crews had cleared more than one thousand acres and he began thinking about ways to ease the laborious task of trimming timber and rolling it by hand into piles for burning. His answer was to use oxen, an untried farming method in those days, author Peter Cook wrote in *Massey at the Brink: The Story of Canada's Greatest Multinational and its Struggle to Survive.*

In the meantime, Massey was busy building a family. In 1820, he married Lucina Bradley; a year later a daughter was born, and in 1823, son Hart Almerrin arrived. By age seven, Hart was handling teams of horses and making trips to the local grist mill. Daniel, meanwhile, was devoting more of his time to tilling the land and had developed an interest in farm mechanization.

In 1840, father and son imported a mechanical threshing machine — the first in Upper Canada — from Watertown, which reduced from twenty to eleven the number of workers needed to handle threshing. Soon, the large barn on the Massey property was being used as a work-shop; eventually, Massey, forty-nine, and a partner purchased a small foundry near the village of Newcastle, Ontario that had been used to produce ploughs and sugar kettles. They named their enterprise the Massey Manufacturing Company. The company soon expanded with a new building, new equipment, and more employees.

In his early 50s, Massey grew tired and was having trouble keeping up with the workload, so he asked Hart to join the business. The twen-ty-eight-year-old brought with him ambitious plans to import and sell the latest farm machinery, much of it imported from the U.S. Together, the Masseys developed a reputation for innovation and excellent work-manship, and four years after Hart came on board, Daniel retired. A year later, in November 1856, Daniel Massey died at age fifty-eight, leaving behind a company that had grown fourfold in just ten years.

With Hart at the helm, Massey Manufacturing used mergers, spir-ited sales and advertising techniques, and entry into foreign markets to become a dynamic farm-implement producer that would transform the productivity of Canadian agriculture. "If you ate a loaf of bread in the early 1920s, it's safe to say the grain was planted by a Massey seed driller," says Franz Klingender, curator at the Canada Agriculture Museum in Ottawa.

Massey Manufacturing became the first North American firm to successfully enter foreign markets. It relocated to Toronto in 1879 and in 1891 merged with its chief competitor, A. Harris, Son & Company, to form Massey-Harris Company Ltd., of which Massey was president until his death in 1896. Four sons, Charles Albert, Frederic Victor, Walter Edward, and Chester Daniel later were active in the company, which plunged into the tractor business in 1928 with the purchase of the J.I. Case Plow Works.

In 1953, Massey-Harris merged with the Ferguson Companies, operated by eccentric Irish inventor Harry Ferguson, to form Massey-

Harris-Ferguson. The name Massey-Ferguson was adopted in 1958 and in 1987 the corporation was reorganized into Varity Corp. In the early 1990s, Varity sold its Massey-Ferguson division to AGCO Corp., an American farm machinery maker.

Over the years, three members of the Massey and Harris families achieved considerable fame. Hart Massey's grandson Charles Vincent was president of Massey-Harris Company Ltd. from 1921 until 1925 and later became Canada's first native-born governor general. Another grandson, Raymond Massey, was an actor best remembered for his roles as Abraham Lincoln and Dr. Gillespie in the *Dr. Kildare* television series. Lawren Harris, son of Thomas Morgan Harris, secretary of the Harris farm machinery company, was a landscape painter and a member of Canada's Group of Seven self-proclaimed modern artists.

Massey Hall, on Shuter Street in downtown Toronto, was built by Hart Massey as a gift to the city.

Name Dropper

Alanson Harris, a native of Ingersoll, Ontario, was a sawmill operator in Brant County before buying a foundry in Beamsville, Ontario in 1857, where he began manufacturing farm implements. In 1872, he moved to Brantford, Ontario and seven years later began marketing his products in Western Canada. His company merged with the Massey Manufacturing Company in 1891 to become Massey-Harris Company Ltd.

Andrew, Harrison, and Wallace McCain

McCain Foods

The New Brunswick village of Florenceville is named in honour of Crimean war heroine Florence Nightingale. But it could just as easily have been called McCainville or McCaintown after Andrew McCain and two of his sons, who have turned the community into the french fry capital of the world.

The McCains began farming the St. John River Valley in the 1830s but didn't begin their march toward family dynasty status until 1940, when teetotalling Baptist Andrew McCain pioneered the export of seed potatoes from Canada, began assembling parcels of prime potato-growing land, and earned a bundle on the stock market.

A.D., as he was known locally, hoped to become a doctor but became a farmer instead. In 1909, he and his father Hugh and two partners started a produce company in Florenceville. In 1914, when the McCains bought the partners out, they changed the name of the company to McCain Produce Co. Ltd.

A.D. was a careful man who always went to work in a dark three-piece suit, stiff white collar, and black dress shoes, even if he was meeting a local farmer. He ran unsuccessfully for the provincial Liberal party in two elections, served as school board chairman, and co-ordinated assistance for people in need during the Depression.

He and his wife Laura had four sons and two daughters. In the late 1950s, about three years after A.D. died, sons Harrison and Wallace used their inheritance, local property tax concessions, and provincial government funding to begin building a frozen food empire that would elevate the McCains to the status of one of Canada's most successful and influential families. They settled on the french fry business after noticing that General Foods in neighbouring Maine was using New Brunswick potatoes to make frozen fries under the Birds Eye label.

The McCain boys opened their first french fry processing plant in Florenceville in February 1957, back when an eight-ounce bag of frozen fries sold for thirty-nine cents and average annual consumption in North America was less than three pounds per person. Thirty years later, that average had jumped to eleven pounds of fries each per year.

Out of their low-rise headquarters in Florenceville, population one thousand, the pair (Harrison was thirty, Wallace was twenty-seven) grew the company from a thirty-employee operation with $152,000 in revenue in 1957 to an international powerhouse with more than sixteen thousand workers in thirteen countries and global sales of $6 billion a year.

As the company broadened its product line in a bid to become king of the freezer case, Harrison became McCain Foods' visionary leader while Wallace was known more for his attention to detail and ability to oversee the company's daily operations. The men are university educated, and are said to be gregarious and charming, but like the Irvings, another wealthy New Brunswick family, the McCains are secretive and rarely give interviews. They combined their fierce work ethic with generous government grants to build and acquire french fry plants in several countries, including the United States. In the 1970s and 1980s, the company diversified into juice, cheese, frozen pizza, vegetables, appetizers, desserts, trucking, farm equipment, and fertilizers.

The McCain empire remains fiscally strong but in the early 1990s was dealt a serious blow during a bitter battle over who would succeed Harrison and Wallace as the leaders of McCain Foods. Although the brothers had shared the same bedroom, owned houses beside each other on a hill over the Saint John River, and seemed inseparable as builders of the largest frozen french fry producer in the world, Wallace was forced out of the company's executive ranks in October 1994 and moved to Toronto, where he bought control of food-processing conglomerate Maple Leaf Foods Inc. Harrison stayed on as chairman of McCain Foods.

In 2001, *Forbes* magazine ranked the still-estranged brothers as among the five hundred richest people in the world, with a net worth of more than $1 billion (US).

Name Dropper

Harrison and Wallace McCain once worked for another wealthy New Brunswick clan, the Irvings. Harrison was Atlantic sales manager for Irving Oil and Wallace managed an Irving-owned hardware business. Years later, the two families became embroiled in a tiff when the Irvings added potatoes and other food products to their portfolio.

John McClelland and George Stewart
McClelland & Stewart Ltd.

A teetotalling Irishman and a bible salesman meet up in Toronto.

It sounds like the start of a joke, but the partnership they formed was no laughing matter; the pair launched what became Canada's best-known and arguably most prestigious publishing house.

John McClelland, born in Glasgow, Scotland and of Irish descent, came to Toronto in 1882 as a young boy. He was a fervent Orangeman who went to work as a teen to help out with his family's financial difficulties. He landed a job at the Methodist Book and Publishing House (later called Ryerson Press after its founder Egerton Ryerson). According to *Jack, A Life With Writers: The Story of Jack McClelland*, by James King, John McClelland eventually became manager of the library department and evaluated manuscripts. He was instrumental in having Robert Service's *Songs of a Sourdough* published by the firm.

In the spring of 1906, at age twenty-nine, McClelland and another Methodist Book employee, Frederick Goodchild, formed their own publishing company, called McClelland & Goodchild. Among their successes was *The Watchman and Other Poems* by Canadian author Lucy Maud Montgomery.

In 1913, George Stewart, who had a reputation of being the best bible salesman in the country, left his job at Oxford University Press to come on board and helped create McClelland, Goodchild & Stewart. When Goodchild left in 1918 (rumour had it that McClelland had discovered him cavorting with nude women), the company became McClelland & Stewart.

The publishers initially thrived by acting as distributors for British and American publishing houses, but they realized the need to establish Canadian authors as well. Between the two World Wars, McClelland & Stewart published such Canadian writers as Bliss Carman, Stephen Leacock, Frederick Philip Grove, and L.M. Montgomery. The company struggled through the Depression, selling only $196,000 worth of books in 1936 (compared to more than twice that in 1919), but McClelland & Stewart was able to survive.

John McClelland and George Stewart

McClelland, a teetotaller and strict non-smoker, worked long hours, hustled business, and along with Stewart, who was more affable and fun-loving, managed to make the company prosperous. McClelland's son, Jack, was not initially interested in joining the firm, and in fact, the company had an agreement that no partner's child could take charge. But the agreement only lasted a year, and with Jack eventually deciding that publishing was what he wanted as a career and Stewart's only child, a daughter, not interested, the stage was set to pass the company to a new generation.

John McClelland stayed in charge until 1952, but would remain an advisor and sometimes thorn in the business side of his son for many years after. He died in May 1968. Stewart had died in 1955, and shortly afterward Jack bought 49 percent of the founding partner's shares from his widow for $65,000. Jack McClelland had begun working at the firm in 1946 and would eventually become the most famous publisher in the country, championing many Canadian writers and publishing some of the most successful books in this nation's history.

Avie Bennett bought the firm in 1986 (McClelland retired in 1987), acquired some other publishing houses over the next several years, and in June 2000, announced that he was making a gift of a large portion of the company to the University of Toronto. As Bennett said at the time, "What better way can there be to safeguard a great Canadian institution, a vital part of Canada's cultural heritage, than by giving it to the careful stewardship of another great Canadian institution."

Name Dropper

The list of authors over the years published by McClelland & Stewart is a virtual who's who of Canadian literature: among the company's many authors are Margaret Atwood, Mavis Gallant, Alistair MacLeod, Alice Munro, Michael Ondaatje, and Leonard Cohen.

Kenneth and Carl McGowen

Mac's Convenience Stores

The Mac behind the Mac's Convenience Stores chain is actually two people — Kenneth and Carl McGowen.

In April 1962, the McGowen brothers opened their first convenience store in Toronto, where jug milk, cigarettes, and bread were among the big sellers. The business was known as Mac's Milk.

"Presumably, the name Mac's was taken from the first few letters of their last name," says Dale Pettit, vice-president and treasurer at Mac's Convenience Stores, as the company is now known. "As the stores evolved, they became known for jug milk, quick in-and-out service, and their yellow and red banner, which became a beacon in many neighborhoods."

Under the McGowens, Mac's grew to about twenty stores. In 1965, Silverwood Dairies Limited bought a 40 percent interest in Mac's; in 1968 Silverwood purchased another 40 percent and in 1972, took over the rest of the company, which at that point had grown to 378 outlets. Ken and Carl McGowen eventually left the company; Ken went on to found the Hasty Markets chain.

In 1978, Mac's amalgamated with Silverwood Industries Ltd, which later became Silcorp Ltd. In April 1999, the company was taken over by Alimentation Couche-Tard of Laval, Quebec, owners of the seven-hundred-store Becker's convenience stores chain. In 2002, Alimentation Couche-Tard owned 800 Mac's stores in Ontario and Western Canada, as well as 550 Alimentation Couche-Tard stores in Quebec and a chain of 200 convenience stores in the United States.

Albert E. Silverwood

Silverwood Dairies Ltd.

Albert E. Silverwood, who for years put milk, ice cream, and butter onto Canadian dinner tables, started his working career as a teacher in the Lindsay, Ontario area before shifting into the food business. The native of Oakwood, Ontario was born in 1876, and after teaching for five years, he landed a job with produce company Dundas & Flavelle Brothers. In 1903, he moved to London, Ontario, where he started his own dairy some years later, according to the book *When Milk Came In Bottles*. When Silverwood died in 1961, Silverwood Dairies Limited was Canada's largest dairy.

John McIntosh

McIntosh Apple

In the spring of 1811, John McIntosh stumbled upon a handful of apple tree seedlings while clearing land near Prescott, Ontario where he planned to establish a farm. Instead of tossing the tiny trees onto a pile of brush that would later be burned, he transplanted them to a nearby garden. McIntosh and his farm in Dundas County south of Ottawa were about to take their place in Canada's history books.

By the following year all but one of the trees had died. He nursed it and it slowly grew, eventually producing a red, sweet, and crisp fruit with a tart taste.

So began the story of the McIntosh apple, which by the 1960s, accounted for nearly 40 percent of the Canadian apple market and continues to be the most widely grown and sold Canadian fruit. In fact, the Mac has become accepted worldwide and is responsible for much of Canada's domestic and export apple growing industry. Today, more than three million McIntosh apple trees flourish throughout North America, all stemming from the single tree discovered by McIntosh.

Fifteen years earlier, McIntosh, the son of Scottish Highland parents, had immigrated to Upper Canada from New York State. Eventually he married Hannah Doran and set out to tame the land he had traded with his brother-in-law.

McIntosh's discovery, near what would eventually become the village of Dundela, would not have been significant if John, and later his son Allan and grandson Harvey, had not nurtured, propagated, and marketed the apple named after his family. In 1835, Allan McIntosh learned the art of grafting and the family began to produce the apples on a major scale.

Despite Allan and his brother Sandy's efforts, it was many years before the McIntosh Red became prominent. In fact, not until 1870, nearly a quarter of a century after John's death, was it officially introduced and named. The Mac made its first appearance in print six years later (in *Fruits and Fruit Trees of America*) and began to sell in large numbers after 1900. The Mac's hardiness, appearance, and taste made it a contender from birth, but it was only when turn-of-the-century advances in the quality and availability of sprays improved its quality that it realized its incredible commercial potential.

By that time things had changed at the McIntosh farm near Dundela, Ontario. In 1894, a fire burned down the family home and badly damaged the original tree. Though Allan made extensive efforts to nurse it back to health, the historic tree produced its last crop in 1908 and died two years later. Allan died in 1899 and Sandy in 1906, leaving grandson Harvey at the helm when the family apple became world-famous.

Early in the twenty-first century, the Mac accounted for more than half of the seventeen million bushels of apples produced in Canada every year, making it Canada's most commonly grown fruit. In the U.S. it ranked behind only the two Delicious varieties and has a personal computer named for it; overseas it is one of the few successful North American varieties.

Name Dropper

To this day no one is certain how the orphan tree discovered by McIntosh arrived on his property. Experts speculate that it likely grew from the seeds of an apple core tossed onto the ground by a passerby.

William Church Moir
Moir Chocolates

From the beginning, few doubted William Church Moir would find his pot of gold.

The native of Halifax, Nova Scotia was born into a family that had developed a prosperous bakery in the centre of Halifax in the early 1800s. When Moir's father Benjamin died in 1845, William, then twenty-three, took over the business and transformed a small workshop into a factory, where he revolutionized the traditional Halifax trade of breadmaking.

Under the name Moir & Co. Steam Bakery & Flour Mill, he imported British and American steam-baking technology in 1863 and 1864, which dramatically improved production of hard bread, crackers, dough, and soft bread.

In the early 1870s, he and his eldest son James William diversified into candy production. It was a move that years after the elder Moir's death would lead to the introduction of the company's flagship product, Pot of Gold chocolates, Canada's leading brand of boxed chocolates. In 2002, it was the product responsible for the bulk of the company's production.

Folks who knew Moir in the latter half of the nineteenth century would hardly be surprised at his success.

In the 1880s and 1890s, Moir, the father of four sons and two daughters, was widely regarded as one of the most energetic and enterprising businessmen in Halifax. Despite financial problems related to his over-ambitious expansion, repeated conflicts with his workforce over wages and hours of work, and several fires, including one that destroyed his Halifax premises, Moir persevered and built a business that became competitive nationally. James Moir became president and general manager in 1890.

Moir, Son and Company was one of the few Maritime industries able to withstand the pressures that brought much of the region's economy under the control of capital based in central Canada.

When William Moir died in Halifax in July 1896, the company employed 265 workers, produced 11,280 loaves of bread a day, and made more than 500 types of confectionery, which were sold from coast to coast. Pot of Gold chocolates were introduced in 1920 and for many years after William Moir's death the aroma of chocolate from his plant mingled with the smell of salt water rising from the harbour. Eventually, the company dropped its bakery lines.

In 1974, a new two-storey plant equipped with robotic equipment in neighbouring Dartmouth replaced the Dickensian ten-storey factory on Argyle Street at the foot of historic Citadel Hill. The modernization, coupled with new ownership, first Nabisco, and in 1987 Hershey Canada, reduced costs, improved productivity, and kept prices competitive.

In the mid-1990s, Hershey/Moir introduced Pot of Gold to chocolate lovers in the United States. The U.S. experiment was an instant success, causing the company to add staff and bump production from one to three shifts.

Name Dropper

When Moir's son James suggested the company diversify into candy production, William Moir had this to say: "What do you want to mess around with a lot of this sticky taffy for, Jimmy? If you're going to fool around with this candy business, you had better take a corner over there and get on it with."

John Molson

Molson's Brewery

John Molson was an eighteen-year-old farm boy with few skills when he arrived in Montreal in 1782. Thirty years later, he was an established entrepreneur who helped Montreal develop into a major Canadian city.

Though known to most Canadians as the name behind beers such as Molson Canadian and Molson Export, the founder of North America's oldest operating brewery was also involved in lumber, distilling, steamboats, a railway, a foundry, banking, politics, public libraries, hotels, and the founding of Montreal General Hospital.

Molson's pioneering efforts laid the foundation for one of Canada's most enduring and well-known business dynasties, a multi-million-dollar conglomerate with interests that later would include hockey, auto racing, music, building supplies, chemicals, and office products.

The eldest son of an English gentleman farmer, Molson was born on December 28, 1763 in Lincolnshire, England, where it appeared he was destined for a life in the country. That changed in 1772 when he was orphaned and became the head of his family at the tender age of eight. Eventually, he became the sole beneficiary of his father's small estate.

When Molson stepped onto the shores of the New World, his ambition and thirst for opportunity more than made up for his lack of skills. His introduction to brewing began by sharing duties at a small brewery owned by Thomas Lloyd (also spelled Loid), a fellow Englishman who was twenty years

John Molson

Courtesy of the National Archives of Canada/
C115899

his senior. The combined malting and brewhouse was strategically located on a forty-foot plot of river frontage where a broad rapids known as St. Mary's Current met the St. Lawrence River, just east of what was then the walled city of Montreal. With a population of about eight thousand, Montreal was the market centre of the fur trade, the colony's principal export.

At the time, the economics of brewing were especially attractive. Land was cheap and the water, barley, and hops needed to produce beer were readily available at little or no cost. Locally brewed beer was not subject to tax or duties and most sales were made for cash. These factors, plus the lack of competition, attracted Molson to the brewing trade.

In January of 1785, Molson secured title to the property from Lloyd. He then returned to England to liquidate his assets and buy equipment for his new brewing enterprise, returning to Montreal in June of the following year. He brought with him forty-six bushels of barley and seeds, a small quantity of hops, wooden casks, brewing equipment, and a copy of *Theoretical Hints On An Improved Practice of Brewing*, written by John Richardson in 1777.

Test runs on the ale started in September, and by Christmas, Molson began brewing. On July 28, 1786, the twenty-two year old officially opened his brewery in Montreal. Brewing was limited to four months of the year during winter. Over the summer, because there was no refrigeration, the ale was stored in stone underground vaults kept cool with ice taken from the river in winter. In his first season, Molson produced a modest four thousand Imperial gallons of beer.

At five cents a bottle his ale sold quickly, and thirsty Montrealers clamored for more. Additional property was purchased, buildings were added or enlarged, and a new stone building was erected to house more brewing equipment brought from England. By 1791, Molson was brewing about thirty thousand gallons a year.

In 1801, after several years in a common-law relationship, he married Sarah Vaughan, with whom he had already had three sons, John Jr., Thomas, and William.

In the years leading up to his marriage, Molson had begun a pattern of diversification which later generations of Molsons continued long after he was gone. He started a lumberyard on his brewery property; launched the *Accommodation*, Canada's first steamboat; formed the St. Lawrence Steamboat Company, also known as the Molson line; and owned a large hotel. He was involved in a profitable family banking business, which in the 1850s became Molsons Bank, and from 1826 to 1830, he was president of the Bank of Montreal.

Molson entered politics in 1816 as the representative of Montreal East in the legislature of Lower Canada and that year opened the Mansion House, a large hotel in Montreal that housed the public library, a post office, and Montreal's first theatre. He later invested in the construction of Canada's first railway, the Champlain and St. Lawrence, which ran twenty-six kilometres between Montreal and Lake Champlain so traffic could move freely to and from the Atlantic Coast via the Hudson River.

Gradually, Molson's sons became active in the family's growing enterprises and the business prospered. Soon the Molsons were among Montreal's well-to-do families and were known to have explored almost every business opportunity nineteenth-century Canada had to offer. They were among the largest distillers in British North America, and their interest in steamboats involved heavy manufacturing and a small foundry next to the brewery. It was this diversification, however, that created disagreements that often pitted one brother against the other and father against son.

In 1828, John Sr. retired from his active role in the brewery and a partnership was drawn up between sons John and William, who alternated as brewmasters. Money was invested in new equipment, and a short time later, the senior Molson asked Thomas to return to the business. The brothers were united once again.

John Molson died in January 1836, on the fiftieth anniversary of the brewery's founding. An obituary in Quebec City newspaper *Le Canadien* remembered Molson as "at all times a zealous supporter of every important commercial and industrial enterprise. Few men have rendered better service to their country in connection with its material development."

Following Molson's death, Thomas and William purchased their brother John's interest in the brewery and an agreement was signed to conduct business as brewers and distillers under the company name of Thomas and William Molson and Company. Over the years, other members of the family ran the operation.

The company became Molson's Brewery Ltd. in 1911. By the middle of the century, Molson was producing an average of 1.5 million bottles of beer a day. In 1957, the Montreal Canadiens hockey team was purchased, and between 1968 and 1972 Molson went on a major diversification binge, purchasing Anthes Imperial Ltd., a company that specialized in office furniture and supplies, construction materials and public warehousing; Canada's Beaver Lumber chain; and American companies that manufactured chemical cleansers and other chemical specialty products.

In 1993, the brewing company was partially owned by Australian and American companies, but in 1998, Molson bought out its foreign partners and the the brewery was once again 100-percent Canadian.

In 2001, Molson's sold 80 percent of the beloved Canadiens to a Colorado businessman. Molson Inc. continues to sponsor the Molson Indy car races in Toronto and Vancouver and the family name is also found on the Molson Amphitheatre at Ontario Place in Toronto.

Name Dropper

In his will, John Molson stipulated that an oil painting of himself must hang in the boardroom at the Montreal brewery for as long as the Molson family retained control. His will also states that should the brewery pass into the hands of strangers, the portrait must be removed.

Eugene O'Keefe

O'Keefe Brewery

In a country famous for such brewmasters as Molson, Labatt, and Carling, Eugene O'Keefe is a different case. Though he ran one of the most successful breweries of the late nineteenth and the twentieth century, O'Keefe knew almost nothing about the business when he started.

With banking and accounting as his career specialty, O'Keefe decided to get into brewing because he thought it was an industry with unlimited growth potential. It was a wise move.

The O'Keefe Brewery Company of Toronto Limited made him a wealthy man; in fact, he was one of the wealthiest in that city. Born in Ireland in 1827, O'Keefe came to Canada with his family while still a child. He received a private school education, was an accomplished sportsman, and from an early age had strong ties to the Catholic church — not an enviable position in what was then a predominantly Protestant Toronto.

His shrewdness in business helped make him a successful brewery owner. O'Keefe was innovative and aggressive in introducing new ideas to the business, becoming the first in Canada to install a mechanically refrigerated storehouse and using motorized vehicles to transport his product.

When his son died young in 1911, O'Keefe sold his shares in the business and became as well known as a philanthropist to many charities and the Catholic Church as he was for his beer. He died October 1, 1913, but the brewery that bore his name remained a popular one for most of the rest of the twentieth century. O'Keefe ale is still sold today by Molson's.

Dave Moore

Moores Clothing for Men

Sometimes simple is the way to go when naming a company.

In 1980, a few entrepreneurs were sitting around trying to come up with a catchy name for their new venture, a men's discount clothing store. Finally, someone suggested naming it after Dave Moore, one of the minority shareholders in the business, and Moores was the sign they hung on their first store in Mississauga, Ontario, which is still in operation today.

"I thought why not Moores. It's worked for Eaton's, it's worked for Sears," says Martin Prosserman, one of the partners at the time. "It's a shorter, sharper name. I've never put my name on any of my businesses, but I don't know why."

Dave Moore agrees that "mine was easier to work with. It wasn't an ego thing, but a matter of convenience at the time." Moore, who lives in Oakville, Ontario, chuckles and says that it was flattering to have his name on the store and that his parents were always proud of him because of it.

When the first store opened, Moore had already been in the clothing business for about fifteen years. The Windsor, Ontario native had studied business in college there and was working as a buyer for Jack Fraser. "At the time the discount business was just starting to percolate in the United States. I felt the opportunity was right to do the same thing in Canada."

He hooked up with Prosserman, who had started Golden Brand Clothing in Montreal and had built it into one of the largest suppliers of men's suits in the country by 1980.

The company was successful enough that at its peak about ten to twelve new Moores stores were opened each year. "The stores had the best value (in men's clothing) in the country," Prosserman told us. By 1996, when Prosserman sold the business, there were ninety-eight Moores outlets across the country with about 20 percent of the market. "It was time to sell," Prosserman said from Toronto. "You always want to get out when you're on top."

Ironically, the man who gave his name to the prosperous company had left it long before that. Moore had stayed with the firm for only two years before he went to work as vice-president for Collegiate Sports and then as marketing director at Harvey Woods. For the past fifteen years he's been in the clothing business for himself and supplies Moores stores as one of his clients.

Seeing his name on all those stores after he left the company was initially a shock, but these days he thinks of it as "a neat experience." Though he didn't benefit from the sale of the company, he is "happy for the experience" of starting up a successful new venture. And to this day, he still gets asked about once a month if he's the guy for whom the company was named. "It was my fifteen minutes in the spotlight, but I've had a few more since then."

A U.S. company, The Men's Wearhouse, purchased Moores in 1999. Today there are more than 110 stores in all 10 provinces with over $200 million in annual sales.

Moores Store

Photo by Mark Kearney

Samuel Moore

Moore Corporation

Entrepreneurs around the globe owe Canada's Samuel Moore a big thank-you — in duplicate or triplicate.

In 1882, while a partner at Bengough, Moore and Co. Printers and Publishers, Moore met a drygoods store clerk named John R. Carter, who demonstrated how carbon paper inserted between two pages of a salesbook could give both customer and store proprietor a record of a transaction.

The salesbook would "let one writing serve many purposes," said Carter.

Although others before him had seen the concept, Moore was the first to recognize its potential. His foresight was bang on: The salesbook laid the groundwork for Moore's development of the business form, an innovation that in later years would impact businesses in much the same way as the typewriter, the photocopier, and the computer.

Moore, a native of England who moved to Barrie, Ontario with his parents in the 1860s, started his career in the printing business in 1861 at the *Barrie Examiner* newspaper, where he eventually became local editor. At age twenty, he set out for Texas to find his fortune but soon returned to Canada, where he formed a partnership with J.W. Bengough to publish *Grip*, a satirical paper that lampooned Canadian politics.

With the economy growing by leaps and bounds, Moore's satire soon took a back seat to the salesbook Carter had shown him. Businesses were hungry for ideas that would save time and money and Moore figured this crude version of latter-day business forms was just what the doctor ordered.

Although Moore can't take credit for the concept, he saw how business forms would revolutionize the keeping of accounts and books, which required a legion of bookkeepers, copyists, and clerks to do mundane and repetitive paperwork.

Moore's first counter salesbook, The Paragon Black Leaf Counter Check Book, was enthusiastically received by businesses in Canada, which enjoyed lower business costs and were able to free up employees for work that was far more productive than shuffling paper.

Soon after, Moore realized that vast markets awaited the product in the United States. He and his associates set up the first factory devoted exclusively to the manufacture of salesbooks in Niagara Falls, New York. In 1889, Moore helped establish the Lamson Paragon Supply Co. in London with rights to the salesbook patents and manufacturing know-how throughout Europe and Australia. In 1899, Moore's shares were listed on the Toronto Stock Exchange.

Over the next forty years, Moore acquired nine related businesses in North America, known as the Moore Group, and in 1929 these merged to form Moore Corporation Limited. Products introduced by his companies included zig-zag folded forms for register machines, continuous folded forms, the economical one-time carbon, and the development of web-fed lithography, making quality high-speed mass production a reality.

In 1934, the Sales Book Manufacturers Association heaped praise on Moore, saying "Mr. Moore proved himself a master salesman, as well as a capable organiser and an efficient manufacturer. He was both a correct interpreter of events and the apostle of an idea."

As the book *Wayfarers: Canadian Achievers*, Canada Heirloom Series, later pointed out, Moore's successful business enterprise spawned interests in other endeavours, including directorships in numerous companies. One of these was the Metropolitan Bank of Canada, which he helped found in 1902, and which was later merged with the Bank of Nova Scotia. Moore served as its president, chairman of the board, and honorary chairman.

Business was not all that Moore lived for, however. He often volunteered his time to the Baptist Church and the Young Men's Christian Association (YMCA). He died in 1948 and thirty-one years later was inducted into the Canadian Business Hall of Fame.

Following his death, the company continued to expand and innovate. One of its key inventions was carbonless paper, which was introduced in 1950.

Moore Business Forms and Systems, the Canadian division of Moore Corporation, markets computer supplies and accessories as well as business forms. It has manufacturing facilities and sales offices across Canada and supplies all parts of Canada's corporate sector.

Internationally, the Moore network operates in fifty countries and employs over twenty-six thousand people worldwide. Moore is also involved in bar codes and business equipment, direct marketing and database publishing, and computer services, systems, and supplies.

Henry Morgan

Henry Morgan and Company

A hardworking Scotsman with a flair for innovation created one of the most enduring department stores in Canadian business history.

Henry Morgan and Company was a well-known name in Montreal through the latter half of the nineteenth century and much of the twentieth, and while it may not be as famous nationwide as Eaton's or Simpson's, Morgan's takes its place as one of the most significant retail outlets founded in Canada.

Morgan was born November 14, 1819 in Saline, Scotland and after completing school, he apprenticed with a company in Glasgow that specialized in wholesale dry goods. Like many Scots of the time, Morgan was lured to Canada with the promise of a better life and settled in Montreal in 1844. He established his first retail dry goods store on rue Notre-Dame with partner David Smith.

Selling draperies, fabric, and household linen, Smith and Morgan was a success from the start and made a profit of £800 after the first year. Morgan worked as hard as anyone, arriving at the store at five o'clock each morning and staying until two the next morning. He relied on his brother James, who was their buyer in Britain, to stay on top of fashion trends and to provide quality goods.

After five years, his partnership with Smith ended, and Morgan joined forces with his brother to form Henry Morgan and Company. The firm was so successful that it moved to new headquarters on rue McGill and then expanded again shortly thereafter. By 1853, there were some twenty clerks working for the company. Morgan's nephew James joined the business in 1863, and three years later the company again moved to a new location, this time on rue Saint-Jacques. Another nephew, William, came on board in 1869.

Morgan travelled through Europe to ensure his store and fashions were up to date. In 1872, he pioneered the idea of displaying goods in the window. Until then stores usually tinted their windows to keep competitors from knowing what products they were selling, and shoppers could only get a general idea of what was available from newspaper advertisements. It's also said that Henry Morgan and Company was Canada's first retail department store. Borrowing retail ideas from France and the U.S., Morgan let his managers take responsibility for purchases, sales, and supervision of their respective departments within the store.

Morgan's two nephews effectively ran the operation from 1877, and they were responsible for finding a new location on rue Sainte-Catherine in 1891. Morgan, who never married, died in 1893, but his company prospered as a family business until 1960 when it was purchased by the Hudson's Bay Company.

Name Dropper

Henry Morgan wanted to have happy customers and told his brother to avoid supplying articles with too much green in them because his clients thought the colour was too Irish.

William Neilson

William Neilson Ltd.

In 1867, William Neilson was strolling along Yonge Street in the heart of Toronto's commercial district when he caught sight of an advertisement for homemade ice cream in the window of a tiny retail store.

The twenty-three-year-old native of Almonte, Ontario, near Ottawa, ventured into the shop and was fascinated by the churning machine that turned dairy liquid and flavouring into bricks of ice cream, which the proprietor cut into slabs and sold to customers for use at home.

Neilson's chance encounter would ultimately give Canada a host of confectionery taste treats, including Crispy Crunch, Jersey Milk, Burnt Almond, Cocoanut Joy, and Malted Milk chocolate bars, the Eskimo Pie frozen treat, as well as fresh milk, coffee creamers, and ice cream.

All have been sold under the banner of William Neilson Ltd., the company Neilson founded in 1893, when he and his wife Mary and their son Morden began making ice cream at their Toronto home using three hand-cranked ice cream machines.

Neilson's entrepreneurial success did not come easy. The son of Scottish immigrants John and Agnes Nilson, William began his career as a machinist's apprentice in Toronto and later moved to Brockville, Ontario, where his wife gave birth to four of their five children. He ran a dry goods store there for a short time, then returned to Toronto to open a grocery store, which went bankrupt in 1891. He then joined his brother in North Dakota, where he worked on a farm.

While Neilson was in the U.S., his wife rented a house and four acres of land in Toronto and began making mincemeat and growing and selling vegetables. When Neilson returned, the family added milk and ice cream to its stable of products, which were sold door to door and to grocery stores.

The first block of Neilson ice cream was sold on May 24, 1893 and in the young company's first summer of operation 3,750 gallons went out the door, earning the family more than $3,000. The secret to Neilson's success was the use of pure cream and his insistence that the cream be churned faster as it got firmer. He also adopted pint-sized bricks of ice cream, an astute move at a time when few homes had the means to store ice cream properly.

In 1904, an ice cream plant for the company's twenty-five employees was built on Gladstone Avenue in Toronto's west end. Neilson also built a comfortable three-storey family home on the site.

The tremendous success of the ice cream business nudged milk off the company's product list, but because ice cream was seasonal, the firm went looking for another product to keep its staff busy year round. In 1906, Neilson began producing bulk and boxed chocolate; a year later mincemeat production ended. In 1907, with fourteen years of ice cream production under its belt, and a new foothold on chocolate production taking shape, the business was incorporated as William Neilson Ltd.

When World War I began, Neilson's was churning out one million gallons of ice cream and 563,000 pounds of chocolate a year, according to the book *William Neilson Ltd./Ltee. The First 100 Years*, by David Carr. The company was also producing hard candies and cough drops.

Unfortunately, William Neilson would not live to see the success of a host of other products that would bear his name. In January 1915, he stumbled on a plank at his factory and fell to the floor. A few days later he suffered a stroke and on February 10, he died at his Toronto home at age seventy. His son Morden became president.

With Morden at the helm, William Neilson Ltd. became the largest producer of ice cream in the British Commonwealth and the largest manufacturer of chocolate in Canada. Under his leadership, a handful of new and different products were introduced, including the Eskimo Pie in 1922; the Jersey Milk chocolate bar in 1924, which would become the company's flagship product; and in 1930, Crispy Crunch, which at one time was Canada's most popular chocolate bar.

When Morden Neilson died of leukemia in 1947, the company was sold to George Weston Ltd. for $4.5 million. Members of the Neilson family remained active in the company until 1972, when Morden Neilson's son Harley, who was executive vice-president of personnel, retired.

Under the ownership of George Weston, the Neilson name continued to be found on ice cream, and was connected to a range of popular chocolate and confectionery products, most added as the result of acquisitions, including the 1987 purchase of the Canadian operations of the Cadbury Confectionery Company. These included Sweet Marie, Mr.

Big, Caramilk, and Crunchy chocolate bars, and Neilson's creamers, tiny sealed cups of milk or cream that are poured into coffee and tea.

In 1981, Neilson was back in the dairy business; Weston incorporated three Ontario dairies under the Neilson brand name. George Weston continues to run the dairy business, which operates a super-dairy in Georgetown, Ontario and a plant in Ottawa, under the name Neilson Dairy, but the company is no longer involved in the ice cream and confectionery business.

In 1990, the ice cream operation was sold to Ault Foods. Six years later the confectionery business, then known as Neilson Cadbury, was sold to Cadbury Schweppes in the UK, which began manufacturing Neilson's chocolate bars under the newly created Cadbury Chocolate Canada Inc.

In 2002, chocolate bars with the Neilson name on the label — including Jersey Milk, Sweet Marie, Malted Milk, and PEP — and 145-gram boxed treats such as Macaroons, Slow Pokes, and Cool Mints were being made by Cadbury Trebor Allan Inc. based in Toronto and owned by Cadbury Schweppes PLC in the UK.

Name Dropper

In 1962, an eighteen-wheel tractor-trailer hauling a cargo of Jersey Milk bars through Rogers Pass in the Rocky Mountains became the first commercial vehicle to cross the Trans-Canada Highway "all Canadian route."

Marie Warman

Sweet Marie chocolate bar

Millions of Canadians have enjoyed a Sweet Marie chocolate bar, but how many have recognized its Canadian origins? And whether the Marie who inspired it ever tasted the popular bar is another matter.

The connection between Canada and the chocolate bar that's smothered with chocolate and nuts began in 1893 when American-born author Cy Warman was living in London, Ontario and walked his girlfriend Marie to her home at Queen's Avenue and Colborne Street. The book *The North and The East* by historian John Lutman says Warman then strolled to Victoria Park in the city's downtown and wrote a love poem to her called "Sweet Marie." It opens with the lines "I've a secret in my heart, Sweet Marie/A tale I would impart, love to thee /Every daisy in the dell/Knows my secret, knows it well/And yet I dare not tell Sweet Marie."

A few years later, a composer named Raymon Moore put the words to music, and the result was a hit song that became popular across North America. It was said that Marie was the best-known London resident on the continent thanks to the tune, which was later featured in the 1947 film *Life With Father* starring William Powell and Irene Dunne.

A chocolate company capitalized on the song by naming one of its products the Sweet Marie bar. Today, you can still wander into most shops that sell candy and buy a Sweet Marie, which is made by Cadbury Trebor Allan Inc., based in Toronto, and is about the thirtieth most popular selling chocolate bar in Canada.

As for Marie and Warman? The poet proposed to Marie and they married and settled in London, raising four children. Their house still stands in the city's Old North section on Cheapside Street.

Alexander Ogilvie

Ogilvie Flour Mills Ltd.

When William Van Horne, general manager of the Canadian Pacific Railway, was asked in the 1880s to name Canada's national flower, he replied: "Ogilvie flour, of course."

The great American miller Charles Pillsbury, whose name to this day is found on a host of foodstuffs, once toasted the president of Ogilvie Flour Mills as "the largest individual flour miller in the world."

Ogilvie flour was adopted as the flour of choice by the royal household of King George V in 1911 and the company also found favour with ordinary housewives when it introduced "ready mixes" that took the guesswork out of making cakes, muffins, biscuits, and piecrusts.

The Canadian milling company that has been held in such high regard by so many was launched in 1801 when Alexander Ogilvie, son of Archibald Ogilvie, erected his first grist mill near Quebec City. Alexander, who like his father was a native of Scotland, was followed by a handful of family members who built an international empire whose products found their way into kitchens around the globe.

Alexander launched the business in Quebec after leaving his father's Montreal-area farm. But he soon shipped his millstones upstream to Montreal, where between 1811 and 1837 he was involved in milling ventures with two brothers-in-law.

"He died in 1858, in his eightieth year, a cheerful and kindly gentleman who probably never realized that fame awaited him as a pioneer and founder of a great industry," author G.R. Stevens wrote in his book *Ogilvie in Canada, Pioneer Millers 1801–1951*.

It was Ogilvie's sons, Alexander, William, and John, who would build A.W. Ogilvie & Company into a flour power by building or acquiring mills in the southwestern Ontario communities of Seaforth and Goderich and in Winnipeg and Montreal.

Historians credit John Ogilvie for seeing the potential breadbasket available on Canada's Prairies. In the early 1870s, he ventured to the Dakota Territory and purchased the first parcel of hard spring wheat to be shipped to Eastern Canada, which proved to be of magnificent quality. In his book, Stevens says this success led the Ogilvies to push for the growing of hard wheat in the Canadian West. In 1881 they began a mill in Winnipeg and erected the first of the traditional rectangular pitch-roofed elevators built in Canada at Gretna, Manitoba. The first export of wheat from Western Canada occurred in 1885 when the Ogilvies sent a small shipment from the Winnipeg mill to Scotland.

The push westward was accelerated when the company received a staggering offer from British military for a half-million-dollar shipment. By 1887, the Ogilvies held two million bushels of Manitoba wheat in their elevators, prompting competitors to complain that the company was out to corner the market.

After nearly a century in the milling business, the early 1900s brought a radical transformation to the Ogilvie family. William Ogilvie died suddenly on January 12, 1900. Two years later on March 31, 1902, Alexander Ogilvie passed away.

On May 30, 1902, A.W. Ogilvie & Company and W.W. Ogilvie Milling Company and seventy country elevators were purchased by a Montreal syndicate and renamed The Ogilvie Flour Mills Co. Ltd. In June 1955, the name was changed to Ogilvie Mills Ltd. The new owners expanded the company's product lineup and built mills across Western Canada and in Montreal.

The company changed hands again in 1968 when John Labatt Ltd. acquired the majority of Ogilvie's shares. In July 1992, Labatt sold the flour, starch, and specialty products divisions of the Canadian and U.S. Ogilvie Mills companies to Archer Daniels Midland of Decatur, Illinois.

Since the 1800s, the Ogilvie name has been most commonly seen in Canada on country elevators, flour mills, and packages containing a range of products including all-purpose flour, cake mixes, minute oats, and even baby food. In 1949, the company was processing cereals and strained foods for Gerber Products Company of the U.S.

At one point, Ogilvie was the most important milling operation in the British Empire and the largest private flour mill in the world.

Susannah Oland

Oland Breweries Limited

In the 1870s, female commercial brewers were unheard of in Canada.

So, when Susannah Oland began building her brewing business in 1877, she called her company S. Oland Sons and Company to downplay the fact that a woman owned the business.

As the lifeblood of the operation, Oland built the company into the dominant brewer in the Maritimes. In doing so, she reclaimed a role held by women centuries earlier, when virtually all brewmasters were females.

"For thousands of years, female brewers were priestesses, healers, and respected members of their communities," the Brewers Association of Canada wrote in the November 2000 edition of *Way Beyond Beer, The Many Contributions of Canada's Brewers*.

Although Susannah is known as the founder of Oland Breweries, the company's roots date back to 1867 when the original company, known as Army and Navy Brewery, was founded as a partnership between British army officer Francis DeWinton and Susannah's husband John. The Olands and their six children had immigrated to Canada from England in the early 1860s.

The first brewery — which used Susannah's recipe for beer — was located on a twelve-acre property at Turtle's Cove in Dartmouth, on the east side of Halifax harbour. Soon after, however, John Oland died in a riding accident and DeWinton sold his shares in the company to Susannah before leaving Canada for military service.

Susannah was known as a capable businesswoman, and under her leadership, with the able help of sons John, Conrad, and George, S. Oland Sons and Co. prospered, despite a major fire that gutted the brewery. Gradually, the sons, all of whom had become accomplished brewmasters, began running the operation. In 1886, Susannah died at age sixty-eight while wintering in Richmond, Virginia.

Near the end of the century, the Oland brewery was sold to a large syndicate.

In the twentieth century, first under George and later under his son Sidney and other members of the family, the Oland name would resurface when other regional breweries in Nova Scotia and New Brunswick were purchased or launched. These companies purchased the Alexander Keith Brewery in Halifax and a brewery in New Brunswick which became Moosehead Breweries Ltd.

In May 1971, Oland and Son Limited's breweries in Halifax and Oland's Brewery in Saint John, New Brunswick were purchased for $12 million by John Labatt Limited and renamed Oland's Breweries (1971) Limited. Eight years later, Oland's Nova Scotia and New Brunswick breweries were amalgamated to form Oland Breweries Limited.

Oland Breweries Limited brews Schooner, Oland Export, Keith's India Pale Ale, Keith's Light, Blue, Blue Light, Wild Cat, Maximum Ice, and, under license, Bud and Bud Light.

Name Dropper

In 1963, Oland & Son Breweries commissioned the *Bluenose II* as a tribute to the first *Bluenose*, which was built in 1921 to win the International Fisherman's Trophy from the Americans. The *Bluenose II*, which is a replica of the original ship, is based in Lunenburg, Nova Scotia, where it is used for public tours and festivals. To mark the launch of the new ship, Oland launched Schooner beer, which carried a picture of the original *Bluenose* on the label. An image of the first *Bluenose* is also found on the Canadian dime.

Jim Pattison

The Jim Pattison Group

Comedian Bob Hope once described British Columbia as a suburb of Jim Pattison. Over the years, various media reports have concluded that it's virtually impossible to do business in B.C. without dealing with one of the Vancouver billionaire's many enterprises.

In British Columbia, if you purchase or lease cars, buy groceries and magazines, listen to the radio and watch television, Pattison has probably touched your life. If you live east of the Rocky Mountains, he has influenced your life too.

The next time you're out and about — be it in Halifax, Ottawa, Winnipeg, Montreal, or Saskatoon — there's a good chance you'll see Pattison's name on the billboards and advertising signage found along most busy streets.

Through The Jim Pattison Sign Group and Pattison Outdoor, Pattison's name is found on twenty thousand large roadside signboards and bus shelters in Canada, and he controls the advertising on hundreds of large neon signs, most located next to major expressways in Toronto and Montreal, and more than fifty thousand "poster boards" affixed to transit vehicles in Ottawa, Edmonton, Calgary, and a handful of smaller Western Canada cities.

Chances are, you've probably eaten a tin of Gold Seal salmon or visited a Ripley's Believe or Not! museum, theatre, or aquarium. He owns those too.

With his fingers in all kinds of pies and a personal fortune pegged at $2 billion, Pattison — who's called "Jimmy" by most people — was ranked Canada's seventh wealthiest person in 2002 by *Forbes* magazine. His sole proprietorship company boasts assets of $3.1 billion, sales of $5.2 billion, and a workforce of twenty-five thousand.

Born in October 1928 in Luseland, Saskatchewan, near Saskatoon, Pattison had his first taste of entrepreneurialism at the age of seven when he began selling vegetable seeds after his family moved to Vancouver. As a University of British Columbia commerce student, he paid for his tuition and other expenses by washing cars at a used car lot and selling vehicles to fellow students.

Photos by Randy Ray

Although his father, a car salesman, wanted his son to be a lawyer, the car business was soon in the young Pattison's blood. In the late 1950s he ran a Vancouver car lot where he set sales records and convinced the owner to invest in the largest neon sign in North America. In 1961, at age thirty-three, he purchased a General Motors automobile dealership in Vancouver, with a $40,000 loan. Four years later he bought struggling radio station CJOR in Vancouver and was well on his way to fulfilling the vow he made to his wife Mary — that he'd be a millionaire by age forty.

Over the years he has gained a reputation as a charming and generous man and a shrewd businessman who has built his company by acquisitions and diversification. He's also been referred to as a hardboiled softy, ruthless, God-fearing, greedy, and slightly tacky.

On the back of the book *Jimmy: An Autobiography*, the late broadcaster Peter Gzowski calls Pattison "a curious man, part altruist, part egoist, partly private, partly show-off."

The Pattison empire started in the car business, which in 2002 included twelve dealerships in Victoria and the Vancouver area, several of which bear his name, as well as Jim Pattison Lease, a national vehicle leasing company based in Calgary with offices in Vancouver, Victoria, Edmonton, and Toronto.

Companies he's acquired on various buying sprees (and in some cases later sold) include one of the biggest coal ports on the West Coast; the Canadian Fish Company, Canada's second-largest producer of Pacific salmon and herring roe; Overwaitea and Save-On-Foods, Canada's largest western-based foodstore chain; Crush International, which bottles Orange Crush; and airlines, trucking companies, and a manufacturer of mobile homes. The Pattison sign group is the world's largest custom electric outdoor sign company, and he owns twenty radio stations and three TV stations in Alberta and B.C. Also under his control is The Jim Pattison News Group, one of North America's largest wholesale magazine distribution companies, as well as export and financial services companies and packaging firms.

On the way to the top, Pattison has always had three loves — money, cars, and his prairie sweetheart, Mary Hudson. The couple were married in 1951 and have a son and two daughters.

Despite his great wealth and success, life in business hasn't always been smooth sailing: In 1969 he almost went bankrupt when one of his

Photos by Randy Ray

holdings, a company called Neonex, attempted to take over Maple Leaf Mills, one of Canada's largest flour mills. Over the years he has battled with the unions that represent his workers, been slammed because one of his companies distributed pornographic magazines, and, according to author Russell Kelly, in his book *Pattison, Portrait of a Capitalist Superstar*, he has raised the ire of employees, shareholders, and business partners over the years for engaging in "blackmail bargaining" and breaking promises.

Though he may not be a household name across Canada, Pattison gained a degree of fame during the early 1980s, when Bill Bennett, premier of B.C. at the time, hired him to salvage Expo 86 in Vancouver, which was so far behind schedule it was in danger of being cancelled. Pattison earned a token dollar a year for his stint at Expo and managed to bring the $1.6 billion project in at $32 million under budget.

After that, it was back to business. By the summer of 1998, he owned 148 companies with operations in twelve countries and his empire continued to grow as Pattison reached his mid-70s. In 2002, he owned fifty-nine companies.

During a speech several years ago in his hometown, Pattison attributed the beginnings of his company's success to the values of caring and integrity that he and his parents got from the small prairie community.

With investments in Canada, the United States, Mexico, Europe, Asia, and Australia, The Jim Pattison Group is Canada's third largest privately held company, and was ranked as Canada's forty-first largest firm in a *Financial Post* survey. Pattison was appointed to the Order of Canada in 1987, and the Order of British Columbia in 1990. A devout Baptist, Pattison spends most of his time in Vancouver.

Name Dropper

Pattison is notorious for his personal shopping sprees, which have included the purchase of Frank Sinatra's former home in Palm Springs, California, for US$4.6 million; John Lennon's psychedelic Rolls Royce for US$2.3 million, and a US$1 million collection of Marilyn Monroe memorabilia.

Yves Potvin

Yves Veggie Cuisine

In 1985, a light bulb went on under Yves Potvin's chef's hat.

Why not come up with a healthy and tasty fast food that would appeal to active, health-conscious consumers who were concerned about cholesterol and fat intake?

Drawing on his practical experience as a French chef and catering company owner in his home province of Quebec, Potvin conceived a healthy alternative to conventional fast foods. After long hours of research, the end product was a line of familiar eats such as burgers and hot dogs that appeal to North American tastebuds using all-vegetable soy-based protein in place of meat.

At the age of twenty-eight, the meat-eating Potvin started a company in Vancouver with $10,000 of his own money and $30,000 borrowed from family and friends. "I like a good hot dog," Potvin told the *Globe and Mail* in 1999. "But don't tell me what's inside."

Yves Fine Foods Inc., later renamed Yves Veggie Cuisine, began as a one-man operation with Potvin working seven days a week manufacturing, packaging, marketing, selling, and distributing his products.

Today, Yves Veggie Cuisine produces a full line of low-fat fake meat products, including pepperoni, ground beef, deli slices, and bacon, that are sold fresh in food stores across Canada and the United States. The

Chef Yves Potvin

Courtesy of Yves Veggie Cuisine

company operates from a modern manufacturing facility in a suburb of Vancouver and has offices and warehouses in Montreal, Toronto, and several American cities including Los Angeles and Atlanta.

The meat-free products have hit the spot with consumers: In the early 1990s, Potvin's tofu wieners were sold at San Francisco Giants baseball games; in 1993, high-profile vegetarian Linda McCartney made the company the official supplier of veggie hot dogs on her husband Paul's North American concert tour; and the company has a pantry full of international awards.

In 2001, with twenty-four products garnering annual sales of $50 million, Yves Veggie Cuisine was purchased by natural foods giant Hain Celestial Group Inc. of Uniondale, N.Y., whose lineup includes Weight Watchers products.

Name Dropper

Yves Veggie Cuisine sells two million cases of its products per year. That's enough wieners, if strung together, to stretch fifty-six hundred kilometres, or the distance from New York to London, England.

Richard Corman Purdy
Purdy's Chocolates

In the early 1900s, Vancouver entrepreneur Richard Corman Purdy was at the heart of many a love affair on Canada's West Coast. It wasn't that Purdy was a great lover, but rather that those who were smitten loved his chocolates.

"To receive a box of Purdy's was to know that one was the one and only girl of one's current crush," a Vancouver newspaper reminisced in 1943 after the pioneer confectioner died at age sixty-six.

Purdy (who in some references is referred to as Norman Richard Purdy) was a native of London, Ontario who started a chocolate-making business in 1907 with a small candy store on Robson Street in downtown Vancouver. He later moved to a building on Granville Street, where he opened a candy kitchen in the basement, sold chocolates on the main floor, and operated the Devon Cafe upstairs.

Because of his insistence that only the finest quality ingredients were to be used in his products, Purdy soon became one of the best-known chocolate makers on the West Coast. An undated document unearthed by the City of Vancouver Archives said Purdy's Granville Street outlet kept "good goods; splendid goods and had a fine restaurant, as good as any in the city in its day … he was famed for Purdy's Chocolates."

Unfortunately, Purdy ran into a string of business and personal problems that took the sweetness out of his candy business. Details are sketchy, but it is believed his troubles were related to his finances, debts related to gambling or the stock market, and at some point, the sale of chocolates containing liquor.

Court documents show Purdy's company and two other defendants were prosecuted for "unlawfully keeping for sale, liquor, contrary to the Liquor Control Act … the defendants kept for sale chocolates known as liqueur chocolates." The outcome of the case is not known.

An unsigned document, also from the Vancouver archives, states: "…something happened; let us say about 1925. Some litigation started; there was an internal disturbance I think over finance, operation, or something, and it was rumored around town that there was trouble in the company and Mr. Purdy had been hard done by. Also, it was said that Mr. Purdy himself was partly to blame."

In 1925 the company was acquired by Hugh Forrester, who kept the business and the Purdy name alive through the Depression and war years. At some point Purdy sold the rights to his name and is believed to have started another candy store known as Window Made Candy on Hastings Street in Vancouver. Obituaries written following his death on February 8, 1943, remembered Purdy as "one of Vancouver's most prominent businessmen" who was "very active in community work." Purdy was married but there is no record of children.

In 1963, Purdy's Chocolates had four Vancouver stores and a three-thousand-square-foot factory kitchen. But faced with financial difficulties, the company was sold by the Forrester family to Charles Flavelle of Vancouver. In 2002, Purdy's Chocolates was run by Flavelle's daughter Karen, who continued to make chocolates with some of Norman Purdy's original recipes.

The company makes about one hundred different types of chocolates, which are sold at more than forty-five retail outlets in Alberta and British Columbia.

John Redpath

Redpath Sugars

Life was sweet for John Redpath long before 1854 when the Montreal businessman built Canada's first sugar refinery on the banks of the St. Lawrence River.

After immigrating to Canada in 1816 as a skilled stone mason, Redpath in the 1820s and 1830s earned a fortune as a building contractor who helped build the new Notre-Dame church, several buildings at McGill University, and the Lachine Canal, all in Montreal, as well as parts of the Rideau Canal.

Not bad for a guy who got his start digging outhouses in Montreal.

After the Rideau Canal opened in August 1831, linking Ottawa and Kingston, the native of Earlston, Scotland returned to Montreal as a wealthy and respected businessman. He began putting his money and time into various investments and directorships involving the Bank of Montreal, the Montreal Assurance Company, the Montreal General Hospital, and the Ottawa Steamboat Line. He purchased plots of vacant land in Montreal and elsewhere and served as an alderman for the City of Montreal for several terms.

But what helped Redpath stand out from many of his equals in Montreal was his decision to construct a sugar refinery in what was then the Province of Canada. The seven-storey factory and its towering smokestack, located

John Redpath

in an industrial belt next to the Lachine Canal, became a city landmark and ensured Redpath and his family a place in Canada's history books.

Nearly 150 years later, Redpath brand sugar is a mainstay in restaurants, kitchen pantries, and grocery stores. Although the company has been out of the Redpath family's hands since the 1950s, a refinery in Toronto bearing the founder's name was producing twenty-four hundred tonnes of sugar a day in 2002.

Redpath decided to enter the sugar business in 1849 when he recognized that income from his investments would not secure his family's financial future, says Richard Feltoe, curator at the Redpath Museum in Toronto and author of the book *Redpath: The History of a Sugar House.* After investigating various aspects of manufacturing, including a cotton mill, an iron foundry, copper works, and a steamship line, he settled on sugar refining because there were no competitors inside Canada.

After studying the business in Great Britain and Scotland, Redpath, now fifty-seven years old, used his skills as a contractor and stone mason to oversee the construction of a refinery, which opened for business in Montreal on August 12, 1854. The John Redpath Canada Sugar Refinery was owned by Redpath and managed by George Alexander Drummond, who later would become his brother-in-law and lifelong friend.

Within a year, Redpath had more than one hundred employees, and, using cane sugar from the West Indies and Central America, was producing nine hundred thousand pounds of refined sugar per month for the Canadian market. In 1859, Redpath brought his eldest son Peter into the firm. The corporate name was changed to John Redpath & Son, Canada Sugar Refinery and that year the company reported a profit of nearly $90,000 as sugar became a highly visible staple relied upon by households for cooking and preservation of fruit and some vegetables.

In 1861, Redpath's son John James and George Alexander Drummond were taken into the business as partners. Over the years the refinery was upgraded and the company broadened its investments to include holdings in slate and telegraph companies, several mines, a copper smelting works, and two sailing vessels, which marked the company's entry into the field of transportation.

In 1867, following a trip to England and Scotland, Redpath returned to Canada in ill health and in 1868 handed the presidency to his son Peter. John Redpath suffered a stroke in April 1868 and died on March 5, 1869, at age seventy-three.

He left a legacy that went far beyond the sugar business. He was married twice, to Janet Mcphee and later to Jane Drummond, and fathered seventeen children, five of whom died as infants. He was a charitable man who supported established institutions such as the Montreal General Hospital and the Montreal Presbyterian College, and he helped found and served on the boards of several community organizations. Some were the beneficiaries of considerable sums of his money.

Redpath is also remembered as one of the leaders of a Montreal association of merchants, which in 1849 promoted Canada's split from the rule of Britain and annexation by the United States. Some members of Montreal's Molson family were among the signatories to a petition which supported an ill-fated bid for a union with the U.S.

With his father gone, Peter Redpath ran the refinery until he retired at age sixty, at which time Drummond became president. The company merged with its former rival, the Dominion Sugar Company, in 1930, and became the Canada and Dominion Sugar Co. Ltd., which later was renamed Redpath Sugars. It remained under the control of the Redpath family until 1959, when Tate & Lyle Sugars Group of England began buying shares. The company acquired control of Redpath in the 1980s.

Redpath's original Montreal refinery was closed in 1980, the victim of a severe economic downturn. Sugar from the Toronto facility is sold predominantly in Ontario and Quebec for use by consumers, but also for use in a huge variety of industrial and commercial products including explosives, gasoline additives, paints, baked goods, jams and preserves, candies, ice cream, juices, soft drinks, canned fruits and vegetables, cosmetics, pharmaceuticals, and plastics.

Name Dropper

The Redpath logo, consisting of John Redpath's signature, is believed to be the oldest continuously used trademark in Canada.

Herman and Sarah Reitman
Reitman Canada Limited

It wasn't exactly rags to riches, but like many prosperous Canadian companies, Reitmans, the large chain of women's wear stores, had humble beginnings.

Herman and Sarah Reitman were both born in Romania and came to Canada for a better life. In the early 1900s, they operated a small shop called American Ladies Tailoring and Dressmaking Company in Montreal. It catered primarily to the dressmaking needs of ladies, specializing in made-to-measure garments.

About 1914, they decided to move away from the dressmaking field and turn their business into a dry goods general store. They sold hosiery, gloves, some house furnishings and housewares, clothing, fabrics, and ribbons by the yard, all from a small department store of about fifteen hundred square feet.

Their second store in 1926 was located on St. Lawrence Blvd. in Montreal, and the couple got help from their children, Louis, Sam, John, and Jack. It soon became apparent that the most popular items in the dry goods store were hosiery, gloves, and lingerie, so the Reitmans decided to specialize in ladies' wear.

It was a good decision. Under the simple name Reitmans, the store prospered and by 1929, the family had four outlets in Montreal. The company continued to expand, and in 1936 it ventured outside of the city, first to Ottawa, and then three years later to Toronto. By this time, Reitmans had twenty-two stores with annual sales of almost $1 million.

Herman died in 1941, while Sarah's death came nine years later, but the company was firmly in family hands. In 1947, with sales exceeding $2 million, the company went public and was listed for trading on the Montreal Stock Exchange. By 1950, Reitmans had fifteen stores in Quebec and twenty in Ontario. A year later the head office and distribution centre was moved to a twenty-five-thousand-square-foot facility at 3510 St. Lawrence Blvd., across the street from the first store.

Reitmans opened its first store in Western Canada in 1958 in Calgary and the following year moved into Eastern Canada with an outlet in Halifax. The company continued to grow and prosper from the 1960s onward, opening Smart Set stores and acquiring others such as Pennington's, which caters to larger-sized women. Today, president Jeremy Reitman oversees an operation that has about six hundred stores, of which more than three hundred bear the Reitmans name. Annual sales are in excess of $20 million.

George Richards

George Richards Big and Tall Menswear

Before he grappled with the challenge of supplying large men with properly fitting clothing, George Richards had already made a name for himself in the wrestling ring.

The Toronto-born entrepreneur, who originally wanted to be a doctor, took up pro wrestling as a young man to help support his family after his father died, according to his son Michael.

Richards was a good athlete and, standing a bit taller than six foot one and weighing 225 pounds, he was a fairly big man for the 1920s and 1930s. Though not the greatest wrestler on the scene, Richards knew his way around the ropes and succeeded at the sport throughout Canada and the U.S. Wrestling was more of a sport and less of a show in those days, but Richards would still take on different names in various cities if it would boost gate receipts. If promoters wanted to attract Jewish fans in New York City, Richards might wrestle under a name like Benny Stein; in Boston, he might step into the ring using an Irish name to entice the fans.

Richards wrestled and worked out with some of the top names in the sport, including Lou Thesz, whom Michael says was the greatest wrestler who ever lived. Matches back then might last up to an hour so "you had to be in really good shape."

Richards, who was born to Jewish immigrants in 1914 in Toronto, enlisted in the air force during World War II and helped train troops on the ships going from Halifax to London. On the return trip, he'd be in charge of German prisoners of war who were being transported to Canada so that they'd be as far from the battlefield as possible. By the war's end, Richards was getting too old for wrestling and decided to buy a men's store at the south end of Yonge Street. He had always been a snappy dresser and interested in clothes, so it seemed a good career move. Being Jewish, Richards still faced discrimination in the WASP environment of Toronto at the time and had only so many opportunities available, Michael explains.

When colleagues from his athletic days began dropping in to buy suits and slacks, Richards realized that if he could provide larger-sized men with well-tailored clothes he might develop a garment goldmine. Some stores in the U.S. catered to large and tall men, but the Canadian market was wide open.

The business prospered, and Richards moved first to a larger store at Bay and Bloor streets, and then in the early 1960s to a six-thousand-square-foot building at Yonge and Roselawn in north Toronto. "It was in the middle of nowhere" back then, Michael says, and many questioned Richards's move. But the customers followed, and with on-site tailoring, attention to service, and a healthy mail order business, the George Richards shop thrived. Richards, who supplied clothes for large athletes in the Canadian Football League, the National Hockey League, and wrestlers such as Lord Athol Layton and Whipper Billy Watson, built up a terrific following with his shop and his catalogue.

Michael graduated from university in 1972 and joined his father's business. He suggested that Richards expand outside Toronto and create a series of chain stores in communities where their mail order business was strong. Over the next decade, several George Richards stores opened across Canada. Grafton-Fraser bought a 50 percent share in the business in 1977 and purchased the balance of the company in 1981.

Richards retired after the sale while Michael worked in other ventures. Until then, Richards had spent most of his time with his business, but always continued to work out. Even in his mid-80s, Richards was leading exercise classes for seniors, and in early 2002 at age eighty-seven, he was still working out four times a week, says son Michael.

Name Dropper

Richards took on other odd jobs early in life to make ends meet. On the opening night of Maple Leaf Gardens, November 12, 1931, Richards was there selling programs. He'd later wrestle in the Gardens.

Edward S. Rogers

Rogers Communications Inc.

Edward Rogers began his march toward broadcast industry stardom long before he started shaving and years before his family name became synonymous with Canadian telecommunications.

Rogers was born in 1900 into a wealthy and highly respected Toronto family descended from Quakers. His parents wanted him to become a business executive, but as a youngster he was enthralled by radio and eventually set up a laboratory in the family garage.

At age eleven, he was broadcasting in Morse code from one of Canada's first licensed amateur radios. In 1913, when he was thirteen, he won a prize for the best amateur-built radio in Ontario and that year was the subject of a feature article in the *Toronto Telegram* newspaper that discussed how he was able to pick up a report of a shipwreck in Ireland on his telegraph set. A year later, he picked up Germany's declaration of war on a homemade radio.

After studying engineering at the University of Toronto for two years, Rogers in 1921 became the first Canadian to transmit a radio signal across the Atlantic Ocean. The signal originated in Newmarket, Ontario and was sent to a receiving station in Androssan, Scotland, near Glasgow.

Published articles about Rogers' accomplishments referred to him as the "Wireless Wizard." In his early 20s, Ted, as he was known to his friends, launched Canada into the age of electronic information and entertainment when he invented the radio amplifying tube.

Stamp featuring Edward S. Rogers

The device revolutionized the radio industry by eliminating the need for cumbersome, leak-prone acid batteries, enabling consumers to operate their radios on the alternating current from wall plugs. His invention also drastically cut the cost of radios, making them far more popular. He was well on his way toward achieving his vision of radio as an electric pipeline that would reach into people's homes to entertain, inform, and educate.

In 1925, he began manufacturing the Majestic five-tube batteryless radio, which despite its hefty $260 price tag was an immediate success because it eliminated an annoying hum that plagued battery-operated radios. In 1927, the year he received a patent for his invention, Rogers founded Toronto radio station CFRB, which was Canada's first all-electric radio station and later became one of the country's most influential and successful broadcasting companies. Among the many entertainers the station showcased were Guy Lombardo and his Royal Canadians and orchestra leader Percy Faith.

Rogers was granted the first Canadian television licence in 1931, foreshadowing the dominance in cable television that would be his legacy. Eight years later, while working on the development of radar, Rogers died of a bleeding ulcer. The Rogers estate floundered and CFRB was sold by his wife Velma.

Twenty years later Rogers' son Edward Samuel, also known as Ted, picked up where his father left off. He purchased Toronto radio station CHFI and over the years built a tremendously successful communications empire. Known as Rogers Communications Inc., the Toronto-based company's vast holdings have included radio and televisions stations, cable TV services and channels, movie theatres, newspapers, magazines and periodicals, Internet service on cable, wireless communications, and football and baseball teams, including the Toronto Blue Jays.

Name Dropper

The call letters for Toronto radio station CFRB stand for Canada's First Rogers Batteryless. When Rogers founded the station, it was originally known as 9RB.

Harry Rosen

Harry Rosen Inc.

Harry Rosen's sense of style and design in men's clothes can be traced to lunchtime pinochle games when he was a high school student.

Rosen worked summers at a clothing manufacturer in Toronto and wanted to find out more about clothing design. That area of the business was off limits to most employees, but Rosen said he liked "sticking [his] nose into everything that was going on." He started playing cards over lunch with the company's designer and peppered the man with questions about how to make suits and what made for a good shirt.

By the time he returned to school, Rosen was starting to think the clothing business might be the right fit. The following summer he branched off into retail and "inside of a few weeks I was able to compete with the hotshot salesman on the floor. I made it my business to understand what the features (of a clothing item) were that the consumer would see as a benefit, and I knew how to articulate it."

Harry Rosen

Courtesy of Harry Rosen

Sam Lelo, the store's owner and Rosen's mentor, wanted him to stay on staff, but the young man had another dream — to run his own shop. With a $500 loan from a relative, Rosen opened a small clothing store in 1954 on Parliament Street, which at the time was not the best location for that type of business because it didn't have the kind of shops that would attract high-end shoppers. His brother Lou soon joined him.

Rosen, who was born in Toronto on August 27, 1931, had not been a clothes horse as a child, but once he got into the business he approached it with passion and zeal. In his first year of business, he did about $70,000 in sales as word spread about the store's quality and service.

He soon met up with people in the publishing and advertising businesses who brought their money to his store and made it something of a hangout. Rosen recalls how they'd gather in late afternoons to "tell lies, drink coffee, and have a fitting. It was a warm, hospitable place."

Rosen was adept at following up prospects and soon customers from outside Ontario started showing up. By 1961, Rosen had moved to larger, more upscale headquarters on Richmond Street. As the company prospered, Rosen's name and quality men's wear attracted attention across North America and beyond. Among his more famous clientele were actors Alan Bates and Christopher Plummer and newscaster Peter Jennings.

In 1982, he expanded outside of Ontario by opening a store in the West Edmonton Mall, and five years later opened his flagship store on Bloor Street in Toronto, introducing the idea of grouping clothing lines together in kind of a shop-within-a-shop concept that has been copied by others many times since.

Having dealt with customers for more than forty-five years, Rosen says men today are more self-assured about their style, but "are still learning a lot about clothing. Men are essentially lazy, they don't care to shop." Harry Rosen Inc., which has more than twenty stores across Canada and sales of about $200 million annually, carries such designers as Hugo Boss, Armani, and Versace.

Rosen himself prefers the Kiton line from Italy with its soft, understated look and likes shades of blue, grey, and green/khaki. His business skills have led him to be on the advisory board of the Richard Ivey School of Business in London, Ontario, he was named Retail Marketer of the Year in 1987, and he received the Lifetime Achievement Award from the Retail Council of Canada in 2001.

When he's not selling clothes, Rosen likes to read, play chess, study history, and play the mandolin, "an instrument I love." He works out daily and as of 2002 still found pleasure in being on the shop floor.

"I delight in looking after customers. I remember what most of them purchased from me." Then he adds with a laugh, "I don't remember my wife's birthday, but I remember the wardrobes I've provided to people over the years."

Name Dropper

Rosen's successful Ask Harry ad campaign, which continues today, was introduced as a way of answering men's questions about how to select and buy clothes. Because of his contacts in the business, Rosen was able to get top-notch advertising early on by bartering clothes. "I got the finest talent money could possibly buy for two suits per ad," he says with a chuckle.

Jacob Schick

Schick Dry Shaver Inc.

Claiming Jacob Schick as Canadian might be considered the equivalent of a nationalistic close shave. But the father of the electric shaver not only renounced his U.S. citizenship late in life and settled in Canada, he may also have come up with the idea for his invention somewhere in British Columbia.

Some sources say Schick was in Alaska just before World War I when he came up with the idea of trying to shave without water, but others say it may have been while he was prospecting in B.C. Regardless, the story goes that Schick was in a mining camp and it was so cold outside he couldn't collect snow to melt for his morning shave. He persevered with the idea until the Depression when he came up with the Schick Dry Shaver, the product that would make him a wealthy man.

Schick was born in Ottumwa, Iowa in 1878, the son of Valentine Schick, who had come to the U.S. from Bavaria and served with the Union Army in the Civil War before discovering a copper mine in New Mexico. Jacob was sixteen when he began working on building a railroad to a nearby coal mine his father had opened to provide fuel for a copper smelter.

Schick began prospecting in Alaska in the late nineteenth century and then joined the army to fight in the Spanish-American War. Despite bad health, Schick was promoted up the army ranks until it was suggested he return to Alaska because the cold climate would be better for his health. He worked out of a mining office in Seattle, taking trips north to prospect. It was on one of those trips that he sprained his ankle, found it too cold to melt water for his shave, and started thinking about the idea of an electric shaver.

Schick resigned from the military in 1919 and began his work on various shavers before patenting one in 1928. He set up a manufacturing plant in Stamford, Connecticut that employed about one hundred people. Though he had spent much of his life serving the U.S. and making his fortune there, he renounced his citizenship in 1935 to move to Canada.

Apparently, then-president Franklin Roosevelt was incensed by Schick's move and accused him of leaving the country to escape income and inheritance laws. But Schick's friends claimed he moved to Canada and its colder climate on the recommendation of his physician.

Unfortunately, the change in climate and country didn't help. Schick died after complications from a kidney operation only eighteen months after he moved here. He was survived by his wife Florence and two daughters, Virginia and Barbara, and is buried in Montreal's Mount Royal Cemetery.

Name Dropper

Though the electric razor today seems like a brilliant idea, it didn't enjoy overwhelming public acceptance right away. Times were so tough for the Schick company in the early 1930s that Florence had to mortgage their home for $10,000 to keep the business going.

J.M. Schneider

Schneider Foods

From button manufacturing to the butchering business.

It's a strange shift in careers, but for J.M. Schneider, whose name today is found on hot dogs, cold cuts, sausages, and other products, it was the route to fame and fortune. John Metz Schneider was born February 17, 1859 in Berlin (now Kitchener), Ontario. He grew up on a farm, looked after the livestock, and helped his parents slaughter and dress the hogs.

As an adult, he found work on the assembly line of the Dominion Button Works earning a dollar a day and working six days a week. When he was twenty-four, he married Helena Ahrens, and they began raising a family. In 1886, Schneider had an accident at the button factory that kept him away from work for about a month. With his hand in a bandage, Schneider, his wife, and his mother began grinding up meat and creating German sausages in their kitchen as a way of earning extra money.

Schneider sold those first sausages door to door, and though he went back to work making buttons, he began building up loyal customers who liked the taste of his sausages. After his long days at the factory, J.M. and Helena would work well into the night trying to make their new venture successful. Eventually J.M. started selling sausages to

J.M. Schneider

Courtesy of Schneider Foods Archives, Kitchener, Ontario

market butchers and grocers until he reached a point at which he had to choose between the security of buttons or the uncertainty of a new business venture.

When he decided to plunge into the meat business, Schneider turned his house into company headquarters and had a wooden shanty built in the backyard for butchering hogs. By 1891, he had saved enough to build a storey-and-a-half structure in which to operate his business and paid an annual licence of $20 to run it. Schneider's timing was good. Berlin was booming and described around that time as "the most rapidly growing and liveliest town west of Toronto."

But the early days were still tough, leading Schneider to offer his business for sale. He changed his mind, however, and in 1895 hired a skilled German-trained butcher named Wilhelm Rohleder, who would play a significant role in the company's growth over the next forty-five years. The hard-working Rohleder developed several recipes for Schneider products that made them popular, and he was so secretive about the ingredients that he didn't even tell J.M.

Schneider, meanwhile, was a hands-on owner from the beginning. He sold his products personally and took the lead in purchasing livestock. When not working, he led a quiet social life playing cards, devoting time to church activities, and enjoying his family. He knew all his workers by their first names and was not one for putting on airs or dressing ostentatiously.

Schneider's sons followed him into the business when they were old enough and watched it expand in the early twentieth century as electricity and refrigeration became essential to the industry. By 1910 Schneider was a wealthy man, but it was the years around World War I that saw the company expand twentyfold to become a million-dollar business. Despite his wealth, Schneider continued to show up for work every day into his early 80s. He died in 1942, and his epitaph reads "to live in the hearts we leave behind is not to die."

These days Schneider Foods Inc. remains a mainstay of the Kitchener economy and is a multi-million-dollar enterprise producing a wide range of products across Canada. Its sign on Highway 401 near Guelph, known as the "wiener beacon," is one of the most recognizable advertising landmarks in southern Ontario.

Bruce Druxerman

Druxy's

For Bruce Druxerman, the recipe for a successful deli was buns, salami, and experience in banking.

When Druxerman graduated with a degree in science, commerce, and business administration, he worked in the New York office of the Mercantile Bank of Canada. But later, after he switched his attention to the restaurant business, the Belleville, Ontario native decided that owning a chain of delis was the way to make his riches. According to *The New Entrepreneurs* by Allan Gould, Druxerman tried to rent some space in the Royal Bank Plaza in Toronto in 1976, but was told by a realtor that it couldn't happen because he had no track record.

Druxerman then phoned the bank's chairman, who was an acquaintance of his father, and the deal was made within a day. The first Druxy's (Druxerman's dad had been given the nickname by a neighbour) opened in the fall of 1976, and a profusion of pumpernickel has been served up ever since. Within three years there were thirteen Druxy's in Toronto. Druxerman's brothers joined the firm, and by the mid-1980s Druxy's was doing about $20 million in business. There are about fifty Druxy's locations, mostly in Ontario, with a few in Calgary.

Joseph E. Seagram

Seagram's Spirits & Wine

Even if he'd only stuck to politics and horse breeding, Joseph Seagram would probably be well remembered today. It was his wizardry with whisky distilling, however, that made the Seagram name world famous.

Joseph Emm Seagram was born April 15, 1841 near New Hope, Upper Canada, the son of an English immigrant who owned two farms and a tavern in the area around what is now the southwestern Ontario city of Cambridge. Seagram's father died when he was seven and his mother died just four years later, which put Joseph and his brother Edward in the care of a nearby Anglican clergyman.

Seagram studied at a business college in Buffalo for a year before taking a job as a junior bookkeeper at an axe-handle factory in what was then Galt, Ontario. He had a fist fight with another bookkeeper, however, and left for other jobs. When he hooked up with Wilhelm Hespeler a few years later in a milling operation, Seagram got his first taste of the distilling business. It was also where he met his future wife, Hespeler's niece, Stephanie Urbs.

In 1868, seeing the potential for the distilling business, he bought out Hespeler's share in the business and then acquired another partner's share a few years later. He changed the name of the business to Seagram and Roos (named for William Roos, another partner), and then two years later owned the company outright. He renamed it the Joseph Seagram Flour Mill and Distillery Company.

By the 1880s, Seagram had developed his best-selling brand, Seagram's 83, and also sold Seagram Old Rye and Seagram's White Feather. His distillery prospered, and he began selling to customers in the United States and Britain. His success south of the border soon surpassed the business in Canada.

By 1911, the company, then known as Joseph E. Seagram and Sons Limited, was established firmly as a family-run business. In fact he had a special whisky blend created, known as Seagram's V.O., which stood for "very own," to celebrate his son Thomas's wedding.

Thanks to his business success, Seagram was able to pursue his hobby of horse racing and breeding throughout the late nineteenth century and into the twentieth until his death. He imported horses from the U.S. and Britain to improve the quality of animals in Canada and had several winners. By 1900, he was dubbed "perhaps the greatest Canadian horse-breeder."

He also entered politics beginning in 1881. Starting as a member of the Waterloo Town Council, Seagram eventually became a federal MP and an MPP for Ontario. It was said that his campaign contributions against a young William Lyon Mackenzie King in 1911 were a major reason for King's defeat that year.

Seagram also had his philanthropic side, supporting the Berlin and Waterloo Hospital and the local branch of the Canadian Association for the Prevention of Tuberculosis. He remained active in his business and hobbies until his death on August 19, 1919. In 1928, the Seagram company was bought by the Bronfman family of Montreal, who led it to even greater prosperity. Among the products they introduced was Crown Royal, which was commissioned in 1939 in honour of King George VI and Queen Elizabeth's visit to Canada that year.

In December 2000, it was announced that Seagram's Spirits & Wine was sold to a consortium of Diageo plc, based in London, England and Pernod Ricard of Paris, France for $8 billion. At the time of the announcement Seagram's was generating revenues of $5.1 billion annually and its products were sold in 190 countries and territories around the world.

Name Dropper

Joseph Scagram's success as a horse breeder was never more evident than at the Queen's Plate. He first tasted victory there in 1891, and his horses would win the renowned race ten times before his death.

Francis Rundell Seaman

Seaman's Beverages

Francis Rundell Seaman can credit his mother for putting the fizz into his life; Prince Edward Islanders can thank him for quenching their thirsts since 1939.

In 1920, after farming near Ebenezer, Prince Edward Island for fifteen years, Lydia Seaman opened a men's boarding house on King Street in Charlottetown. At age fifteen, F.R., as he was called, became acquainted with one of their boarders, Carl Zercher, who was the production manager for local bottler the J&T Morris Soft Drink Company.

Zercher was impressed with the young boy's drive and ambition and hired him as a labourer in his warehouse. F.R. started out stacking cases of soda and later landed an office job with Morris's distributor, DeBlois Brothers, where licking stamps was a large part of his duties. He also learned how to handle the books and eventually returned to J&T Morris as a bookkeeper, later working his way into the job of selling soda to smaller customers.

In 1938, F.R. decided it was time to start his own business. "At the end of the year I decided I was going to quit my job and start my own business, even if I had to start it in my mother's garage on King Street," he once said.

Francis Rundell Seaman

Courtesy of Seaman's Beverages Ltd.

With broad beverage industry experience on his resume, he borrowed $2,500 from a cousin and travelled to Montreal to buy used bottling equipment and supplies, and then patented his personally-developed soda recipes for Iron Brew, Ginger Ale, Orange Thrill, and Root Beer.

In the spring of 1939 he rented space in a run-down brick building on Water Street in Charlottetown, where he also lived. It was here that he began producing sodas for about thirty customers. In 1940 he married his long-time love, Jean MacLeod of Charlottetown, who contributed a strong instinct for business and good judgment. Together they developed new flavours such as Lime Rickey and Grapefruit & Lime, Jean's favourites, all aimed at satisfying thirsts during the Island's hot summers.

Over the years there were many hardships. During the mid- to late-1940s, competition was stiff among the more than thirty-five soft drink makers in Prince Edward Island. Sugar rationing during World War II made it difficult and sometimes impossible for producers to afford their much-needed sugar. But the company never lost sight of F.R.'s words: "Do the very best for your customer and they'll always be there for you."

Many competitors bottled their soft drinks in inferior packages to lower production costs but Seaman's insisted on delivering only premium products in a premium package. Seaman continued using refillable bottles and expensive ingredients.

In 1984, Rundell Seaman Jr. became president of the company after twenty-five years of working his way up in the business. F.R. remained active until he was eighty-six, and passed away in 1994 at age eighty-nine.

The present-day Seaman's Beverages employs one hundred people and produces more than one million cases of soda per year for Prince Edward Island and customers in Ontario, Quebec, and Atlantic Canada out of a sixty-five thousand-square-foot bottling plant in Charlottetown.

Seaman's has increased annual production by more than 7,000 percent since 1939. Further evidence of the company's growth can be seen in the number of franchises and takeovers assumed by the company over the years, including Red Rock Cola, Pepsi Cola, Mountain Dew, Canada Dry, Hires Root Beer, Orange Crush, and 7 Up.

In addition to soft drinks, the company developed its own natural spring water brand, Prince Edward Springs. In 1995, the company acquired Gulf Vending, a full-service Island-wide vending business. In April 2002, Seaman's announced the sale of its Charlottetown plant, product line, and family recipes to Pepsi Bottling Group Inc. Seaman's had been the exclusive bottler for Pepsi in Prince Edward Island since 1952.

Laura Secord

Laura Secord

Generations of Canadians have associated her name with candies and chocolates, but Laura Secord was much more than just a name on a pretty box of treats.

Secord, as many know, was a heroine during the War of 1812 who warned British troops of an American surprise attack and thus prevented a potentially devastating defeat for Upper Canada. This is especially interesting when you consider that she was born in the United States and that her father had supported the rebels during the American Revolution. Her husband, James Secord, however, was a Loyalist.

Secord was born Laura Ingersoll on September 13, 1775 in Great Barrington, Massachusetts. Though her father sided with rebel forces to gain independence from the British, he found business tough in post-Revolutionary times. When he heard of land being offered to settlers willing to relocate to Upper Canada, he moved his family to Queenston. Laura was eighteen when the Ingersolls arrived there.

Here she met a Loyalist named James Secord, and they married around 1798. Secord did well as a merchant, but in 1812 the Americans declared war on the British and made several attacks on what is now Canadian soil. In June 1813, it's believed that some American troops billeted in the Secord house began talking about a plan to surprise the British at nearby Beaver Dams. Laura supposedly overheard them, and because her husband had a bad leg, she decided to make a thirty-kilometre trek behind enemy lines to warn Lieutenant James FitzGibbon of the impending attack.

Secord travelled through bush, swamp, and rough terrain and managed to get word to FitzGibbon, allowing him to capture the Americans and thwart their plan. Fear of future reprisal from Americans led the Secords to remain silent about Laura's role in the encounter. For many years, she received little or no recognition for her bravery, but thanks to others, including FitzGibbon, Secord's trek soon became public knowledge, and in 1860 she received £100 from the Prince of Wales who heard about her story. Secord died in 1868.

So what does this have to do with chocolate? In 1913, a century after Laura's heroic walk, Frank P. O'Connor opened a candy shop on Yonge Street in Toronto and named it after Secord. In addition to that year being the one hundredth anniversary of Secord's heroism, it's thought that O'Connor chose her name for the enterprise because it represented courage, loyalty, and devotion to Canadians.

O'Connor began making his own products on site and when demand grew he opened more shops in Ontario and Quebec. By the 1930s, there was a Laura Secord office in Winnipeg, but rationing during World War II meant shops could only stay open for four hours daily. Laura Secord shops boomed in the 1950s, and there were operations coast to coast by 1969. The company has been owned by several firms since then, and in 1999 became part of the Archibald Candy Corporation, an American firm with headquarters in Chicago. There are approximately 180 Laura Secord shops across Canada selling chocolates, ice cream, and other candies.

Name Dropper

Laura Secord's father wasn't the only supporter of rebels in the family. Her great-nephew, Dr. Soloman Secord, left his home in Kincardine, Ontario to enlist in the Twentieth Georgia Infantry as a surgeon during the U.S. Civil War. He fought for the South, even though he opposed slavery, possibly because he had friends in Georgia. When he died in 1910 in Kincardine, a monument was erected in his memory, perhaps the only such tribute in Canada to a Confederate officer.

Robert Simpson

Simpson's Department Stores

For the better part of one hundred years you couldn't mention Eaton's department stores without mentioning Simpson's in the same breath. Eaton stores continued on until 2002, but the Simpson's name disappeared before the twentieth century ended.

Robert Simpson was born in Speymouth, Scotland in 1834, the son of a general store owner. When he was about twenty, he arrived in Upper Canada having apprenticed to a shopkeeper in his homeland. He worked in a general store in Newmarket, Ontario, and in 1858 he and two others bought the business and sold dry goods, boots, hardware, and groceries. It was the trend at the time to deal only in cash, and the partners offered the lowest prices around.

The partnership only lasted four years, but Simpson soon linked up with another businessman, M.W. Bogart. Two fires caused damage to the enterprise and in the mid-1860s Bogart left Simpson to run the business on his own. Fortunately economic times were good during that decade, and Simpson opened a new shop said to be the finest north of Toronto.

Hurt by still another fire and some slack accounting, Simpson once again regrouped before selling his store to a cousin in 1872. He moved his family to Toronto and opened a dry goods store, this time on Yonge Street north of Queen. Simpson's business grew along with Toronto, which was becoming increasingly industrialized during those years. Like his rival Timothy Eaton, Simpson established a wholesale operation to complement his retail store. By 1881, however, he had abandoned the wholesale business and concentrated on his retail business in premises that were adjacent to Eaton's.

Though the two competed for business, both were able to prosper in busy Toronto, and by 1885 Simpson's employed sixty clerks and sold a variety of goods. Simpson, who was reportedly a heavy drinker, managed to keep his firm profitable through the rest of his life. When he moved the company into new headquarters in 1896, there were five hundred staff, a restaurant on the premises, and a mail order department.

Simpson died suddenly on December 14, 1897. Eaton and his son attended Simpson's funeral and flew flags at their stores at half-mast that day. Simpson had a daughter, but in those days business usually didn't get passed on to females. So without a son to inherit the business, Simpson's was sold a few months later to three Toronto businessmen.

Simpson's thrived as a major department store with outlets across the country for most of the twentieth century. It was bought by the Hudson's Bay Company in 1979 and some years later the Simpson's name was removed from the storefronts. But for older shoppers the name remains memorable as one of the most famous retail stores in Canadian history.

John H. Sleeman

Sleeman's Brewery

The Sleeman's Brewery story has as much flavour as the beer that has been embraced by Canadians from coast to coast.

It's a tale of a brewery started by a man who came to Canada in the nineteenth century from Cornwall, England and of a company that stayed in the family for several generations.

But it also has the plot twist of a business almost destroyed for good by a descendant caught smuggling during 1930s Prohibition, and then resurrected by a great-great-grandson because of the persistence of his aunt.

John H. Sleeman, born in 1805, was an ambitious young brewer when he came to Canada in 1834. He originally started brewing near St. Catharines, Ontario, but by 1851 he had switched operations to Guelph, Ontario, where the company was known as the Silver Creek Brewery.

Sleeman's original Guelph brewery was twenty-four feet by forty feet, and he could brew 320 gallons of beer a week. Within ten years, he was producing sixteen thousand gallons annually and making a yearly profit of more than $1,300. By the time he retired in 1867 and passed on the business to his son George, the brewery had several agencies set up throughout southwestern Ontario. John H. Sleeman died near St. Catharines on February 24, 1894.

Not a lot seems to be known about him. He did marry three times (his first wife Ann died in 1863) and had several children, and according to his great-great-grandson John W. Sleeman, who owns the brewery today, he was "a man of high principles and hard work, but fairly easy to get along with. He left the relative comfort of England and came over here and took a chance. He was an entrepreneur and a bit of a visionary."

The same was probably not said of his son George, whom John W. Sleeman says was more hard-driving and known as a bit of a "tyrant." George, who became mayor of Guelph in 1880, expanded the business in the late nineteenth century and lived in style in a house he had built in 1887.

It was during George's tenure as owner of the company, in 1898, that the recipe for Sleeman Cream Ale was formulated. The company thrived during the first part of the twentieth century thanks to its fine quality malt, hops, and pure water. But things changed shortly after George died in 1926. George A. Sleeman, who then managed the brewery alongside brother Henry, was caught smuggling beer into Detroit in 1933 during Prohibition. Authorities insisted he pay the beer taxes and get out of the brewing business or lose possession of the brewery. George opted to sell the brewery and pay the taxes.

For years the brewery sat idle, but in 1984, John W. Sleeman was given a leather-bound book of family beer recipes that his aunt had kept for years. Sleeman was working as an agent for some international beers, but had heard little of the family's brewing history when growing up. His aunt believed he should start up Sleeman's again, and in 1985 he reincorporated the Sleeman Brewing & Malting Co. Ltd. "It was because of her insistence that Sleeman's is here today," he says.

The brewery, known primarily for its Cream Ale, Original Dark, and Honey Brown Lager, does about $150 million in sales annually, producing a million barrels of beer each year. "I expect he (John H.) would be pleased and surprised that the brewery is still around," says Sleeman.

Name Dropper

In more ways than one George Sleeman's manor was the house that beer built. Apparently, the sidewalk leading up to the place he lived in was inlaid with upturned beer bottles.

Don and David Ellis Smith

Ellis-Don Construction Ltd.

It started with a small house renovation and construction of a three-room school and grew into a multi-million construction company that counts Toronto's SkyDome, the National Gallery in Ottawa, and Edmonton's Commonwealth Stadium among its projects.

And those Ellis-Don signs seen on construction sites across Canada are also found on huge projects in the United States, Europe, and Asia. So just who are these guys, anyway?

David Ellis Smith was born in Provost, Alberta in 1920; his brother Don was born there in 1924. Their father died in 1930 and the family moved to Toronto, where the brothers grew up during the Depression.

As a child, Don would build model airplanes and other small projects. "I enjoyed the Mechano sets. I liked to build things," he told us in an interview. The two brothers joined forces as builders in London, Ontario in 1951, using their names "Ellis-Don" simply because it sounded distinctive. During their first day on the job they landed a $55,000 contract to build Northdale School in that city. They also took on a house renovation at the same time.

Don never dreamed two small projects would lead to a world-class construction firm. "I never had any ambitions that way. You should try to grow sensibly." And so the company did,

Don Smith

Courtesy of Ellis-Don Corporation

landing more school projects in the London area as it tried to keep pace with the growing baby boomer population. The company started in a small office with the Smiths' mother and Don's wife, Joan, helping with the bookkeeping, and soon attracted bigger and more lucrative projects such as hospitals.

According to company information, Ellis-Don established a name for itself by excelling in the public tender market. Its ability to guarantee prices and completion dates helped it thrive. The firm's officials were risk-takers, but they never forgot that building was what they did best.

Within a few years, however, Ellis, who was overseeing operations in Calgary, left the business when the Alberta operation was closed in 1957. Don bought his brother's shares in the company and assumed sole ownership. Ellis, who was a civil engineer, liked the west and went to work for another company. He died in the early 1990s.

The Ellis-Don name stuck, and Don shepherded the company through a series of expansions from the late 1950s on, including the opening of a branch office in Toronto in 1963. Twenty years later, with the establishment of a Vancouver office, Ellis-Don became Canada's first coast-to-coast building contractor.

According to the book *In the Blood* by Gordon Pitts, Don could be a tough boss. He was a hands-on guy who quickly learned the ups and downs of this particular business. Where others failed, he would take on extra work even when times were good because he knew there would be lulls later. Smith says he's not sure he agrees with the word "tough" to describe him and notes that there are many employees who have been with the company for thirty years or more because he was fair and gave them freedom to do their work. "I couldn't have built all those projects without their loyalty."

He and Joan had seven children, five boys and two girls, six of whom got involved in the family business at an early age. Geoffrey Smith has been president of Ellis-Don since 1990, while Don is officially retired but remains a director.

When he wasn't building, Don became well known in Liberal Party circles as an excellent fundraiser. His wife, Joan, became a councillor in city politics in London before eventually rising to a position in former Ontario premier David Peterson's cabinet.

But it's at construction sites around the world that the Ellis-Don name is most prominent. In addition to projects mentioned above, Ellis-

Don has built many multi-million dollar complexes such as the American Health Center in Anchorage, Alaska; the Olympic Village in Atlanta; the Ontario Cancer Institute in Toronto; parts of Canary Wharf in London, England; several university buildings in Canada and the U.S.; and the convention centre and new entertainment/arena complex not far from where the company got its start in London, Ontario.

Don cites the National Gallery, SkyDome, and the Cami Automotive plant in Ingersoll, Ontario as his three favourite projects because they were interesting to build and necessitated a lot of personal involvement on his part. The Cami contract was given to Ellis-Don without any other competition because of the company's reputation, he said. And though no one believed the firm could build a working retractable roof at SkyDome ("We didn't know it would work, either," he admits), it was the first of its kind in the world.

While the company he founded more than fifty years ago continues to thrive, Don stays busy investing in the stock market, skiing, and fundraising for several organizations such as the Boys & Girls Club in London. He occasionally visits many of the buildings his company constructed over the years. "I get a big kick out of seeing them. Seeing your name on the cornerstone. It brings back memories."

Rolland Dansereau and Napoléon Piotte

RONA *L'entrepôt* / RONA *Warehouse* / RONA *Home & Garden*

The next time you're shopping for two-by-fours at a home improvement centre with RONA on the sign, think of Rolland Dansereau and Napoléon Piotte. The two Quebeckers founded the RONA chain back in 1939, and it's their names — in part, at least — that are in front of retail building supply stores in many parts of Canada. RONA is a combination of the first two letters of each man's first name.

The firm's foundation dates back to 1939 when several Quebec hardware stores led by Dansereau and Piotte formed Les

Marchands en Quincaillerie Ltée (The Hardware Merchants Ltd.). Twenty years later, they incorporated as Quincaillerie Ro-Na Inc. with a mandate to promote business collectively.

The company moved outside Quebec in 1982 by acquiring the Botanix network and negotiating purchasing alliances with Canada's Home Hardware stores and the Do-it-Best chain in the U.S. In 1988, Ro-Na merged with Dismat, which specialized in the building materials sector and the name was changed to Groupe Ro-Na Dismat Inc.

In 1994, RONA L'entrepôt (RONA Warehouse big box outlet) was launched and soon after, the RONA name was officially adopted. Seven years later, RONA purchased Ontario-based Cashway Building Centres and a year after, took over the British Columbia-based Revy Network, which included stores formerly operated in B.C. and Ontario under the Revelstoke, Revy, Lumberland, and Lansing Buildall banners.

Today, the company founded by Messrs. Dansereau and Piotte is known as RONA Inc. and is based in the Montreal suburb of Boucherville. It is the largest distributor and retailer of hardware, renovation, and gardening supplies in Canada, operating stores in eight provinces. RONA and its dealer-owners run a Canada-wide network of nearly 540 home improvement stores operating under fifteen different banners, including RONA L'entrepôt, RONA Warehouse, RONA Home & Garden, RONA Revy Home Centres, RONA Revelstoke Centres, and RONA Lansing.

With more than sixteen thousand employees and some ten million square feet of retail space, the stores ring up annual sales of nearly $3 billion. About 62 percent of the company's shares are held by RONA dealer-owners and employees. Dansereau and Piotte have not been associated with RONA since the 1960s.

Ernest D'Israeli Smith

E.D. Smith & Sons Ltd.

As strange as it may seem, Ernest D'Israeli Smith, the founder of one of Canada's leading food manufacturing companies, wasn't fond of eating.

"He never found food very interesting," his great-grandson Llewellyn S. Smith wrote in *The House That Jam Built*, a history of the Smith family and their company, E.D. Smith & Sons Ltd. It might have been because he had digestive problems or "maybe he was just too busy to eat."

Whatever the reason, it wasn't enough to stop Smith from growing fruits and making a variety of food products that filled the bellies of others.

From modest beginnings on a Niagara escarpment farm in the late 1870s, Smith — E.D. as he was known to friends and family — started a company that, under the guidance of successive generations of his family, would manufacture more than five hundred products, including pie fillings, ketchup, jams, salsa, pancake syrups, vegetable juice, and sauces, that have been fixtures on supermarket shelves across Canada.

Smith was born near what is now Winona, Ontario in 1853. He began farming full-time when he took over his ailing father's spread in 1877. Like his mother Damaris, he was a diarist who used his journal to

show where his life was headed. His scribblings reveal that working the land was not his first career choice: He fancied the occupation of civil engineer, but poor eyesight put an end to that. At one point a doctor tried to cure his failing vision by putting leeches on his eyes.

Ernest D'Israeli Smith

Courtesy of the National Archives of Canada. PA305267

After deciding on agriculture, E.D. grew grain, raised livestock, and later diversified into fruit and food manufacturing. Along the way, he served as a local councillor, a member of Parliament and a senator. He and his wife Christina had three children.

The "Fruit King," as he was often called, was known for his honesty and extensive research into the land, crops, and market opportunities. Entries in his diary noted seasons, weather and soil conditions, what he planted and where. "By studying the past, he could plan the future," says *The House That Jam Built*.

Banks never asked for his signature when he borrowed money and most of the deals he made with fellow farmers were based on his word. In 1879, a year after being elected to the local council, E.D. sold his first fruit, 803 pounds of grapes, to a customer in Guelph. He harvested his first strawberries in 1880. With neighbouring Toronto ballooning to a population of eighty thousand and other communities in the area growing fast, fruit became his mainstay. "I believe there will be an almost unlimited market for the next generations," he wrote in his diary. "I believe those who go into fruit at once will reap the largest rewards of anyone engaged in farming."

In 1889, E.D. moved below the Niagara Escarpment to a farm once owned by relatives of Laura Secord, where the climate and soil were better suited to fruit farming. In 1900, he was elected as MP for Wentworth riding and at about the same time, with a glut of fruit in the region, he began production of the first pure jams made in Canada. His first jam factory opened in 1905, with A.M. Cocks, a jam maker brought from England, running the show. Over the years E.D. also operated a nursery that supplied trees to growers in the Niagara Peninsula and elsewhere.

In 1908, he resigned from Parliament because of ill health but still found the energy to build Helderleigh, a huge family home made of stone from a nearby quarry. Until it burned down in 1992, the house "stood within a peaches throw" of the existing E.D. Smith & Sons head office in Winona.

In 1913, E.D. was appointed to the Senate by Prime Minister Sir Robert Borden. His son Armand was by then playing a big role in the business. By all accounts, Senator E.D. Smith was a hard worker with a keen interest in the country's welfare and progress. As might be expected, many of his pet projects were related to the fruit industry. He helped draw up laws, regulations, and improvements for the fruit business; he fought for and won better transportation facilities for fruit on railways and steamships, and he sought protection for Canada's fruit industry in the form of higher tariffs.

As was the case in most industries, the Depression took its toll on E.D.'s company, now known as E.D. Smith and Sons. Sales dropped by as much as 50 percent, wages were reduced, and a handful of employees were terminated but by 1935 the business was again in the black.

When E.D. resigned from the Senate in 1946, he made several prognostications that came true years later: He predicted a "hard concrete road" would be built across Canada; he visualized a great desire of millions of people in Europe to settle in Canada; and he said inventions would lessen the need for manual labour.

E.D. retired from the business in 1946, leaving sons Armand and Leon in charge. He died on October 15, 1948.

After his death, the company was operated by members of the Smith family, most recently Llewellyn S. Smith, who assumed ownership in the company in 1984. In 2002, the manufacturing firm was sold to Toronto merchant bank Imperial Capital Corp. and Smith remained at the helm. According to company literature at the time of the sale, E.D. Smith and Sons was a market leader in own-brand and private-label jams, number one in pie fillings, and number two in ketchup.

E.D. Smith & Sons has about 340 employees at its single site in Winona with annual sales just under $150 million. E.D. Smith Fruit Farms Inc., the original family business, was retained and is in the midst of its largest expansion in fifty years with the planting of fruit trees for the "pick your own" market.

Name Dropper

E.D. Smith was the first senator to resign. He left because he "felt he could not honestly be paid for a job he was becoming too tired to do." While a member of the Senate, he always paid for his own lodgings and train fare to Ottawa and would not allow family members to use passes to events because he felt it was a waste of taxpayers' dollars.

James Smith

Smith Brothers

Next time you have a sore throat you might want to whisper a thanks to James Smith for bringing you relief.

Although the famous bearded brothers on the package of Smith Brothers cough drops are William and Andrew Smith of Poughkeepsie, N.Y., it was their father James, of St. Armand, Quebec, who got the company started.

James, originally from Scotland, was a carpenter by trade, but headed south from Quebec to Poughkeepsie in 1847 to start a restaurant. The story goes that a customer passed on to him a secret formula for making effective but tasty cough candies. James then made his own batch over the kitchen stove and began handing them out to people with coughs and sore throats. One source says that wild cherry bark was the key ingredient in the original recipe.

Demand grew rapidly, and sons William and Andrew began to sell the candies in streets and as far afield at they could manage. Early advertisements for James Smith & Sons claimed the candies could cure coughs, colds, sore throats, and asthma, among other things. One ad read "one of these drops put in the mouth before going to bed, loosens the phlegm and causes the patient to enjoy a comfortable night's sleep."

When James died in 1866, the sons inherited the business and renamed it Smith Brothers. In those days rules about copying products weren't as strict as today, and that meant a lot of competition from similarly named cough drops. In fact, there was even another company called Smith Brothers. To offset all the competition trying to cash in on this growing trade, William and Andrew decided to put their pictures on the envelopes in which they packaged their product.

Coincidentally, the bearded gentlemen appeared above the words *Trade Mark*. That's William's likeness over the word *Trade* and Andrew's above the word *Mark*, and for years the brothers were known to the public as "Trade" and "Mark." The first flavours offered were wild cherry and black licorice, and by the 1870s, the brothers had switched to boxes instead of envelopes to hold the cough drops.

Andrew, who was born in 1836, never married and was known to be carefree with his money, thus earning him the nickname "Easy Mark." William, born in 1830, was something of an eccentric and a militant prohibitionist. Andrew died in 1895, and William stayed on as president almost until his death in 1913. His son Arthur took over the company, and by 1915 the factory making the cough drops could produce about thirty tons of product a day. The business stayed in the Smith family until 1964 when it was sold to the Warner Lambert Company. In 1977, Smith Brothers was acquired by F & F Laboratories of Chicago.

F & F Foods, Inc. still produces Smith Brothers Cough Drops, and William and Andrew can still be found on the candy's packaging.

Sam Sniderman

Sam the Record Man

What do Anne Murray, Tom Jones, Gordon Lightfoot, Tony Bennett, Liona Boyd, and legions of Canadian music fans have in common? All crossed paths with Sam Sniderman at one time or another.

Sniderman is the Toronto retailing icon that turned a job stocking records at his brother's radio store into the legendary fifty-one-store Sam The Record Man chain with its landmark record emporium on Toronto's Yonge Street. Along the way, Sniderman supported a who's who of young and rising musical talents in Canada by promoting their records and concerts and fighting for more airtime for their music.

The Toronto native jumped into the record business in 1937 when he began stocking classical records in his brother Sid's store. It was a tactic to woo the woman of his dreams, Eleanor Koldofsky, and it worked: they were married five years later. When record sales outpaced radio sales in the mid-1950s, the business took the name Sam the Record Man.

Initially, the outlet was a hangout for musicians who were lured by its stock of obscure labels and artists; soon however, Sniderman was drawing enormous crowds of music lovers who couldn't resist his discounted loss leaders.

In 1961, Sniderman changed the face of Yonge Street when he converted a two-storey furniture outlet at 347 Yonge into his flagship store and invested $15,000 in a huge neon sign in the shape of two huge LPs. The sign was designed to trump his arch-enemy A&A records, two doors away, and back Sniderman's claim that the store had the largest selection of retail records in Canada. Over the years, many customers referred to the Yonge Street store as a madhouse, especially during Boxing Day sales when lineups often wound around the block onto Gould Street.

If you lived in Toronto, or even within driving distance during Sam's heyday, it was almost a rite of passage to visit the store. Many baby boomers fondly recall making the trip to Sam's with money ready to spend and hours to kill flipping through endless racks of albums.

In an article in the *Financial Post*, Sniderman credited much of his success to a tip from his mother, who once told him: "You'll always be dealing with the consumer and you've always got to be fair and honest if you want to stay in business." For years he personally handled complaints from his customers. It was his way of ensuring customers kept coming back.

But Sniderman, who during the 1960s smoked two packs of cigarettes and downed twenty-five cups of tea a day, was more than a peddlar of records, tapes, and CDs.

An Order of Canada member and recipient of the Governor General's Award for voluntarism in the performing arts, Sniderman for years lent a hand to up-and-coming Canadian artists like Murray, Lightfoot, Buffy Sainte-Marie, and Joni Mitchell by hyping their records in the media and displaying and playing them in his stores. Back in the days when there was no such thing as a Canadian music industry, he had a significant hand in crafting the "CanCon" regulations that required radio stations to give airtime to more Canadian artists.

One of the highlights of his career was when Sainte-Marie received a Canadian Music Hall of Fame award. "She said that Sam the Record Man was instrumental in her success ... to be recognized in that fashion gave me goosebumps," he told *Profit* magazine.

Sniderman's contributions to the lives of some of Canada's most famous performers are well documented, from badgering record companies on Lightfoot's behalf to finding space on the stage at Mariposa for Mitchell. At one point a disconsolate Anne Murray told him: "Sam, if this record doesn't work, I'm going back to Nova Scotia to be a gym teacher." Murray remains his favourite Canadian singer and her song "You Needed Me," is one he listens to often.

After casting his famous shadow on the world's longest street for forty years, the world came crashing down on the Godfather of Canadian Music late in 2001 when Sam the Record Man declared bankruptcy. In 2002, the Yonge Street store was still operating under a new company operated by his sons Bobby and Jason, but many of the franchised outlets across Canada were closed.

John William Sobey

Sobeys

Carpentry skills and a booming coal mining industry brought John William Sobey to Stellarton, Nova Scotia. But it was his talent as a butcher that led him to settle there and build a business that today is one of Canada's leading supermarkets.

J.W. Sobey was born in England in 1869, the son of a military man who had married a Nova Scotian woman and who lived in a variety of locales before moving back to the province in 1876 to take up farming. J.W. grew up in Pictou County learning how to build with his hands and till the land. He was a deeply religious and quiet teetotaller who married when he was thirty-two.

According to *The Man and The Empire: Frank Sobey* by Harry Bruce, J.W. Sobey quit farming in 1905 to move his family to Stellarton. There, he helped construct a new mine, but when the work was completed two years later, he bought a meat business and started selling his products door to door. Sobey's work day began at 6 a.m., when he would feed the horses, eat breakfast, and then begin cutting meat. His drivers would then take loads of pork, beef, and lamb into the streets of Stellarton to sell.

In 1912, he and his brother, Charles, erected a two-storey shop (known as the Number One store) to handle the growing business. Sobey and his family lived on the top floor. He had one chief competitor at the time, but there were eight other stores in Stellarton selling meat and groceries to the miners, railway workers, and their families.

Though Charles moved to the West Coast a year later, Sobey continued his meat and vegetable business and thrived. In 1924, thanks to the persuasive powers of his son, Frank, the company was renamed Sobey, J.W., Meats & Groceries and began offering customers a wide range of goods such as tea, coffee, cheese, butter, and tinned foods. That first year of expansion generated sales of $35,000 — good money for the time. Sobey was so impressed by his son's business acumen that he made him his partner and began the process of turning the business into a grocery food chain. They operated the business carefully in the Depression, with J.W. drawing a salary of only $50 a week and putting the rest of the money back into the company.

John William Sobey

Grocery stores were not self serve in those days. Each item was weighed and packaged individually, which meant that shoppers had to wait their turn for service. This meant grocery stores were something of a social hangout, a place to get caught up in gossip. Frank spearheaded the construction of six stores over the next decade in various parts of Nova Scotia, followed by tremendous expansion after World War II.

J.W. seemed content to let Frank run the business from the 1930s on, enjoying his days with curling and baseball (he managed the Stellarton Monarchs softball team in 1938), and being an unofficial handyman/adviser in later years. However, his religious beliefs never faltered. When Sobeys was opening its first supermarket in New Glasgow in 1947, J.W., then aged seventy-eight, was so upset to hear that employees were working on a Sunday to get the new store ready that he went to the shop personally and kicked them out.

Though he was sure Frank was making a mistake opening such a large store, J.W. was as thrilled as anyone when the supermarket became a huge success and helped Sobeys become the huge multi-billion-dollar enterprise it is today. He died in November 1949.

Since a $1.5-billion takeover of The Oshawa Group in 1998, Sobeys is the second-largest food distributor in Canada and owns such companies as IGA, Price Chopper, and Lawton's Drugs. Sobeys has more than four hundred corporate stores and one thousand franchise outlets throughout Canada, and generates about $11 billion in sales.

Mac Voisin / Mark Nowak

M&M Meat Shops

Mac Voisin and his then brother-in-law Mark Nowak wanted restaurant-quality steaks that could be bought by regular consumers at supermarket prices.

Mac and Mark pursued their dream and opened their first M&M shop in Kitchener, Ontario in 1980. The first franchise opened in nearby Cambridge two years later and the concept began to take off. Today, Voisin is president of the chain, which has more than 320 stores coast to coast in Canada. In Quebec, where the company expanded in 1992, the shops are called Les aliments M&M. And the company offers much more than meat, with a range of seafood, hors d'oeuvres, desserts, and pizza.

"The trend continues to be that people want to eat high quality foods at home," Voisin, a former owner of a successful construction business, once said in an interview, and that has made dinnertime for Canadians a lot easier and more interesting.

Charles Edward Stanfield

Stanfield's Limited

When Charles E. Stanfield arrived in America in 1855 he had no idea the family business he later founded would put millions of Canadians in his underwear. Nor could he have imagined that Stanfield would become a household name in Nova Scotia.

After a brief stop in Philadelphia, Stanfield, who had learned the wool business in an uncle's mill near Bradford, England, sailed to Prince Edward Island, where he and his brother-in-law, Samuel E. Dawson, founded the Tryon Woollen Mills in the tiny community of Tryon. He sold his interests to Dawson in 1866 and moved to the central Nova Scotia town of Truro, about one hundred kilometres north of Halifax.

In 1870, Stanfield founded the Truro Woollen Mills, followed by the St. Croix Woollen Mills at St. Croix, Nova Scotia; the Union Woollen Mills at Farnham, Nova Scotia; and the Truro Felt Works in Truro, which in 1882 moved to its existing site on the banks of the Salmon River.

An eccentric man with few close friends, Stanfield quickly developed a reputation as a creative genius who was focused on his products and his factories. He was constantly developing new equipment and products, often while puttering in a workshop behind his house on Dominion Street in Truro.

Among his early innovations were the first cardigan jackets in Canada, as well as stockinettes, which consisted of a roll of woollen cloth produced as a tube, which could be cut and sewed into a warm and inexpensive sock. He also introduced Canadians to heavy rib underwear, and legend has it that he invented the "trap door" in men's long underwear, an innovation which earned him the gratitude of millions of Canadian males who have wrestled with long underwear over the years. He also manufactured sweater cloth and knitting yarn.

In 1896, with seventeen workers on staff and ninety-two customers buying his products, Stanfield sold his business to his sons John, who earlier had apprenticed in woollen mills in the United States, and Frank. The boys called their business the Truro Knitting Mills Limited.

After taking the reins, the brothers decided to specialize in knitted merchandise, a move their father thought was unwise. Nevertheless, they felt their success depended on building a reputation in a specific field and on a stable product base.

John and Frank Stanfield discarded many of their father's sidelines and, over time, turned the small family business into one of the largest woollen producers in Canada. They developed the "shrink-proof process" that would make Stanfield's underwear famous. When gold was discovered in the Yukon, the Yukon Klondike Trail of 1898 provided the company with its first big break when Stanfield's "Unshrinkable" Underwear became a byword among the hardy sourdoughs involved in the rush for the precious metal.

"The miner could find no substitute for the warm, heavy, woolly underwear made by the little Truro firm," according to literature provided by Stanfield's.

Charles Stanfield died on December 23, 1900. Six years later, Stanfield's Limited was incorporated, with John and Frank among the seven members of the original board of directors. The company was well on its way to becoming a dominant force in the commercial and cultural life of the Truro area, and, some would say, the province of Nova Scotia.

"In their own, quite different way, the Stanfields were to their province what the Kennedys would later become to Massachusetts," Geoffrey Stevens wrote in his 1973 biography of Robert Stanfield, grandson of Charles Stanfield and a former leader of the federal Conservative Party.

The company acquired other mills, beefed up its lineup of products and introduced new technology, materials, and processes, which, among other things, led to softer fabrics. John and Frank also found time for politics and other business interests.

Although Frank Stanfield was always the active head of the business, he was MLA for Colchester from 1911 to 1929 and was appointed Lieutenant Governor of Nova Scotia in 1930. He also conceived and organized the Acadia Trust Company and Central Agencies Ltd., two successful firms that were sold in 1961. He died in 1931. John was elected three times as a federal Conservative MP in Nova Scotia and after World War I was appointed to the Senate.

Over the years, Frank Stanfield shunned publicity but supported many community projects anonymously. He felt the firm had a very great responsibility to its employees, a policy that probably explains the fact that there has never been a work stoppage at Stanfield's.

In the late 1930s, Stanfield's entered the undershirt and briefs field and was one of the first to package these items in cellophane bags. Knit briefs began the slow and steady replacement of woven underwear. In the 1940s, two-piece winter underwear as we know it, and thermal underwear in the 1950s, gradually took over the winter underwear market. These two trends were the building blocks that provided significant growth over the years.

Today, Stanfield's continues to operate out of Truro, Nova Scotia as a specialist in men's underwear products, competing with American manufacturers such as Jockey, Calvin Klein, and Fruit of the Loom, as well as many private label brands sold in department stores and discount outlets. More than 90 percent of its underwear is sold in Canada.

"We are proud of the fact that unlike our competitors, 99 percent of our products are manufactured in Canada," says company president Tom Stanfield, great-grandson of the founder.

Name Dropper

Stanfield's Limited takes great pride in having been one of the first employers in Canada to pay the same wage to women as to men.

Samuel, Edward, and George Stedman

Stedmans

From hawking newspapers on the streets of Brantford, Ontario as children, Samuel, Edward, and George Stedman built a chain of general merchandise stores that became as much a part of small-town Canada as hockey rinks and county fairs.

Samuel was the first to go into business. Born in the southwestern Ontario community of Ayr in 1881, he moved down the road to Brantford with his parents, Ellen and Edward Stedman, where he was apprenticed as a tailor. According to some reports, he was only nine years old when he began selling newspapers on the street on the same day a notorious murderer was hanged in Woodstock, Ontario. Other accounts, however, say he was sixteen when he went into the newspaper business. Soon afterwards, his younger brothers, George and Edward, started selling papers as well. The Stedman brothers kept up the job through their school days and then did it full time, becoming distributors for such Toronto dailies as the *Globe*, the *Mail*, and the *World*.

They set up headquarters above a butcher shop. In those days, the common practice was to get up around 3:30 a.m., harness a team of horses, and pick up papers at the Grand Trunk Railway station in nearby Harrisburg. Within a few years, the Stedmans were agents for a variety of American magazines and newspapers, and became the largest news dealers in the province west of Toronto.

The sales volume led the brothers to open a book and stationery shop in 1905 on the main street of Brantford. They jokingly cited that the reason for moving indoors was "to get out of the rain." Within a few years they had bought out their main competitor and renamed the company Stedman Brothers Ltd.

Success enabled them to move to better offices and to install a modern printing plant for the production of scribblers, exercise books, and pennants. As trends changed, the Stedmans gradually began expanding their range of merchandise to such products as hardware, dry goods, toys, games, and crockery. They had more than one hundred employees and twelve salesmen working from coast to coast.

Samuel, Edward, and George Stedman

By 1924, the Stedmans decided it would be wise to move closer to their major markets and uprooted from Brantford to move to Toronto. They pruned their merchandise lines to include just their best-sellers and within a year had outgrown their office space. Instead of using salesmen to peddle their goods, the Stedmans began opening associate stores in the late 1920s in locations throughout Ontario and beyond. Even with the Depression in the 1930s, the Stedmans kept expanding and offering greater variety in their stores.

Like many Canadian businesses, Stedmans experienced tremendous growth in the post World War II era. By the early 1960s, there were 138 company-owned stores and 200 associated franchises, with about 2,000 employees. Unlike other chain stores, Stedmans concentrated on small towns and rural areas for their growth. The firm believed its competitive prices and personal service worked better than focusing on expensive surroundings and plenty of advertising.

In 1962, Gamble-Skogmo Inc., a larger retailer based in Minneapolis, bought Stedmans to complement the Macleods stores they had bought earlier. George Stedman remained as a consultant with the new firm until his death in 1967. Samuel had died just two years before (Edward before that). Samuel had been a leading figure at the Board of Trade and Canadian Chamber of Commerce and served as an alderman for three years.

Today, Stedmans stores are still a common sight in small-town Canada where the locals shop for goods ranging from clothing, housewares, and candy to toys, books, and fishing equipment. The chain is operated by Winnipeg-based Tru*Serv Canada Co-operative Inc.

Ida Steinberg

Steinberg Inc.

In 1917, with her husband gone and six children to feed, Ida Steinberg took the advice of friends and opened a small food store in downtown Montreal. Unknowingly, she had planted the seeds for a family business that would help revolutionize the weekly ritual of grocery shopping in Canada.

The company Ida started has been called "the king of Quebec's grocery business," and members of the family have been referred to as "the world's finest merchandisers."

For seventy years, until 1989 when the family's supermarket and real estate empire broke up, the Steinbergs introduced Canadians to such innovations as customer-operated coffee grinders, transparent wrap for fruits and vegetables, and conveyor belts that move groceries toward cashiers, all designed to simplify the shopping experience.

It all began when Ida, the daughter of a poor Hungarian couple, opened her business on St. Lawrence Boulevard in the vibrant heart of Montreal's Jewish community six years after she arrived in Canada with husband Vilmos Sternberg and their four children. During a stopover in Quebec City, a Canadian immigration officer inadvertently changed their name to Steinberg.

Launching the business was a necessity for Ida, whose husband had left, leaving her desperate for money to keep her family together.

Soon after the first store opened, Ida moved to larger quarters, and with $200 worth of merchandise on the shelves, put up the sign, "Mrs. I. Steinberg, Grocer." Her family, now numbering six children — daughter, Lily, sons Jack, Sam, Nathan, Max, and Morris — as well as her two sisters, lived above and behind the business, which was a full-service shop where customers telephoned in their orders for delivery by horse-drawn cart.

Ida, "an industrious one-woman show" and "tireless shopkeeper," according to the book *Steinberg: The Breakup of A Family Empire* by Ann Gibbon and Peter Hadekel, toiled long hours in the store, which operated six days a week from 8 a.m. to 11 p.m.

Ida Steinberg

Her hard work paid off: Before long, the store became popular in the neighbourhood and across the city. Ida knew all her customers by name, let them haggle over prices and buy on credit, and often surprised her clientele by adding an extra apple or cookie to their bag of purchases to build customer loyalty.

Ida's maxims were absorbed by her son Sam, who like his brothers and sister spent long hours working in their mother's store. Blessed with natural talent, drive, and a keen entrepreneurial sense, he would evolve as the undisputed leader of the family and architect of the multi-million-dollar empire that would follow.

By 1930, Ida's original store was a small chain of four grocery outlets and the company was incorporated as Steinberg's Service Stores Ltd. Two more outlets opened by 1931, at a time when the competition for the consumer's food dollar included Dominion Stores and the American chain A & P. Steinberg's followed the lead of Loblaws in Ontario and introduced self-serve food stores to Quebeckers under the banner Wholesale Groceteria.

In 1931, Ida was still working long hours at her original shop but, stricken with angina, could barely cope with the workload, so Sam closed her original shop in downtown Montreal and moved her to another store in western Montreal, which she co-managed with her daughter. Ida retired about two years later, and in 1942 she died after falling ill with pneumonia.

Ida's death changed little for the business, which Sam had been running for more than a decade. In the years that followed he would turn the enterprise into a vast empire, which included grocery stores and Miracle Mart discount department stores located mainly in Ontario and Quebec.

Pushed forward by the spirit of their mother, Sam and his brothers continued to innovate. The Steinbergs are believed to have introduced Canadians to separate coolers for meat and produce, parking lots for customers, magic-eye doors which opened automatically, subsidized taxi services for shoppers, car order depots which transferred groceries from stores to customers' vehicles, midget-sized shopping carts for young shoppers, one-way cart traffic, and merchandise bonuses for early-in-the-week shoppers.

The family also set up a real estate company, Ivanhoe Inc., that financed a huge wave of expansion in the 1950s, including the development of shopping centres, which, of course, contained Steinberg supermarkets.

Sam died in 1978. The company was purchased in 1989 by Michael Aucher of Montreal for $1.3 billion. At the time, the enterprise Ida Steinberg had founded seventy-two years earlier was Canada's twenty-first largest company, with sales of $4.5 billion, thirty-seven thousand employees in Canada, and assets in supermarkets, department stores, restaurants, sugar refineries, and real estate.

It is fitting that many Steinberg family decisions were made beneath a portrait of Ida Steinberg that for years hung in a Montreal boardroom where Sam and other Steinbergs developed their empire.

Michael and Sophie Strub

Strub's Pickles

At the beginning of the Great Depression in 1929, the pantry at Michael and Sophie Strub's home near Hamilton, Ontario was nearly bare. It was enough to convince Mr. Strub, a butcher, to trade a barrel of his wife's homemade pickles to a local grocer for food.

When the pickles sold quickly and the grocer came calling for more, the Strubs knew they were onto something. Michael discarded his butcher's apron and the couple, who came to Canada from Kharkov, Ukraine in 1921, began making pickles full-time in the kitchen and backyard of the family home in which they lived with their three children.

Strub's pickles were originally sold right from the barrel for a nickel apiece, with about 350 barrels produced annually in the early years.

In the early 1940s, with Michael's sons Irv and Dan at the helm, the company took the name Strub Brothers Limited and the pickle operation moved to a small area in the back of a warehouse in nearby Dundas. Michael Strub passed away in 1943; Sophie died in 1949. In 1956, Strub's moved to a larger facility, and in July 1991, a new pickle plant was built in Brantford, Ontario. The plant, which today is the company's headquarters, doubled in size in April 2000.

Strub Brothers is Canada's largest family-owned pickle manufacturer. The company is owned and managed by third and fourth generation Strub family pickle-makers and employs more than one hundred people, some of whom who have been with the company for more than twenty-five years.

The company processes and packs more than sixty million cucumbers a year — compared to about two thousand cukes annually when Michael and Sophie got started — and makes more than three hundred retail and foodservice products for distribution across Canada, the U.S., Australia, and Israel.

Strub's best-selling product is its refrigerated Full Sour Dill in Original Brine, which continues to be made using the family recipe brought over from Ukraine by the founders. Other products include refrigerated herring tidbits, pickled eggs and horseradish, plus home-style dills, pepper rings, sweet gherkins, bread and butter pickles, and zucchini relish and chili sauce bottled under the Willie's name, an Ontario firm purchased by Strub Brothers in 2000.

Members of the Strub family continue to run the company. Great-grandsons involved in pickle-making are Arnie, marketing manager; Marty, vice-president, production; and Andy, vice-president, sales. Their father Leo is company president and provides the link between the old and the new.

"When I was eight years old, I would go to the plant after little league games," says Arnie Strub. "The plant was across from the base-ball diamond and it was my job to pick out the bad cucumbers as they came out of the washer."

The day after Arnie graduated from university, his father asked him to join the business. Marty and Andy also joined after graduation from university.

Arnie Strub credits the company's success and longevity to its dedication to quality from the day Michael and Sophie Strub barrelled their first pickle. The cucumbers used to make Strub's pickles go from vine to brine within twenty-four hours.

Name Dropper

Pickles date back forty-five hundred years to Mesopotamia, where it is believed cucumbers were first preserved. Cleopatra, a devoted pickle fan, believed pickles enhanced her beauty.

Name Dropper

According to Pickle Packers International, Inc., the perfect pickle should exhibit seven warts per square inch for North American tastes — Europeans prefer wartless pickles.

Gordon Tamblyn

G. Tamblyn Ltd.

Long before the days of Shopper's Drug Mart, Jean Coutou, and Pharma Plus, there was Gordon Tamblyn.

The son of a doctor, Tamblyn was born in 1878 in Belwood, a community north of Guelph, Ontario, and attended high school in Markham and Guelph. In 1901, he graduated from the Ontario College of Pharmacy in Toronto, where high marks earned him a gold medal and a scholarship.

In 1904, he planted the seeds for the Tamblyn's drugstore chain when he used $400 in savings to open his first pharmacy, a gaslit shop on Queen Street in Toronto's Beaches neighborhood. The store operated as Cut Rate Drugs and earned $7,000 in revenue in its first year. Business was slow at first, so he set up tables and served ice cream to folks picnicking at the nearby Lake Ontario beaches.

Tamblyn expanded his chain at the rate of about two stores a year and operated the outlets under a green and white banner that

declared: "Tamblyn's Saves You Money." By 1924, he had twenty stores, all in Toronto, with annual sales of $1.8 million; soon after, outlets were operating in most large Ontario cities. G. Tamblyn Ltd. was incorporated in 1928 and its expansion continued after he died of angina in 1933 while playing golf in Toronto.

Gordon Tamblyn

Courtesy of William Tamblyn

A self-taught businessman, Tamblyn is believed to be the first retailer in Canada to develop the "chain store" concept, a group of stores similar in appearance and design, where merchandise that is common to all outlets is sold at the same price.

"The guiding principles of Gordon Tamblyn's business operations were efficient merchandising, quality merchandise at reasonable prices, innovations for the comfort and convenience of the public, courteous service, properly qualified staff, integrity, and reliable drug dispensation," Tamblyn's president A.H. Hutchenson wrote in a 1970s-era memo to staff.

"He was keenly attentive in detail and insisted upon his employees keeping to his strict ideas of good business, which meant giving utmost service with quality in all goods," said a newspaper article written shortly after his death.

Tamblyn is remembered by his son William as a workaholic who spent long hours at his office and who wasn't beyond visiting some of his stores at night, always accompanied by his wife Edna. The company was his key interest, but in his spare time he liked to play golf and watch hockey. He was a member of the Rosedale Golf Club, the Granite Club, the Parkdale Canoe Club, and the Royal Canadian Yacht Club.

The Tamblyns had four children, none of whom followed their father into pharmacy. When Gordon Tamblyn died he was still active in the business, which had become a public company with more than fifty Ontario stores.

After his death, the chain expanded into Western Canada and was eventually purchased by George Weston Ltd. of Toronto. In the 1950s and 1960s, the arrival of discount stores such as Towers and Top Discount cut severely into Tamblyn's sales; despite a remake of the company's image and a renaming of its stores to Super Save Drug Mart in 1970, stronger sales failed to materialize. As a result, Tamblyn's name reappeared on signs that read Tamblyn Supersave and later, Tamblyn Drugmart.

In the late 1970s, with poor sales continuing, Weston Ltd. sold the 147-store chain to Boots the Chemist PLC of Britain, which replaced the Tamblyn's banner with the name Boots Drug Stores. Boots evolved into Pharma Plus Drugmarts Ltd., which is now owned by The Katz Group of Edmonton.

Name Dropper

For Tamblyn, who was known around the chain as "G.T.," cleanliness was a cardinal rule in his stores. A Toronto newspaper once reported that during surprise visits to his pharmacies he would don a pair of yellow rubber gloves and run his finger along the woodwork to check for dust.

Alex Tilley
Tilley Endurables

Alex Tilley had no special love of hats as a boy growing up in such places as Kitchener, Sudbury, and Vancouver. But in his mid-20s, he owned a favourite coat and got someone to make him a "Mississippi Gambler" style hat to match.

Little did he know that years later, hats would earn him a fortune and worldwide acclaim.

In 1980, Tilley was a self-employed art consultant and avid sailor. One day while sailing in his thirty-foot sloop in Lake Ontario, his hat blew off and got soaked — again. Enough, he thought. Tilley put on his thinking cap and started researching ways to make better, long-lasting headgear. With the help of a sailmaker, Tilley came up with the first of more than 1.5 million hats that bear his name.

Shortly afterwards, he tried the hat out on a trip to Belize but still experienced problems when the wind blew. While lying in bed one Sunday morning, Tilley came up with the idea of affixing a cord that went around the back of the head.

Within a year, Tilley had branched into sailing shorts and pants for travellers that would wear well and be comfortable. Today more than thirteen hundred retailers in seventeen countries, including Australia, Finland, and Turkey, sell Tilley Hats. The first one he ever sold, to Horst Berlin of the National Yacht Club in Toronto, is still around.

Alex Tilley

Courtesy of Tilley Endurables

Most of Tilley's clothing is manufactured in Don Mills, Ontario. "The hat represents me," says Tilley of why he put his name on the product. Some two hundred thousand Tilley hats are made in Canada annually and come in more sizes than any others in the world. They're known for their indestructibility; a hat belonging to Michael Hackenberger of the Bowmanville Zoo, for example, was still wearable after being eaten by an elephant three times. Among the celebrities who have worn Tilley hats are legendary mountaineer Sir Edmund Hillary, former U.S. president George Bush, and members of the royal families in Great Britain and Denmark.

And Tilley still owns that Mississippi Gambler hat. "It's interesting that even way back when I was somewhat hat conscious."

Name Dropper

Tilley Hats were worn by all of Canada's armed forces during the Gulf War in 1991 to help protect them from harsh desert conditions, and the U.S. Coast Guard Auxiliary has adopted the product as its official sun hat.

Basil Tippet

Tippet-Richardson Limited

Basil Tippet was a mover and shaker in the world of Canadian business and in the community in which he lived and worked.

A mover, because Tippet-Richardson Limited, the company he founded in 1927, has grown into Canada's largest privately owned moving company, over the years transporting the possessions of thousands of Canadians, including former prime minister Lester B. Pearson.

A shaker, because his contributions to the North American moving industry and the community are legendary. Tippet dedicated long hours to children and young people by helping organizations such as Big Brothers and the YMCA. He was also president of several business organizations.

"He was ahead of his time as a businessman. His philosophies are responsible for putting us at the top of the industry," says Peter Naylor, who in 2002 was president and principal shareholder of Tippet-Richardson.

Tippet was born in Saint John, New Brunswick in 1896 and attended elementary and high school in Montreal before launching a career as

a registered cost accountant. He joined the Merchant's Bank in 1913 and in 1918 was hired by Howell Warehouses Limited in Toronto, where he transformed the company by reorganizing staff, adding modern equipment, and improving service

Basil Tippet

Courtesy of Tippet-Richardson Limited

levels. He became company president in 1924 after founder George Howell died, and held the position until 1947 when the firm was sold.

Tippet founded Tippet-Richardson in 1927 with partner C.A. Richardson, a vice-president at Howell Warehouses. The company, which began with a rented warehouse and one van, was launched as a direct result of Tippet's involvement in charitable work.

While Tippet was working with the Big Brothers, a young man fresh out of prison convinced him to finance a truck that would help put the ex-con's life back on track. "He vamoosed and left me with the truck," Tippet told the *Financial Post* in the 1950s. "I then decided in order to stave off the unkindly and numerous criticisms of my friends to put the truck to work. This was the beginning of Tippet-Richardson Ltd."

Tippet and Richardson were partners until 1934 when Tippet bought Richardson's share of the company. Tippet and his wife Doris had no children.

In the 1930s, Tippet's moving company adopted the slogan "the friendly mover," a phrase still found on the company's trucks, letterhead, and promotional literature. Over the years he formed several other companies, including the Eastern Forwarding Company, Canadian Freight Forwarding Company, and Hamilton Freight Forwarding Company.

Along the way, he became one of Canada's foremost experts on moving and warehousing. Tippet, who was president of the Canadian Warehousemen's Association, was renowned for his knowledge of cost control, pricing strategies, and employee relations, which enabled his and other moving and storage companies to be profitable and efficient. His principles were adopted by the National Furniture and Warehouseman's Association in the United States and are still in use today.

"He always had an interest in his people," recalls Naylor, who spent summers moving furniture for the company before rising to the position of branch accountant in Hamilton, Ontario. "In the '30s and '40s, he distributed newsletters to keep employees and their families informed. He also set up programs to reward employees for their hard work. He was very good at motivating people to perform better."

Away from the office, Tippet held a variety of positions in the community, including president of the Rotary Club of Toronto and the Toronto Board of Trade, first president of the Young Men's Club of the Board of Trade, a member of the central board of directors of the YMCA, and president of the Big Brothers organization. He was a Freemason and was prominent in church activities such as teaching Bible classes. His company consistently donated a percentage of its profits to the community, including $10,000 to finance a children's wading pool in Toronto.

Tippet was Tippet-Richardson Limited's major shareholder until he died in December 1959 at age sixty-three. He was remembered in an obituary as one of the "most exciting and inspirational leaders of the household goods moving and storage industry."

After Tippet's death, the company was taken over by brothers Russell and Walter Naylor, both Tippet-Richardson employees who had been minority shareholders since 1934. In 1976, when Russell Naylor died, his sons Peter and Bruce began running the firm.

Today, under the leadership of Peter Naylor, Tippet-Richardson is a broad-based national moving and storage company with 250 full-time employees and 200 trucks and warehouses across Canada. Its services include local and long distance residential and office moving in Canada and the United States, overseas moving and storage of household goods, and storage and management of business records.

AMJ Campbell Van Lines

A man named Campbell is a key player in the history of AMJ Campbell Van Lines. But truth be known, his name is not AMJ Campbell. In 1977, Tim Moore, original owner of the company, bought a small Barrie, Ontario moving firm owned by M.J. Campbell. Moore put an A in front of the name to give it better placement in the Yellow Pages, and today, Toronto-based AMJ Campbell is one of Canada's busiest movers of households and offices, with annual revenues of $110 million.

Herb Title

Herbie's Drug Warehouse

As a young man growing up in Toronto, Herb Title thought of studying medicine, but as a "middle-of-the-road student," he knew he didn't have the marks for medical school and decided to become a druggist instead.

Turns out he was much better than middle of the road when it came to pharmacy; he built one of the most successful drugstore chains in Ontario. And yes, the company logo of a portly, smiling gentleman wearing half glasses does bear a resemblance to the real Title.

"I discovered I had a strong talent in pharmacy marketing and merchandising. I truly learned to love it," he says from his Mississauga home. "I was extremely fortunate that I never separated work from pleasure. Work was pleasure."

Title graduated with a pharmacy degree from the University of Toronto in 1949. He was able to apprentice while studying to help pay for his education — even if he earned only $16.60 a week. In 1954, he opened his first drug store, Medical Centre Pharmacy, on Brown's Line in west Toronto.

The prospect of Sherway Mall opening up in his area, however, spurred him to establish Economy Fair Discount Stores, and by the time the mall became reality he was already operating a string of shops. These weren't the Herbie's stores that would make him famous later, but he now knew what it took to succeed.

After many years of prosperity, Title visited stores in the United States and realized that operating large discount drugstores could work in Canada. But he didn't want to lose the personal touch he believed was essential in the pharmacy business. He opted to name the new operation for himself. "Because of the size of the store, I recognized there was potential to lose that personal relationship. That concerned me very much." His first Herbie's store opened in Hamilton in 1984 and took off. "Our inventory selection and discount structures were extremely well received."

So, too, was the company logo. Title says the character resembles him a bit, especially the glasses, but the face is chubbier to give it a happier look.

Herbie's marketed itself aggressively from the start and offered a wide selection of goods, including grocery items not normally found in drugstores. Title also used TV ads, primarily in Barrie, Ontario, to reach customers. "We wanted to sell the idea that Herbie was a real person and a druggist. We had a lot of fun doing those commercials."

At its peak, Title had ten Herbie's outlets in Ontario and employed about one thousand people. The flagship store in Kingston was sixty thousand square feet, making it the largest drug and food warehouse in the country, according to Title.

But in 2000, at age seventy-four, he decided to sell the business to Rexall Drugs, which continues to use the Herbie's name and may eventually expand it beyond Ontario. "The timing was right," says Title. "I always wanted to retire by the time I was seventy-five."

He continued to work, however, setting up Title & Jones Investments Inc. with his son-in-law, and exploring various business ventures. He also hung on to two retail outlets (not Herbie's stores) in the Muskoka area.

Title is proud the Herbie's name lives on, especially because his grandchildren can see the stores he created. "I've loved my life," he says. "I'm so lucky."

Name Dropper

When Title disposed of his stores, he also sold his airplane. He'd been flying for about thirty-five years and would often see communities first from the air to determine whether they might make good sites for his stores.

Karim Hakim

Hakim Optical

Karim Hakim has been helping people see more clearly since he was nine years old.

The founder of Hakim Optical got his start as a young boy in Iran, grinding magnifying glass from old windows to help support his family. He was obviously skilled at it because by age nineteen, Hakim was working in Germany grinding lenses for various instruments. He did the same work in Switzerland before immigrating to Canada in the mid-1960s.

Hakim set up a lab in the old Elmwood Hotel in Toronto and eventually began selling his lenses to opticians and optometrists. When people wanted to buy lenses directly from him, he saw a business opportunity and began making frames as well. Today, there are more than eighty Hakim Optical outlets in Ontario, Nova Scotia, New Brunswick, and Florida selling as many as one thousand pairs of glasses a day. In fact, since he began operations in Toronto, Hakim has sold more than fourteen million pairs of glasses.

Now that's a man with a vision.

Rose-Anna and Arcade Vachon
Vachon Cakes

The company that brought Canadians Jos. Louis snack cakes and a variety of other tasty pastries was launched by a modest family with a dream, a bank loan, and a brood of hard-working children.

From its beginnings as a mom and pop bakery operated by Arcade and Rose-Anna in Quebec's Beauce Region, Vachon Cakes evolved into a multi-million dollar operation, which was referred to by one media commentator as a "treasured morsel of the province's food industry heritage."

In 1923, Arcade, fifty-five, and his wife, who was ten years his junior, left Saint-Patrice de Beaurivage, Quebec, after spending twenty-five years as farmers there. Under the direction of Rose-Anna, the couple borrowed $7,000 and bought the Leblond Bakery in Sainte-Marie de Beauce, about sixty kilometres from Quebec City. They had $15 in the bank at the time.

Their first employee was their son Redempteur, who made bread, and with his father criss-crossed the surrounding area in a buggy selling loaves for six cents apiece.

Arcade and Rose-Anna Vachon.

Courtesy of Tourisme Sainte-Marie.

Rose-Anna and Arcade Vachon

As a way to boost sales, Rose-Anna two years later diversified into other baked goods, including donuts, sweet buns, shortbread, cakes, pies, and even baked beans, which she made in the wood oven in the kitchen of the family home. Simone, one of two daughters, helped sell the tasty treats after school. In 1928, two of the Vachons' six sons, Louis and Amédée, returned from the United States to help out. The business prospered when it began exporting to Quebec City.

By 1932, sons Joseph, Paul, and Benoit had also joined the company, which by then had ten employees and had introduced the Jos. Louis, which soon became its most popular cake. As business grew, trucks were purchased to make deliveries, and trains transported goods to more distant customers. By 1937, the company was peddling its products in Ontario and the Maritimes.

Several significant events occurred between 1938 and 1945: On January 15, 1938, at age seventy, Arcade Vachon died. His wife and sons kept the company running and moved to a former shoe factory, where an eight-thousand-square-foot extension was built and modern production equipment installed. In 1940, the family decided to focus exclusively on snack cakes.

In 1945, at the age of sixty-seven, Rose-Anna retired and sold her interest in the company to her sons Joseph, Amédée, Paul, and Benoit, who broadened the product line to 111 different items. Rose-Anna died on December 2, 1948. Two years later a new company, Diamond Products Limited, was founded to produce jams for the bakery. It was later sold to J.M. Smuckers of the United States.

In 1961, with its sinfully sweet pastries being sold in most of Canada, the company changed its name to Vachon Inc. By 1970, following several expansions and an acquisition, the company had twelve hundred employees. That year, 83 percent of Vachon shares were sold to Quebec banking co-op Mouvement des caisses populaires Desjardins, leaving 17 percent in the Vachon family's hands.

Montreal-based food giant Culinar Inc. bought the company in 1977; in 1999, Culinar and Vachon were acquired by dairy and grocery products company Saputo Inc. of Montreal. Despite the corporate shuffle, the Vachon family name is still found on a handful of products made famous by Arcade, Rose-Anna, and their children, including Jos. Louis and May West snack cakes.

The Vachon home in Sainte-Marie de Beauce, Quebec, where

Rosa-Anna did her bookkeeping and used her own recipes to bake breads and snack cakes, is a historic monument and museum.

Name Dropper

Some snack lovers believe the Jos. Louis is named after the legendary American boxer Joe Louis. In fact, the chocolate cake's moniker is a combination of the names of two Vachon sons — Joseph and Louis.

Hiram Walker

Hiram Walker & Sons Limited

It was nineteenth-century prohibition that caused Hiram Walker to cross the border from Detroit to Windsor and start up his famous distillery. And it was American insistence that he identify his products as being Canadian that led to the creation of one of the most famous names in the whisky business.

Hiram Walker was born on the Fourth of July, 1816 in East Douglas, Massachusetts, one of four children. He moved to Boston in 1836, worked in the grocery business, and two years later headed west to Detroit, which at that time was a fur trading centre and army post. Walker continued in the grocery business and also had a partnership in a tannery, but made his money mostly from the sale of grain, liquor, and vinegar.

What sealed his fate in coming to Canada and starting one of the most famous distilleries in the world was the Ironclad Prohibitionary Law of 1853, which stated that only druggists could sell liquor in Michigan. Though Walker was making a good living selling grain and vinegar, he purchased land across the Detroit River near Windsor and began a milling and distilling business in Canada in 1858.

He also crossed the border because real estate and building supplies were cheaper, the Upper and Lower Canada Railroad was in place to ship to other parts of Upper Canada, and there were no other distillers in the area. The whisky he made here was lighter than American booze, and he didn't shy away from packing it in barrels that bore his name, something that was innovative for the time. Walker's whisky was enjoyed by gentlemen members of clubs in the area, so he decided to label it "Club" to distinguish it.

As his business grew, Walker built large headquarters in what was to become known as Walkerville, near Windsor, and hired a salesman, John McBride, who successfully drummed up new business in the area.

By the 1880s, Walker's whisky was so popular in Canada that he decided to tackle the American market. Distillers south of the border, however, didn't want their customers to think that Walker's whisky was similar to what they produced and lobbied the government to get him to indicate the country in which his liquor originated. And so, in

1890, Canadian Club was born. Today it is sold in more than 150 countries and is one of the best-known brands in the world.

Walker transformed the Windsor area with his business success. A man of action with incredible stamina, he raised livestock, had the railway extended to his stockyards, built a church, and established a ferry to and from Detroit for commercial use. He and his wife Mary had several children, though some died at an early age.

Walker was known as a charitable man who took care of his employees during hard times, when they were sick, or when they needed financial support. During a depression in 1874 it was said that Walker distributed some $5,000 worth of bread and staples to help families in Walkerville, Windsor, and Detroit get through the winter. Though he spent much of his life in Canada, Walker remained a U.S. citizen.

After Walker died on January 12, 1899, his sons ran the business for another twenty years and later passed it on to their sons. Hiram Walker & Sons Limited was acquired by the U.K.-based firm Allied Domecq PLC in 1987.

Jack Warner

Warner Brothers

Some might think it a bit of a stretch to claim the renowned Hollywood film company and its famous movie mogul Jack Warner as Canadian. The famous producer of Warner Brothers fame was born in London, Ontario in 1892, but only lived there for the first two years of his life before his family moved to Youngstown, Ohio.

Still, in 1960, Warner received the Order of the British Empire and in a 1973 interview talked about being from Canada along with so many others from Hollywood's earliest days.

Jack Warner was the only one of the famous brothers born in Canada. His father Ben had emigrated from Poland in 1890 and settled in Baltimore, Maryland. He got a job as a cobbler and sent for the rest of his family. Eventually Ben changed trades and became a peddler, a job that brought him eventually to London. Jack apparently had no birth certificate, but later chose August 4 as his birthdate. Ben's business didn't thrive in the southwestern Ontario community, so the family pulled up stakes and moved.

Warner and his brothers got their start when they opened a theatre in Pennsylvania to show films. One account says they had to borrow chairs for the theatre from an undertaker, which meant patrons had to stand if a funeral was taking place while a film was showing. The Warners' first Hollywood effort was in 1917–18, but they would produce thousands of films over the next five decades, including the popular Bugs Bunny cartoons and several award-winning movies.

Known as a gambler and a "no-good sonofabitch" who often clashed with famous stars, Warner nevertheless won Oscars for such films as *Casablanca*, *The Life of Emile Zola*, and *My Fair Lady*. He was apparently proudest of *The Jazz Singer*, the 1927 film that helped usher in the sound era, and for which he later received a special Academy Award. In his retirement years before he died of inflammation of the heart in 1978, Warner said "you're nothing if you don't have a studio. Now I'm just another millionaire, and there are a lot of 'em around."

Warner Brothers is still one of the best-known studios in the business, having merged with the Time Inc. in 1990 and then becoming

AOL Time Warner in 2001. It is one of the biggest media/entertainment conglomerates in the world, producing such recent films as *The Matrix* and *Harry Potter* and TV shows such as *ER*, *Friends*, and *The West Wing*.

Louis B. Mayer

MGM

Many Canadians besides Jack Warner have been involved in Hollywood's movie industry from its early days. Another one in the spotlight was Louis B. Mayer, one of the M's in MGM studios.

Mayer was born in Minsk, Russia in 1885, but came to Canada with his family when he was three, settling in Saint John, N.B. Mayer's father was involved in the scrap metal industry, a business young Louis entered when he quit school. At nineteen, he moved to Boston, eventually bought into some nickelodeons (early movie theatres), and began producing films. He moved to California in 1918, cofounding Metro-Goldwyn-Mayer (MGM) in 1924.

In addition to producing a wealth of movies during his long career and overseeing the careers of hundreds of Hollywood stars, Mayer was also a key figure in creating the Academy Awards. He devised the scheme partly as a way to keep labour unrest in the movie business from getting out of hand.

Mayer was a major force in motion pictures until the 1950s and died in 1957. Though Canadian-raised, Mayer not only became an American citizen but falsely claimed he was born on the Fourth of July, American Independence Day. Mayer received a special Academy Award in 1950.

Joe and Ben Weider

Weider Health and Fitness

In the 1930s, a slightly built boy named Joe Weider and his younger brother Ben couldn't make it home from school without being picked on by tough guys who patrolled the streets in their Montreal neighbourhood.

Tired of being the proverbial ninety-pound weaklings, the Weiders decided to add some strength by using a calisthenic program popularized by American strongman Charles Atlas. When their muscles failed to expand and the bullies refused to let up, the brothers tried lifting weights made with materials found in a railroad yard.

They soon discovered that lifting weights enlarged their biceps and triceps, and more importantly, built self-esteem, which they discovered was the real key to beating bullies. With new-found muscles, the boys were convinced they were onto something and began sharing their secret. From the living room in their parents' home, they launched a fitness empire that would result in successful careers for both men and ultimately impact the lives of millions and turn bodybuilding into an international sport.

By age eighteen, Joe became the strongest kid in the neighbourhood, a feat that led him to win Quebec's weightlifting competition, the most important weightlifting event in Canada at the

Ben (left) and Joe (right) Weider

Photo by Robert Reiff (MagicLight Productions), Marina Del Rey, California.

I KNOW THAT NAME!

Name Dropper

Ben Weider is recognized as an expert in Napoleonic history after cowriting three books and conducting extensive research that helped prove French Emperor Napoleon Bonaparte was poisoned to death 1821 instead of dying of cancer, as indicated in previous history books.

---

time. Sixteen-year-old Ben was not far behind in his enthusiasm for bodybuilding.

Joe dreamed of publishing his own fitness newsletter to promote the physical and psychological value of working out and, with $7 in his pocket and a mimeograph machine, he began publishing *Your Physique*, a twelve-page instructional magazine. By 1943, the circulation of *Your Physique* (later known as *Muscle Builder* and now called *Muscle and Fitness*) reached across Canada. So many readers wrote in for information on weight equipment that Joe began his own equipment mail order business with the help of Ben, who had recently returned home from duty in the Canadian army.

By 1946 there was such a community of weight training devotees that the Weiders organized the first Mr. Canada contest. Unlike the exploitive carnival and vaudeville contests of the time, in which participants had to perform such stunts as bending steel bars or biting through steel, the Weiders' competition was respectful of the individual and of the discipline of lifting. They developed a sport by having competitors pose in front of judges to determine who had the most balanced muscular build.

The following year, Ben, who like his brother had completed public school — the extent of both boys' education — visited Europe and Africa to spark interest in the growing sport of bodybuilding. Eventually he travelled the globe and established the International Federation of Bodybuilders, which has grown to include more than 170 member nations and is recognized by the International Olympic Committee. By the 1950s, Joe Weider was publishing sixteen magazines and was a millionaire.

In the 1960s, Weider Sports Equipment and Weider Health and Fitness led to the formation of Weider Nutrition International. The company eventually moved its American base to California. Shortly after, the Weiders moved bodybuilding from cult to mainstream by appointing a spokesperson who would be a living, breathing symbol of the virtues of the sport. That spokesperson was a young, charismatic Austrian champion named Arnold Schwarzenegger.

The Weiders moved Schwarzenegger to California from his hometown of Grauz, Austria in 1969 and paid him $200 a week and bought him an automobile to write about his training and diet in *Muscle Builder* magazine. Joe also took the young bodybuilder under his wing by managing his daily training schedule and tutoring him in real estate investments, media relations, and the arts. In return, Schwarzenegger told readers about the benefits of using Weider supplements and equipment.

Soon, Schwarzenegger's personable manner, wit, and charm captivated audiences and helped dispel the notion that big muscles equated with little brains. The release of the motion picture *Pumping Iron* in 1977 made Schwarzenegger a household name and boosted the sport. By the early 1980s, bodybuilding and the healthy lifestyle associated with it were ingrained in the public consciousness, thanks to the Weiders' marketing skills.

The success of the Weiders' publishing efforts and products had made it possible for the brothers to realize their goal of making bodybuilding lucrative for the athletes and recognized as a sport. As a result of their strong beliefs in the concept of liberty and equality, the brothers have done their share to open the sport to all people, regardless of gender, race, religion, or politics.

Name Dropper

The Weiders were ahead of their time in waging campaigns against the tobacco and alcohol industries. As early as the 1930s, the brothers were educating people about the pitfalls of both addictions. To this day, all ads from these industries are not accepted for publication in their magazines.

By putting women bodybuilders on the cover of their magazines, writing articles about them, and promoting women's competitions, the Weiders have made the image of strong women acceptable to society at large and marketable to boot. ESPN, Fox, and other cable contracts have brought both men's and women's competitions into millions of living rooms across North America and around the world.

Today, Weider Nutrition International rings up sales of more than $350 million worth of vitamins, nutritional supplements, and sports nutrition products, which are sold in health food stores, pharmacies, health clubs, and gymnasiums in more than eighty countries. Weider Publications continues to publish seven magazines in more than fifteen different languages. The Weiders' companies operate out of Montreal, Los Angeles, Salt Lake City, and New York.

In 2002, Ben, seventy-nine, and Joe, eighty-one, are still involved in the various Weider enterprises. Ben, who has four honorary degrees and is married to Huguette, is president of the Montreal-based International Federation of Body-Builders and continues to work out four times a week in Montreal. Joe and his wife Betty are living in Los Angeles, where Joe works out regularly in his home gym. In 2002, the brothers completed a book titled *The Edge*, which provides cutting-edge scientific research on the use of supplements and nutrition for sports, as well as training secrets and illustrations of various bodybuilding exercises.

Name Dropper

The Weiders had their share of critics, including American Charles Atlas, who once told Joe he was "an idiot" for selling barbells to build strength. Nevertheless, the brothers persevered and eventually created the Weider Triangle of Peak Performance, based on exercise technique, nutrition, and bodybuilding, to enhance athletic performance in activities like swimming, cycling, and all other sports. They also created speed-training programs to develop fast twitch muscle fibers aimed at increasing speed for specific sports.

George Weston

George Weston Ltd.

From the beginning, it appeared George Weston was destined for a career in the food business.

Though his father was a labourer, packer, and bookkeeper, one of his brothers was a butcher, another worked in the baking trade, and a third went into the confectionery business.

The native of Oswego, New York moved to Toronto with his parents in 1869 when he was four years old. By age twelve, he was working at a small bakeshop owned by Charles J. Frogley on the fringe of Toronto. In the pre-dawn hours, Weston's tasks included cleaning mixing basins and mixing flour, water, yeast, and sugar into bread dough. He also hauled 120-pound sacks of flour, tended the hand-driven kneading machine, and stoked the wood-fired oven.

While working ten hours a day, six days a week, Weston was unknowingly taking an extensive course in the delicate chemistry of bread-making that would eventually make him and his family very wealthy. After three years with Frogley, he continued his apprenticeship with another small baker and confectioner, G.H. Bowen, who taught him how to make everything from plain biscuits to almond cakes.

By putting Weston out on his bread routes, Bowen gave the young lad his first exposure to sales and marketing. Every day, he would carry his wood and metal tray filled with an assortment of bread and cakes up to the kitchen doors of his prospective customers. Because most housewives made their own baked goods, landing a sale was challenging. So was the competition: In the early 1880s, fifty-eight bakers and fifty-nine confectioners were fighting for a piece of the baking business in Toronto.

Rising to the task before him, Weston in 1882 scraped together enough money to buy two of Bowen's bread routes, making him an independent entrepreneur at age seventeen. As his routes expanded, he was baker, bookkeeper, deliveryman, janitor, and stable boy. He also demonstrated an innovative streak that would help propel his company to greater heights: In the 1890s, Weston introduced what he called the "home-made loaf," which sold for pennies and convinced pressed-for-time homemakers to spend less time tending their ovens.

Around 1890, while working one of his routes, Weston met Emma Maud Roberts, a native of London, Ontario, who worked as a maid for one of his customers. They married shortly after and had six children.

Weston's formula for business success was fourfold: He had to out-hustle rivals and gradually take over their customers before buying them out for the lowest price possible; he preached quality; he paid his employees as little as possible, just as his bosses had once done with him; and he recognized that baking was undergoing a technological revolution. Between 1850 and 1900, he transformed a small-scale manual business into a mechanized assembly-line operation that could operate in a large factory.

To keep pace with change, Weston in 1897 opened what became known as the "Model Bakery," an imposing two-storey building in Toronto's Grange area. With a staff of forty and fourteen horse-drawn delivery wagons, the new state-of-the-art plant could turn out thirty-two hundred loaves a day. Two years later, he had thirty wagons for city and suburban delivery and Weston's Home-Made Bread was available in five hundred stores.

For five years Weston ran Model Bakery Co. Ltd. with partner Lawrence Spink before winding up the company in 1907, and at age forty-six, merging his bakery interests into the newly formed Canada Bread Company Co. in 1911. In the meantime, he continued to run a successful cake and biscuit business in downtown Toronto. At one point he was featured in a publication entitled "Men Who Made It" as one of Toronto's most successful businessmen, which declared Weston was a "name known to every householder in the city."

In 1919, Weston's son Garfield returned from France and began working in his father's biscuit plant, and in 1921 Weston purchased the H.C. Tomlin bread bakery at 420 Bathurst Street, right across the street from the Canada Bread Company. That same year the Weston family had advanced up the city's social ladder, rating mention in the *Torontonian Society Book*, which was known as the "authoritative directory of elite Torontonian families."

During a spring snowstorm in March 1924, George Weston decided to walk home from his factory. He caught a cold, which deteriorated into pneumonia, and died on April 7.

George Weston Ltd. was taken over by his son Garfield, who over the years would turn the company into a national and international business powerhouse with holdings on both sides of the Atlantic, which have ranged from Canadian grocery chain Loblaws, and paper maker E.B. Eddy to Neilson Dairy, National Tea of Chicago, the Tamblyn Drugstore chain, and Connors Brothers Ltd. fish processors of New Brunswick.

Today, the company oversees an assortment of more than seventy-five companies, boasts sales of more than $20 billion, and is headed by Garfield Weston's son Galen.

Name Dropper

In the 1910 civic election, George Weston was elected a member of Toronto city council and was re-elected in three subsequent votes. Never a force at city hall, he sat at the council table when the city dealt with issues such as the building of a new train station, introduction of hydro-electric power from Niagara Falls, and funding for the construction of a subway system.

Wilbert C. Wood

W.C. Wood Company

Next time you're in the market for a freezer you can dazzle the salesperson with the story of Wilbert Copeland Wood, whose name is not only on Wood products but is behind those of Frost Queen, ArcticAire, Danby, and others.

Wood was born on December 6, 1896 in Ontario, a time when many people were still clearing land for farming. In 1909, Wood moved to Saskatchewan with his family to try homesteading and later graduated from the University of Saskatchewan with a degree in agricultural engineering. He worked as a research engineer with Massey-Harris in Toronto until 1929, when the Depression forced the company to lay off employees. Looking for other opportunities, Wood determined that the rising use of electrical power in Ontario provided an ideal chance to help farmers who had to transport feed to and from mills for grinding.

It wasn't a freezer that caught his fancy at this time, but an electrical grain grinder, which he assembled on the back porch of his landlady's house in Toronto. He started up his own business, thanks to a Brampton-area farmer who gave him $150 for the grinder.

He and a sixteen-year-old assistant started machining their own castings in an empty candy shop on Howard Street, and by 1934 the W.C. Wood Company had moved to a larger factory on Dundas Street. The manufacture of appliances was still a few years away as the company concentrated on making an oat roller, a farm milking machine, and farm milk cooker. It was the refrigeration system designed for the milk coolers that led Wood to make freezers and eventually other appliances instead of farm equipment.

In 1941, Wood moved into a twenty-five-thousand-square-foot factory in Guelph, Ontario. Over the next fifteen years, the company became so successful that it moved to a new location in that city that offered ninety thousand square feet. That was the size of the plant when son John came onto the working scene in 1964. Today, the company has four plants in North America with a total of more than 1.2 million square feet. Throughout its history the company has manufactured more than ten million appliances.

Wilbert C. Wood

John Wood, company president for more than thirty years, his wife Barbara, children Susan and David, son-in-law Alex, and nephew Daniel Wood are all active in this still family-owned business. W.C. Wood died in 1987.

Wood freezers are a common sight in appliance stores today and the second-biggest retail brand in the country. The company also makes other brands of refrigerators and dehumidifiers and has markets in Canada, the U.S., and Mexico.

Name Dropper

We say zed, they say zee, but another difference between Canadians and Americans is that more than 80 percent of freezers sold in Canada are chest style, while in the U.S., where warmer weather means fewer homes have basements, upright style freezers claim nearly 50 percent of the market.

Charles Woodward

Woodward's Ltd.

For most of his life, Charles Woodward was plagued by bad luck and failure. But despite repeated setbacks as a farmer and retailer, the spunky farmer's son became the millionaire owner of Western Canada's Woodward's department store chain.

The son of English immigrant John Woodward, Charles was born in 1852 on the family farm near Orangeville, Ontario. After quitting school at fourteen, he showed a knack for marketing his father's produce by selling grain and vegetables more cheaply than competitors and posting clear signs at the local market to advertise price and quality.

Years later, he'd use those skills as a businessman but not before a handful of money-making endeavors turned sour.

Charles's first stint in the mercantile trade went bust when his boss wouldn't let him deal with customers at his store near Arthur, Ontario, where the Woodward family was living in 1873. Later, land he bought north of Toronto and on Manitoulin Island turned out to be unsuitable for farming. His first Woodward's store, a trading post opened in the mid-1870s in a log cabin in the Manitoulin Island community of Bidwell, did well, but the area's seasonal market didn't produce enough business to support him.

A general store started with his brother-in-law on Manitoulin Island in 1877 would have gone bankrupt had his father not come to the rescue. While he owned a general store in Thessalon, Ontario, his manager accumulated huge

Charles Woodward

debts, which he managed to overcome. Unfortunately, the store burned down in 1890.

With these and other misadventures behind him, Woodward, now married and the father of eight children, moved to Vancouver where he built a general store that opened on March 1, 1892 on Westminster Avenue. Although the downtown business prospered during the economic boom caused by the Klondike gold rush, bad times continued. Between 1892 and 1900, his wife Elizabeth and three of their children died; soon after, he and several merchants who opened a larger store on Hastings Avenue in 1903 were at each other's throats over the store's poor performance.

But as always, the ever-industrious Woodward persevered. At age fifty-two and nearly broke, he scraped together enough cash to buy out his partners, take control of the company, and make yet another fresh start. This time, he told a business associate, he was going to make a million dollars. And he did. Between 1907 and 1912, Vancouver's population more than doubled to 129,000 and cash registers at Woodward's were ringing madly. In 1912, with twenty departments and a mail order business under his control, Woodward was a millionaire.

With family members helping run the business, Woodward and his second wife Alice retired and began spending time in California, though he continued to have a say in the operation of the store.

In 1925, with two of his sons handling much of the management responsibilities, Woodward was elected as a member of the Legislative Assembly for British Columbia's ruling Liberal Party. During his four-year tenure as an MLA, the interests of Vancouver were among his top priorities, though he often tangled with the premier and other members of his own party over issues such as timber policy, the Pacific Great Eastern Railway, and the government's close ties to brewers. Woodward's career as an MLA ended in 1928 when he became alienated from the party.

In the years leading up to his death in 1937, Woodward's opened a store in Edmonton and completed various additions to the Vancouver store. After Woodward died, his son Billy was appointed president, and in ensuing years other members of the family ran the company, including his grandson Charles Namby Woodward, who was chief executive officer and chairman of the board until 1979.

In 1986, Woodward's Ltd., which at one point operated travel agencies, twenty-six department stores, and thirty-three discount stores in Alberta and British Columbia, posted annual sales of $1.1 billion. But recessionary times and competition from specialty stores soon cut heavily into its revenues.

The Woodward family sold its majority share in the company in 1989. In 1993, the chain was taken over by the Hudson's Bay Company, which pulled down the Woodward's name and converted most of the stores into Bay or Zellers outlets.

Name Dropper

Despite his great wealth, Charles Woodward was known as a penny-pincher who never owned a car and never tipped more than five cents. But he did have a generous side: although a department manager once sued the company for wrongful dismissal and lost, Woodward later rehired him.

Walter P. Zeller

Zellers

Walter P. Zeller was obviously a man who believed in company policy.

In 1955, when he turned sixty-five, he followed his firm's retirement policy and tendered his resignation as president of the corporation that bears his name. By that time, Zellers was a well-established company in Canada approaching its twenty-fifth anniversary. Zeller continued his close association with the firm, however, remaining chairman of its board of directors.

Zeller was born on October 21, 1890, on a farm in Ontario's Waterloo County. According to information from the Hudson's Bay Company Corporate Collection, his family was of Swiss origin and had been living in southwestern Ontario since 1831. Zeller finished high school and got a job as a stock boy in a variety chain store in Chatham, Ontario. He was hard-working and energetic and was soon promoted to a variety of positions with increasing responsibility. He worked in Canada and the U.S. and had a wide range of experience in retailing by the time he decided to launch his own business.

Zeller's Limited was incorporated on July 13, 1931 with the power to deal in "goods, wares, materials, commodities and merchandise and arti-

cles and objects of commerce of every kind and description whatsoever." In its first year, Zellers opened twelve stores, the first being in London, Ontario. Zellers started off solidly by purchasing the assets of another chain store company and managing to reach $2 million in sales by the end of the first year.

Walter P. Zeller, from 1942 Zeller newsletter.

From Hudson's Bay Company Corporate Collection

Zellers Store

Photo by Mark Kearney

With the slogan "Retailers to Thrifty Canadians," Zellers was able to weather the economic storm of the Depression as well as the goods shortage created by World War II. Zeller believed his stores should always carry an assortment of merchandise, such as moderately priced fashion and staple items that were usually only sold by larger department stores and specialty shops. This philosophy enabled Zellers to expand and thrive, especially in the postwar years.

A key turning point occurred in 1952, when Zellers purchased the outstanding shares of another Canadian chain, Federal Stores, and renovated and relocated some of their shops. The company also began an affiliation with W.T. Grant Company, a general merchandise chain in the U.S., that same year. In a message to shareholders in 1953, Zeller wrote "through this affiliation Zellers will have available new sources of supply … and the extensive experience of the Grant Company on matters of real estate, store development and general administration." By 1959, W.T. Grant had acquired 51 percent of Zellers Ltd. common stock.

Zeller, who was also known for his charitable work, particularly for underprivileged boys, died in 1957, just two years after he retired. Following his death, Zellers continued to grow, and by 1981 was owned completely by the Hudson Bay Company. Over the next dozen years, Zellers sales would hit $3 billion and several Woodward's stores would be renovated and converted to the Zellers name. Today, there are 350 Zellers stores across Canada and located in every province.

Selected Bibliography

Bata, Thomas J. and Sinclair, Sonja: *Bata Shoemaker to the World*, Stoddart Publishing Co. Ltd., 1990.

Berton, Pierre: *Great Canadians, A Century of Achievement*, The Canadian Centennial Publishing Company Limited, 1965.

Boulton, Marsha: *The Just a Minute Omnibus*, McArthur & Company, 2000.

Brandt, E.N.: *Growth Company: Dow Chemical's First Century*, Michigan State University Press, 1997.

Bruce, Harry: *The Man and The Empire: Frank Sobey*, Macmillan of Canada, 1985.

Carpenter, Thomas: *Inventors: Profiles in Canadian Genius*, Camden House, 1990.

Carr, David: *William Neilson Ltd., The First 100 Years 1893 — 1993*, William Neilson Ltd., 1993.

Chalmers, Floyd S.: *A Gentleman of the Press*, Doubleday Canada, 1969.

Chartrand, Maurice and Provost, René: *Provigo: The Story Behind 20 Years of Entrepreneurial Success*, Prentice Hall Canada Inc., 1989.

Condon, George: *75th Anniversary, A Celebration, Loblaws Companies Limited*, Canadian Grocer, 1996 (special supplement).

Cook, Peter: *Massey at the Brink, The Story of Canada's Greatest Multinational and its Struggle to Survive*, Collins, 1991.

Dare Foods Limited: *Dare: The First Century, A Corporate History of Dare Foods Limited, 1892-1992*, 1992.

Davies, Charles: *Bread Men, How the Westons Built an International Empire*, Key Porter Books, 1987.

DeMont, John: *Citizens Irving, KC Irving and His Legacy, The Story of Canada's Wealthiest Family*, Doubleday Canada, 1991.

Donaldson, Gerald and Lampert, Gerald: *The Great Canadian Beer Book*, McClelland and Stewart, 1975.

Drushka, Ken: *H.R.: A Biography of H.R. MacMillan*, Harbour Publishing, 1995.

Folster, David: *The Chocolate Ganongs of St. Stephen, New Brunswick*, Macmillan of Canada, 1990.

Francis, Daniel: *The Encyclopedia of British Columbia*, Harbour Publishing, 2000.

Francis, Diane: *Controlling Interest: Who Owns Canada?* Macmillan of Canada, 1986.

Franklin, Stephen: *The Heroes, A Saga of Canadian Inspiration*, McClelland and Stewart Limited, 1967.

Fuller, Alfred Carl: *A Foot in the Door*, McGraw-Hill, 1960.

Gibbon, Ann and Hadekel, Peter: *Steinberg: The Breakup of a Family Empire*, Macmillan of Canada, 1990.

Gillen, Mollie: *The Masseys, Founding Family*, Ryerson Press, 1965.

Gould, Allan: *The New Entrepreneurs: 80 Canadian Success Stories*, McClelland and Stewart-Bantam, 1986.

Grant, Tina, ed.: *Canadian Company Histories*, Gale Canada, 1996.

Grant, Tina, ed.: *International Directory of Company Histories*, St. James Press, 1996.

Grescoe, Paul and Pattison, Jimmy: *Jimmy, An Autobiography*, Seal Books, 1987.

Griggs, Tim and Horton, Lori: *In Loving Memory: A Tribute to Tim Horton*, ECW Press, 1997.

Hambleton, Ronald: *The Branding of America*, Yankee Books, 1987.

Harker, Douglas E.: *The Woodwards, A Family Story of Ventures and Traditions*, Mitchell Press Limited, 1976.

Harrison, Robert E.: *Theodore Pringle Loblaw* (Loblaw & Stevenson) Family Study, 1996.

Humber, Charles, ed.: *Canada: From Sea Unto Sea*, Loyalist Press Ltd., 1986.

Hunter, Douglas: *Open Ice: The Tim Horton Story*, Viking, 1994.

Hunter, Douglas: *Molson: The Birth of a Business Empire*, Penguin Books Ltd., 2001.

Johnson, Leo. A.: *History of Guelph, 1827–1927*, Guelph Historical Society, 1977.

Jorgensen, Janice, ed.: *Encyclopedia of Consumer Brands* (several volumes), St. James Press, 1994.

Kelly, Russell: *Pattison, Portrait of a Capitalist Superstar*, New Star Books, 1986.

King, James: *Jack, A Life With Writers: The Story of Jack McClelland*, Alfred A. Knopf Canada, 1999.

Lee, Laura: *The Name's Familiar: Mr. Leotard, Barbie, and Chef

Boyardee, Pelican Publishing Company, 1999.

Liepner, Michael, De Jordy, Herve, and Schultz, Michael: *The Entrepreneurial Spirit*, McGraw-Hill Ryerson, 1991.

MacDonald, Larry: *The Bombardier Story*, John Wiley & Sons, 2001.

MacKay, Donald: *Empire of Wood, the MacMillan Bloedel Story*, Douglas & McIntyre, 1982.

MacLeod, Kenneth O.: *The First Century: The story of a Canadian Company: Henry Birks & Sons*, Henry Birks & Sons Inc., 1979.

Marsh, James, H.: *The Canadian Encyclopedia*, Year 2000 Edition, McClelland & Stewart, 1999.

Mayer, Roy: *Inventing Canada, One Hundred Years of Innovation*, Raincoast Books, 1997.

McGrath, Molly Wade: *Top Sellers USA*, William Morrow and Company, 1983.

McQueen, Rod: *The Eatons: The Rise and Fall of Canada's Royal Family*, Stoddart, 1999.

Meurer, Susan and Sobel, David: *Working at Inglis: The Life and Death of a Canadian Factory*, James Lorimer & Company, 1994.

Newman, Peter C.: *The Canadian Establishment* (Vols. 1 and II), McClelland and Stewart, 1989.

Newman, Peter C.: *Titans: How the New Canadian Establishment Seized Power*, Penguin Books, 1998.

Pitts, Gordon: *In the Blood, Battles to Succeed in Canada's Family Businesses*, Doubleday Canada, 2000.

Smith, Ken: *No Mean Business, A Hundred Years of Real Estate from The 1880s To The 1990s*, Toronto Real Estate Board, 1989.

Smith, Llewellyn S.: *The House that Jam Built*, Baby Boomer Press, 1995.

Sneath, Allen Winn: *Brewed in Canada*, The Dundurn Group, 2001.

Stanton, Ray: *A Legacy of Quality*, J.M. Schneider Inc., 1989.

Stevens, G.R.: *Ogilvie in Canada, Pioneer Millers 1801–1951*, McLaren, 1951.

Stevens, Geoffrey: *Stanfield*, McClelland and Stewart Ltd., 1973.

Thomas, Dave, and Marchant, Bob: *When Milk Came in Bottles: A History of Toronto Dairies*, Cowtown Publications, 1997.

University of Toronto Press: *Dictionary of Canadian Biography*, various editions.

Waldie, Paul: *A House Divided: The Untold Story of the McCain Family*, Viking, 1996.

Watson, Patrick: *The Canadians, Biographies of a Nation*, McArthur & Company, 2000.

Woods, Shirley E. Jr.: *The Molson Saga, 1786–1986*, Doubleday Canada Ltd., 1986.

Index

Index

Index

Acknowledgments

Although we spent more than a year researching and writing about many famous Canadian names, we couldn't have done so without the help of other not-so-well-known names who dug up information, answered our questions, and pointed us in the right direction when we were stumped.

We'd first like to thank all those in the book whom we interviewed and who spent time telling their stories or those of their relatives, ancestors, and colleagues who are featured here. We're also grateful to the many company officials, public relations officers, association spokespersons, and archivists who had a wealth of information for us or told us who might. We'd be remiss in not naming a few of them, including Stuart MacCuaig at the Hamilton Public Library; Gloria Pare, Haldimand County's Genealogy Research Coordinator; Carol Haber at the City of Vancouver Archives; Glenda Todkill of the Black Photo Corporation; Jane Holland at Lewis Carroll Communications; and Nellie Swart at Labatt Brewing Company. Thanks also to Hudson's Bay Company for the use of their copyrighted material.

We owe a big thanks to Laura Lee of Albany, New York, whose book *The Name's Familiar* was an inspiration and blueprint for ours. Laura first suggested we do a book like this featuring Canadian names, and we're glad she did.

We're especially thankful, as always, to our wives, Janis Ray and Catherine Blake, for their support, advice, and ideas about what this book should cover and how we should complete it. Both deserve kudos for listening to us patiently as we repeatedly said, "hey, did you know this?" or "have you heard about that?" And they never tired as we pointed out names on billboards, transport trucks, and store shelves that made their way into the book.

A tip of the hat to all the writers and friends on the PWAC-L listserve who not only suggested names from across the country that we should explore, but were also helpful in suggesting titles for this book.

As always, we want to acknowledge the staffs and excellent collections of the Ottawa Public Library, the London Public Library, particularly Pat Tripp and Arthur McClelland, the University of Western Ontario, and the National Archives in Ottawa. We'd still be working on this project today if it weren't for them.

Other friends and colleagues who offered ideas and support for this book include John Firth, Ed Janiszewski, Doug Chaudron, Wayne Skinner, Jane Rideout, Carl Kent, Simonne LeBreton, Barb Steep, Arthur McCudden, Jane Widerman, Harold Wright, George Brimmell, Louise Rachlis, Bryan Ray, Brian McAndrew, Richard Patterson, David Dauphinee, Don MacDonald, Carl Dow, and Paul Cassidy.

Thanks also to those people who have supported our previous books in many different ways: Bas and Shirley Kearney, Kim Kearney, the late Barbara Blake, Lenore Hawley, Marg Munhall, Gary Michaels, Jim Richards, Peter Garland, Jayne and Cliff Anderson, and reporters, columnists, and broadcasters too numerous to mention. We also want to acknowledge the late Harry Barberian: The downtown Toronto restaurant that bears his name has been our regular hangout over the years, a place where we've hatched ideas and discussed how to write our books, often fuelled by Harry's fine food and wines, the odd martini, and on occasion, by his charm and friendly company.

Finally, we also appreciate the special attention from the folks at The Dundurn Group, particularly Tony Hawke, Kirk Howard, Jennifer Scott, Jennifer Bergeron, Barry Jowett, Kerry Breeze, and Beth Bruder. Their enthusiasm and professionalism from the start was a big plus.

Mark Kearney and Randy Ray